T0367591

A MASSACRE
of
INNOCENTS

A MASSACRE

of

INNOCENTS

Loren Abbey & Pamela Zibura

iUniverse

A MASSACRE OF INNOCENTS

iUniverse books may be ordered through booksellers or by contacting:

iUniverse
1663 Liberty Drive
Bloomington, IN 47403
www.iuniverse.com
1-800-Authors (1-800-288-4677)

Because of the dynamic nature of the Internet, any web addresses or links contained in this book may have changed since publication and may no longer be valid. The views expressed in this work are solely those of the author and do not necessarily reflect the views of the publisher, and the publisher hereby disclaims any responsibility for them.

Any people depicted in stock imagery provided by Thinkstock are models, and such images are being used for illustrative purposes only.
Certain stock imagery © Thinkstock.

ISBN: 978-1-4917-6025-3 (sc)
ISBN: 978-1-4917-6024-6 (hc)
ISBN: 978-1-4917-6023-9 (e)

Library of Congress Control Number: 2015903019

Print information available on the last page.

iUniverse rev. date: 05/20/2015

ACKNOWLEDGMENTS

The authors wish to express their deepest gratitude to the many unselfish background toilers who contributed their efforts in the research and writing of this book and without whose kind assistance could not have been written.

Judy Anderson of the Plumas County Sheriff's Office was extremely generous in offering her assistance by allowing us to examine investigators' actual contemporary notes, relevant but long forgotten documents, and police photos which had never before been made available to the public and which, due to legal restrictions, can be viewed only on www.amassacreofinnocents.com.

The administrative staff at the Sacramento Public Library's Periodical Department helped us re-discover decades of old contemporary newspaper accounts allowing us to follow and reconstruct events as though they were taking place in real time. We are more than grateful for their help.

The kindness shown to us by the administrative staff at the California Supreme Court in San Francisco and the Superior Courts in Quincy and Sacramento was a most welcome contribution. By their allowing us to browse the minutes of the Grand Jury proceedings in Plumas County, as well as the court transcripts of the trials in Los Angeles and Quincy, we were able to describe the trials fully and accurately. For that too, we are most appreciative.

We are grateful to Director Marilyn Quadrio of the Chester-Almanor Museum and in Quincy, Curator Scott Lawson at the Plumas County Museum; both of whom were most considerate in sharing with us the historical information that had accumulated in their respective museums over the past half century with special emphasis on how the township of Chester and Quincy were affected by the massacre of four of their own.

Special thanks to our beloved editor, the indomitable Ann Fisher whose unflinching support helped to keep us motivated. She was always there to offer not only her invaluable editorial expertise but even more importantly, her inspiration and her encouragement. We'll always be grateful for that.

Acknowledgments

Keith Sauers and Anne Greene of the Doris Foley Library for Historical Research in Nevada City, California, were especially helpful to us in conducting our research, as was Christal Young's sister Geraldine Walters who was kind enough to provide details about the extended Young family in a way that was so much more personal than any we could have obtained from other sources.

Sondra Gay, the tragic event's sole survivor, was interviewed on several occasions during which she was able to provide precious insights into the Young family's experiences following the Chester tragedy and their resettlement in Utah—insights which added a texture to the narrative and without which this book in its present form, would not have been possible.

Our thanks to Tony Zibura for his dogged patience and eagle eye in ferreting out those ubiquitous typos and other inadvertent but inevitable errata.

We're also grateful to Dan Colson whose constructive critique was a major contributor. As a former California judge, Dan's legal expertise and advice was most invaluable.

We also wish to thank Samantha Keeling, a Chester resident who generously volunteered her time and energy while acting as tour guide during our research visits to Chester. Her interest in the book's subject matter, her keen knowledge of the local geography as well as her many personal acquaintanceships were extremely helpful as we sought out interviews with locals who may have been living in Chester at the time the murders were committed.

Our deepest gratitude to all.

CONTENTS

PREFACE

MASSACRE! Screamed the headlines in huge capital letters, reminiscent of the day Pearl Harbor was bombed. Headlines like that were very hard to ignore. That there are people in this world who, without a second thought or trace of moral compunction, would—or even could—visit this kind of horror on other human beings, let alone four totally innocent and defenseless children was, to most rational people, beyond comprehension. That there could be people walking among us who are capable of such barbarity was simply unthinkable. This was something one might expect to see in some low-budget Hollywood production—certainly not in Northern California's bucolic Sierra Nevada foothills. Certainly not in the placid, serene community of Chester.

But this was no movie.

What is the catalytic force that brings together two small-time hoodlums who, as individuals, during the first forty or fifty years of their miserable lives had limited themselves to petty larcenies, burglaries, check-kiting schemes, car thefts, or an occasional strong-arm robbery, only to see them suddenly morph into brutal killing machines? Neither of these individuals had a known history of violent behavior, much less the kind of gratuitous brutality as was exhibited in this rampage. One might wonder if their murderous symbiosis could have been one of those rare examples of the whole being greater than the sum of its parts.

True sociopaths, i.e., remorseless individuals completely unburdened or unconstrained by conscience, according to at least one noted clinical psychologist, comprise as much as four percent of the American population. But how many among that four percent are capable of the acts that are described in this book, especially when the ages of these particular victims are taken into account? If the math is correct, four percent of the American population means that there are 480,000 of these monsters living among us; rubbing shoulders with us, standing next to us in elevators; on trains, in line at supermarket check-out counters, all while appearing to be perfectly normal people.

Dr. Robert Hare, creator of the Hare *Psychopathy Checklist,* or *PCL,* the psychologist's bible, in his clinical study of the criminal mind, *Without Conscience: The Disturbing World of Psychopaths Among Us,* notes that *". . . . psychopaths tend to live day-to-day, to change their plans frequently. They give little previous thought to the future and they worry about it even less."* It's a psyche once exemplified by the notorious murderer Gary Gilmore, executed by firing squad in 1977. When asked why he committed the two murders for which he was being executed, he said, *"I wasn't thinkin'; I wasn't plannin'; I was just doin'."*

Hare explains: *Psychopaths' lack of remorse or guilt is associated with a remarkable ability to rationalize their behavior and to shrug off personal responsibility for actions that cause shock and disappointment to family, friends, associates and others who have played by the rules. Usually they have handy excuses for their behavior and in some cases they deny that it happened at all.*

Research for *A Massacre of Innocents,* conducted over sixty years later, included interviews with Chester residents who had lived through the horrific events but had retained only the dimmest of memories. Most of the key players in this drama had either moved from the area and were un-locatable or had died. Key documents such as trial transcripts, had been lost, misfiled or inexplicably destroyed.

The authors were, however, able to meet with and interview sole survivor Sondra Gay Jones, nee, Young, and while she continues to bear both emotional as well as physical scars, remarkably, she was still able to recall and share with us bits and pieces of the horror to which she and her family were subjected on that day so long ago.

* * *

A Massacre of Innocents might best be described as a non-fiction *True-Crime novel,* a genre originally pioneered by Truman Capote with his magnum opus *In Cold Blood,* and expanded on by two-time Pulitzer Prize winner Norman Mailer. It was more recently fine tuned—and probably perfected—by contemporary "true-crime" writers such as Joseph Wambaugh, Ann Rule and Dominick Dunne.

Bob Colacello's introduction to *In Cold Blood* defines the narrative non-fiction style as *novelistic journalism*; a writing style that allows the author, when writing about historical events, to take certain liberties not permitted the "hard news" journalist. When writing *A Massacre of Innocents*, although some dramatic license was taken in order to reconstruct portions of dialogue between participants, the authors have taken extreme care to be able to assure the reader that every fact and significant event as depicted in this book is true.

Our purpose in deciding to write *A Massacre of Innocents* was not to make some kind of morality statement or to present a clinical commentary on criminals such as Jack Santo and Emmett Perkins, but rather to give readers a small snapshot of the history of crime in our home state of California. It's a dark and storied history that— among many others—would include the sensationalized Black Dahlia murder of the '40s, the unsolved San Francisco Zodiac killings in the '60s, the Manson Family's rampage of the '70s and the double murder for which O.J. Simpson was tried and acquitted in the '90s and which still, even today, remains officially unsolved.

But most readers are probably unaware of many of the state's less notorious crimes: the Laurel Canyon murders, the nearly forgotten Chicken Coop murders and the Keddie quadruple murders which, incidentally, also took place in Plumas County, not far from the scene of the Chester massacre.

These crimes, though every bit as horrific as their more infamous counterparts, have now become so obscure as to have been virtually expunged from the history books.

The quadruple murders that took place in 1952 in Chester, California were just such a crime.

"Nobody gets hurt, unless someone decides not to cooperate."

ONE

Prelude

Over sixty years ago, on a winding Northern California mountain highway, two men sat in a beat-up green Ford pickup as it careened down historic State Route 49. Neither of the men was aware that, on this sunny but cool October afternoon, one of the most horrific chain of events ever to occur in the state's long and storied criminal history was beginning to unfold.

The panoramic scene of lush pine forests, flower-blanketed meadows and pristine lakes scrolled past as the old pickup gained speed, weaving and lurching from side to side on the narrow, sometimes twisting, but always precipitous blacktop.

The two men, a husky, baby-faced, twenty-seven-year-old named George Boles was behind the wheel and beside him sat Emmett "Perk" Perkins, with his beady little eyes, large prominent ears and receding hairline. Perkins was a wizened gnome of a man who looked considerably older than his forty-five-years. He wore a menacing scowl that George was sure had been engraved on his pasty visage the day he was born.

As they drove, neither man paid the slightest attention nor bothered himself with a second glance at the passing scenery. This pair of self-absorbed lowlifes was concerned only with the far more sinister business at hand.

By now, George had become familiar with the larger-than-life yarns that Perkins was so fond of spinning. Perkins tells of how, as a teenage boy, he had been brought from his native Texas to California by his doting mother, and because he'd never lost his Texas persona, when his tales were told in that deep Texas drawl, the effect always seemed to add a flavor of authenticity.

George was painfully aware that the slightest hint of encouragement would launch Perk into another of his trademark narrations which would never fail to include stories of a long and wide-ranging criminal career, his boom-or-bust exploits speckled with armed robberies, burglaries, check scams, gold thefts, kidnapping and even an occasional murder. Without a sign of remorse or regret, Perkins would brag proudly—although not always truthfully—of his participation in various acts of mayhem committed against those he considered to be his own personal quarry—the "saps and suckers" of the world.

George had been there too but for a much shorter stretch of time, and although he was certainly no Boy Scout, he had yet to exhibit that same breadth of viciousness. He'd seen his share of action and now, since that last job, he could even add a killing to his resumé. He wasn't looking for trouble but he had made his bones and if that same situation should ever present itself and with no other way out, he'd have no problem doing it again.

This was the life he had consciously chosen for himself. It was a life that promised excitement and action and most importantly, if done right, would provide him with the comfortable living that no lunch-box job could offer in a hundred years.

Although he knew Perkins would probably not agree, in a rare moment of self- introspection, George mused that despite the perceived "benefits," it was also a life that would, more than likely, end badly for both.

Casting a quick, furtive glance at his stone-faced passenger, George could sense in him a kind of stiff-lipped anticipation and resolve that seemed to flow between them. His head swam with visions of adventures he was sure, lie just over the horizon; thoughts that brought a sudden rush of adrenalin and made him realize more than ever before, that this was why they did what they did. George could visualize this new world awaiting him as he traveled about in the company of men like Emmett Perkins and the man they were on their way to meet, Jack Santo.

George leaned on the accelerator with a heavy right foot and as the engine roared, the truck surged ahead, creaking and vibrating with each turn of the wheel. The wind blowing through the rolled down windows combined with the loud roar of the engine made verbal communication between the pair almost impossible.

"Where the hell is Higgins Corner anyway?" George shouted.

"It's not that far," Perkins yelled back. "We should be there in less than an hour."

"What do you figure Jack's got in mind for us this time?" George was referring to Jon Albert *Jack* Santo, the self-appointed ringleader of a group of motley misfits he had fashioned into his own gang of brigands and cutthroats. The last few jobs that Jack had sent them on, for one reason or another, had fizzled out and they had come away empty-handed. Now he had a new plan and he's called them down to his bar to discuss it.

"I hope it's something good," George said. "Man, I can sure use the money."

"Hey, Perk," George shouted over the rumbling noise of the engine while trying to make conversation. "You know anything about the gold mining history around this neck of the woods?"

"Not too much," Perkins replied. "What's to know? A lot of gold, not enough suckers. Come to think of it though, me and Jack's first job together was in this area. It was some kind of a gold deal as I recall." He thought for a moment. "But that's about it."

"Well, if you think there's a lot of gold around here now, you should have been here a hundred years ago," George said. "There was more gold in Grass Valley than there is in Fort Knox. The road we're on right now used to be called the Old Gold Rush Trail."

"Is that so?" Perkins drawled, his curiosity piqued.

Anxious to let Perk know he wasn't just some uneducated street thug, George took the opening. "This was the site of the famous Empire Gold Mine. It was the biggest, deepest, longest and, get this; the richest—fucking gold mine in the history of the world—three hundred sixty miles of tunnels, criss-crossing all over the place."

"That's pretty big, all right; so what's your point?" Perkins asked.

"Do you know how much gold they pulled out of there, Perk?"

"No, but I'm sure you're going to tell me."

"About five, six million ounces of gold. Not ore, Perk, I'm talking about pure, unadulterated gold. They say at today's market value, that would have been worth more than six billion dollars. The now animated George went on. "Six fucking billion dollars! How would you like to have a shot at some of that?"

"Yeah," Perkins replied after a moment's thought. "Looks like I was born about a hundred years too late."

George, with visions of gold bars and stacks of large denomination bills, dancing around in his brain, pushed a little heavier on the gas pedal and the truck lurched forward. Reaching into his jacket's inner pocket he brought out a pint-sized bottle of bourbon and while keeping one hand on the wheel, he somehow managed to unscrew the cap after which he took two long swigs before offering the bottle to Perkins.

Perkins angrily snatched the bottle from the startled George, and in the same sweeping motion, flung it through the open window.

"What are you—stupid?" Perkins raged over the roar of the engine. "Are you trying to get us killed?" Perkins was beginning to think this kid must have some kind of a death wish. "You're already driving like a dammed idiot! We sure as hell don't need booze to make it worse!"

George, his eyes fixed firmly on the road ahead, merely grunted and lit a cigarette.

"Perk, you worry too much, you know that? There's something you guys need to learn about me. I know how to control myself."

"Is that right?" Perkins snarled. "Just like you controlled yourself on the Hansen job, right?"

George shot a glowering glance at his passenger. "I was wondering how long it would be before you brought that up again."

"Don't sweat it, Perk," he brightened. "You're not starting to lose your nerve in your old age, are you?" he asked with a grin.

To Perkins, this kid's cocky arrogance could prove to be dangerous. Jack had even remarked about it but instead of expressing concern, to Perk's dismay, he regarded George's sometimes reckless behavior as an asset.

"Maybe this job will turn out to be our jackpot," George shouted. "I've been eyeing a slick little Chevy convertible. Sure would look nice sitting in my driveway. What're you going to do with your cut, Perk?"

"I'm going to wait until I get it before I decide what to do with it, kid," Perkins said. "I advise you to do the same."

George just shook his head at Perkins' lack of enthusiasm. "You need to get out a little more, old man. There's a whole big world out there."

In real life, while entertaining fantasies of himself as arch-desperado, George filled his regular work day, not by scheming on how to rob banks or knock over gas stations, but instead, by performing menial tasks as a lab assistant at Weimar Sanitarium, a small hospital for tuberculosis patients located about a hundred miles west of Reno.

George was a reasonably bright—some would say good-looking—wishful thinker who, before taking his current job, had drifted aimlessly up and down California in search of that elusive pot of gold. He had even tried his hand at more intellectual pursuits, at one time working as a cub reporter for a tiny weekly newspaper in San Rafael. The editor of that paper had once commented on George's short tenure as a reporter: "George didn't turn out to be a very good reporter," she recalled, "but he had a flair for excitement and he wrote the most marvelous stories. Only we couldn't print them—libel, you know."

George's acquaintanceship with Emmett Perkins began a year earlier when, during a poker game in which he had won a considerable sum of money—most of it from an unsuspecting Idaho shoe salesman who was so drunk he couldn't tell a king from a jack. After stripping the poor sap of his last nickel, George tossed him out on the street, leaving him without so much as street-car fare.

Emmett Perkins had always admired people who had the balls to kick a sucker when he was down. It warmed the cockles of his heart to see this fuzz-faced kid respond with such malevolent firmness, and he had taken an immediate liking to him.

But for right now, Perkins was still steaming over the way things had gone during the Hansen job. George knew that Perkins didn't have a whole lot of confidence in his ability to keep his cool in a tight spot and he knew also that this was a concern that, if he didn't get it fixed, could exclude him from some of the better jobs that Jack might be planning. Then again, that was the first time he'd been in a situation like that. Even the most experienced guys could lose their cool—maybe even panic—if faced with the same kind of situation.

Besides, he didn't really mean to kill the guy—the gun just kept going off and he couldn't stop it.

To Emmett Perkins, it wasn't so much that killing someone was all that big a deal. He had nothing against killing someone. It's just that this was one time it didn't need to happen, especially when there was a witness left to tell about it. All George should have done to stop Hansen from running out the back door was just cold-cock him. He didn't need to put six bullets into him. Not only was that totally unnecessary—it was stupid.

Only a month before the Hansen fiasco, Boles and Perkins had done the Andy Colner job over in Folsom and that one got screwed up, too. Santo had somehow got wind that Colner, a big time gold dealer who, had a bad habit of hiding large amounts of cash and gold around his house. He had sent Perkins and Boles in to find it and get it.

So after strapping Mr. and Mrs. Colner to a couple of straight backed chairs and while Mrs. Colner watched, Perkins burned the bottoms of the old man's feet with lighted matches until the pain got so unbearable he finally coughed up four grand in cash and gold. They were all feeling pretty good about that four grand score until Jack learned through newspaper accounts that the "cagey old bastard," as Jack had called him, had snookered them by stashing another twenty grand underneath the house. Jack still hasn't come down from the ceiling after that one.

* * * *

No one had ever confused Emmett Perkins with being a choirboy. He began his nearly thirty-year criminal career in 1924, when he was arrested for stealing a car. Instead of jail, authorities placed him in a hospital where he could undergo treatment for a venereal disease. He promptly escaped but was quickly recaptured, returned for treatment, and released six months later. Within eight months he was back in the slammer for stealing another car. At the state's reformatory for juvenile delinquents, even though he had exhibited a propensity for anti-social behavior, Perkins was now becoming an expert at gaming the system and he was paroled a year later.

He was sentenced to ten years in San Quentin after being arrested in 1929 on an armed robbery charge only to be paroled again in 1930. Two years later he was back in prison—this time it was Folsom, the state's only maximum security facility—doing a twenty-year jolt for his part in a $53,000 bank robbery.

After serving fewer than ten years of that twenty-year sentence, he was inexplicably paroled in 1942, only to be returned to San Quentin three years later on weapons charges. He was paroled yet again in 1950 and although having been involved in a steady string of car thefts, burglaries, strong-armed robberies, home invasions and assaults, Emmett Perkins, since 1950 had somehow managed to stay out of prison—obviously not because his behavior had changed, but only because he hadn't been caught.

Den of Thieves

Jack Santo had been the de facto owner of the Higgins Corner Bar and Café since 1945, but because of a strictly enforced California law that prohibits the granting of bar and liquor licenses to convicted felons—which of course, Santo definitely was—the establishment had to be sold and licensed to Harriet Henson, his paramour, common-law wife and sometime partner-in-crime. It was at Higgins Corner where Jack and Harriet first met when she wandered in one day looking for a job.

Harriet was an unsophisticated twenty-six-year-old naïf who had been completely swept away by this brash, swaggering man of the world. Fantasies of a movie script kind of life filled with adventure and romantic moonlit nights had somehow morphed into the reality of a frenetic, run-for-your-life existence, where today it might be champagne and filet mignon, but tomorrow, it would be back to weenies and beans.

Harriet did a reasonably competent job of managing the bar's day-to-day operation but there was never a question as to who was the actual boss. Harriet was completely under Jack's thumb and could always be counted on to do exactly as she was told whenever he told her to do it.

As things would turn out, *The Corner* became the perfect setting in which to transact illicit gold deals or to plot other nefarious activities. Its clientele consisted mainly of local mine workers, loggers and an occasional fishing or deer hunting party.

Jack Santo worked behind the bar, at least on those days when he worked at all, which wasn't all that often. A hand-lettered sign tacked against the back bar announced: "Your host, Jack Santo - nightly at the cash register", but because the cigarette smoke was so thick, few were actually able to read it.

Jack didn't mind putting in a shift every now and then since, as bartender, other than wash and polish glasses, open beer bottles, fill pitchers with beer, or shake bar dice with a customer for his drink, the bartender didn't really have a lot to do. In an establishment like *The Corner* it wasn't very often that he'd be asked to serve anything more complicated than a shot and a beer.

The green Ford pickup pulled into the gravel covered parking lot that fronted the Higgins Corner Bar & Café, a creaky, ramshackle wooden structure that could have been lifted right out of an old Western movie lot. All that was needed to complete the picture was a couple of hitching posts. With its somewhat shabby countenance and weather-beaten front sign, notable only for the missing "C" from the word *Café, The Corner* was definitely not the kind of place where busloads of tourists were apt to stop off for a bite to eat or to enjoy a martini or two.

The two men stepped through the dusty entrance and once inside, hesitated momentarily while their eyes became adjusted to the cavernous darkness. George squinted through the dim light until he could almost make out the tall figure behind the bar.

"Hey, Jack," he called out, oblivious to the groups of startled customers who looked up to see who was intruding on their quiet conversations. "How about a little service here?"

Recognizing George, Jack smiled broadly and yelled back, "Hey, George, it's good to see you." Then, as Perkins emerged through the smoky darkness, Jack shouted, "Perk! Glad you guys made it. How the hell you been?"

Instinctively, he grabbed a couple of frosted mugs from the cold box under the back bar and after placing them one by one under the big Lucky Lager tap handle, he watched the glasses overflow with cold, foamy, amber liquid.

Jack Santo was a bigger-than-average guy: ex-professional prize fighter, ex-rodeo and ranch hand roughneck and ex-garage mechanic whose mere presence in some circles could be more than a little bit intimidating. At fifty-two, with a six-foot, two-inch frame, mostly muscle and a deep stentorian voice, he could dominate a conversation simply by being a part of it. The fact that he wore large black horn-rimmed glasses and sported a pencil-thin moustache didn't in the slightest detract from this aura of authority; in fact it was an advantage he would often exploit to good effect.

Throughout his adult life, Jack had always rejected the idea of working for someone else. His aversion to being on anyone's payroll other than his own was evidenced by the string of businesses in which he had been engaged, most of them—for whatever reason—ending in failure. At age sixteen, after completing the eighth grade, he dropped out of school and traveled around the West and even into Mexico, finding work as a ranch hand or sometimes as a mechanic's helper. But there were other occasions when, no doubt tempted by the allure of what looked like easy money, he found himself drifting into a life of petty crime.

In the early 1920s, a keen interest in automobiles had led Jack Santo into his first business venture—an automobile repair shop in San Francisco, and while it was proving to be marginally successful, his wife had been taken extremely ill, forcing him to sell the business and move to New York where she would be able to obtain specialized medical care. When, after two months, she unexpectedly died, he returned to Southern California where he became the owner-operator of the Santo Stucco Paint and Roofing Company in Pasadena.

Still being dogged by bad luck and with frustrations mounting exponentially, he was forced to sell the business when a competitor reported a previous felony conviction which he had failed to disclose on his contractor's license application and because of which, he lost that license and consequently, his business.

In 1940 he purchased a Northern California hog and cattle ranch but went completely broke three years later when the hog market collapsed. Shortly after that unfortunate circumstance, his seven-hundred acre ranch was totally destroyed in a devastating fire. However this time, all his losses were covered—with money to spare—thanks to a recently purchased insurance policy. At that point, whether due to the vagaries of fate or just plain arson, Jack Santo's fortunes began to change for the better.

Using the proceeds from the insurance settlement, he purchased the Higgins Corner Bar & Café and bought a controlling interest in the Big Chief gold mine. He quickly discovered that there was more money to be made in high-grading and other gold-related larcenies than in just digging the gold out of the rocks. Thus, Jack Santo began "earning" a living by cheating, robbing—even killing—when and if it became necessary.

Emmett Perkins and Jack Santo had first hooked up several years earlier when, after meeting at Perkins' illegal poker room, they pulled off their first criminal collaboration—a gold high-grading venture. Their association gradually evolved into a kind of pecking order where the brutishly dominant Santo would give the orders and his disciple Perkins, a man devoid of even a trace of moral compunction, would dutifully carry them out.

On that day when the weak-minded and conscienceless Emmett Perkins crossed paths with Jack Santo, no less a predatory criminal sociopath in his own right, the perfect criminal storm was born. The coming together of these two individuals of disparate criminal backgrounds and whose crimes were of almost no newsworthiness in themselves would be the forerunner of events so utterly appalling, they would rattle the foundations of the California criminal justice system.

The men made small talk while they polished off their beers and after the final couple of swallows, Jack pointed through the smoky din toward the far corner of the room.

"Grab us a booth over there, Perk."

He turned to Harriet who had just walked out of the back office. "Take the bar for a while, will ya, toots? I have to talk to these guys."

"Sure, Jack," Harriet said as she nodded in their direction.

"Hello, boys," she smiled. "Long time no see. How you boys been?"

"Been just fine, Harriet," Perkins answered. "I see you're still looking good."

George smiled half-heartedly but said nothing. "Say hello, George," Jack admonished. "She's not mad at you anymore."

Jack was referring to the torrent of unkind words Harriet had directed at Boles after he had single-handedly screwed up the Hansen robbery. Harriet was the driver on that job and had been expecting a full share of the proceeds. She didn't appreciate it when her money flow is interrupted through the sheer ineptitude of the players. Not a dime for all their effort and things only got worse. A week later, after being hospitalized while trying to recover from wounds suffered in the botched robbery attempt, Edmund Hansen had died.

Harriet's common-law relationship with Jack had introduced her to a life of, if not luxury, certainly one she found much more comfortable than anything she'd known before. As she gradually became involved in Jack's shadier activities, she found that, distasteful as those activities may have been, the money and all the nice things she could buy with it made that distaste a lot easier to swallow.

Jack removed two frosty pitchers from the cold box and after filling them with beer grabbed a cold mug for himself and headed across the room to join George and Perkins in the booth. Peering through the smoke, he satisfied himself that unless a would-be eavesdropper was actually sitting in the same booth, their discussion would be safe from prying ears. This was one conversation that would require complete privacy. Jack sat down, filled all the glasses and came directly to the point.

"I have something good," he began.

"Not like the last one, I hope," George mumbled, eliciting Jack's icy glare.

"You can always pass, kid," Jack said. George understood—the message was clear—they would do the job whether he was in or out.

"Pickings have been kind of lean lately," Jack bemoaned. "It just seems like these days, good scores are getting harder to come by."

"I guess the high-grading business isn't what it used to be, huh, Jack?" George asked.

"Over the years I've made a lot of money high-grading gold," Jack said, "so I don't want to knock it. But you're right. The low price of gold and a lot of new people coming into the business who don't know what they're doing have really put a crimp into the business."

The term *high-grading* had originally referred to the buying and selling of illegally obtained gold and even though the high-grader may have been aware of the gold's dubious provenance, he was willing—sometimes even eager—to deal, but only at a price that was significantly lower than that of the prevailing market. Over the years, the phrase had been corrupted into meaning almost any activity that had anything to do with the illegal gold trade, including salting mines, stealing it, cheating people out of it, robbing it from other high-graders, smuggling it across international borders or selling worthless mining stocks. For a good part of Jack Santo's life, he had earned a considerable income from his activities in all of the above.

High grading, when applied to gold mining, has a long and storied history usually shared by old-time sourdoughs whenever the California Gold Rush comes under discussion. In the 1850s, gold mining companies would employ crews of miners to go down into the shafts and dig the gold ore out of the hard rock walls. Frequently, the miner's means of supplementing his pay envelope—the bulk of which may have been lost in a payday poker game or borrowed from the company as an advance against his next paycheck—he would often slip a few of those rich scrapings into his shirt pocket or dinner bucket to keep for himself. Of course he would rationalize his thievery as just a way of "evening the score" with the boss.

Rumors of employees bringing home fortunes in gold in this manner abounded, and eventually the mining companies finally began to wise up when it was pointed out to them that they could be losing thousands—maybe even millions of dollars. *Changing Rooms* were installed as adjuncts to the mines. Miners would be required to change into company issued uniforms—uniforms of course without pockets or other potential hiding places.

Historians write of ingenious—some would say diabolical—methods the miners would employ to circumvent the companies' *changing room* tactic. They would stash the pilfered ore in double-bottom dinner buckets or they'd sometimes conceal it in wads of chewing tobacco. They might fill their corncob pipes with gold shavings. One miner told of picking up the gold-laden ore scrapings that came off the mine's walls and mixing it in with the piles of manure deposited by the skip (or tram) pulling donkeys and once the load had been brought to the surface, the manure would be screened, separated, and after being extracted, the gold would then be fenced to the high-grader.

"I'm not talking about gold this time." Jack had their attention. "I'm talking about cold, hard cash—spendable."

"OK," he continued looking directly at Perkins. "This is the deal. You remember Larry Shea, my long time hunting buddy down in Chester?"

"Yeah." Perkins recalled. "He's the guy we sold that grey Olds to sometime back—that weasel contractor guy." It was a not very subtle dig to let George know what he really thought of Jack's friend.

"Does he still have that car?"

"Yeah, that's the guy and no, we had to get rid of it. He needed papers and I couldn't come up with any. Shame, too. Damn nice car," Jack said, ignoring Perkins' "weasel" remark.

"So you had to give him back his dough?" Perkins asked. It was a terrible thing, Perkins thought, anytime money had to be returned, especially to someone like Larry Shea.

"Nah, no problem. I just jacked him another one." Jack smiled proudly before turning dead serious. He lowered his voice.

"Okay, listen up," he began. "I've known Larry a long time and I know he can be trusted. He's one of us." He looked around to be sure no one else was listening.

"Larry's been telling me about these two guys he knows that go around packing big bundles of dough. Now remember, we're talking about the town of Chester. Besides it being a good hunting area, it's also logging country and they got this big lumber mill up there."

George was all ears. "Somewhere in this story, you're going to tell us how we end up with all those big bundles of dough, right, Jack?"

"Keep your shirt on, kid, and just pay attention," Jack responded.

"Here's the deal. Each one of these guys owns a big grocery store. In fact they own the only two grocery stores in the whole town. And they do a ton of business, especially when it's payday at the mill. That means they need to keep a lot of cash on hand so they can cash all those mill workers' paychecks."

"Okay, Jack, I think I get the picture," Perkins interjected in his deep Texas drawl. "A small hick town, two grocery stores and a barrel full of money. Now how do we get it? Are you suggesting a couple of stickups?"

"No," Jack replied, just getting warmed up. "Not a stickup like you're thinking," he said as his audience of two leaned in closer.

"Alright, now listen to this, guys. The nearest bank is in Westwood, twelve or thirteen miles down the road from Chester." Jack could feel the anticipation, particularly in George, start to build.

"Next Friday is payday at the mill so, like always, he's going to have to make a run to the bank in Westwood to get the dough to cash those paychecks. Now I've been on that road. It goes right through the woods, not too many people around." He paused to allow his portrayal of the robbery scene to sink in. While George was about to come out of his chair with excitement, Jack sensed that Perk was not completely sold at this point. He picked up the pace.

"So he goes to the bank in Westwood, gets the dough and heads back to Chester."

"And that's when we hit him, right?" George exclaimed.

"Yeah, George, that's when we hit him," Jack continued, hoping that Perk was now convinced. "It'll be like taking candy from a baby."

"Glory and hallelujah!" George was barely able to control his exuberance. "We're talking a twofer—the daily fucking double!"

"Easy there, pardner," Jack admonished, doing his best to avoid attracting attention. "Try to keep it down."

"How much are we talking about?" Perkins asked somewhat dubiously.

"I'm not sure we can do both," Jack said, responding to George's outburst. "It may be a matter of logistics. It'll probably have to be one or the other."

Turning to Perkins, he said, "Larry says that when these guys come back from the bank, they're loaded. He says they're packing anywhere from five to ten grand."

"Okay, Jack, lay it all out for us." Perkins knew that at times Jack could be very persuasive, but today, that wasn't going to be good enough. He wasn't going to let Jack talk him into another one of his half-ass ideas until all the details get worked out beforehand.

The problem with the last two disasters was simply a lack of planning. He was not about to make that mistake again.

Jack looked around at the dozen or so patrons who were still milling about and after satisfying himself that no one was paying the slightest attention to what appeared to be three deer hunters just having a few beers and swapping stories, he cleared his throat and continued.

"We know that next Friday is payday and we know there's going be a big bunch of cash traveling down that road," he said. "I need to get more details from Larry, so Harriet and I will be taking a hunting trip up to Chester. We'll drive up maybe Wednesday or Thursday and stay at Larry's. You guys will show up early Friday morning. In the meantime I'll have the job cased. We'll hook up at Larry's, do the job, and before anyone knows we're there, we'll be long gone with the dough."

Perkins was unimpressed. "You mean we're talking about a job just a little over a week away and you haven't even got the details of the thing worked out yet?"

This, thought Perkins, was typical of the haphazard way most of their jobs were planned and executed. It was clear to him that Jack never put enough thought into these things and because of that, something always went haywire—something he hadn't planned for. And that would have to change. He resolved to himself that they wouldn't make the same mistakes again. This time, he smiled smugly to himself, there would be no witnesses.

Questions swirled in Perkins mind. "Maybe we ought to give it a little more thought," he said to Jack. "Like for instance, what's the situation with the cops? And how come these guys don't believe in armored cars? Or armed guards?"

His cornbread drawl had become noticeably more pronounced as his anxiety level rose. "See, Jack, there's a lot of stuff ya'll are going to need to find out. This time I want to know how much cash we're actually talking about; how is it protected and how do we get away?"

"Larry knows all that stuff," Jack assured him. "He's been watching and he's got it pretty well figured out."

Perkins studied Jack closely as George leaned back in his seat and lit a cigarette. Was this going to be another comedy of errors like the last two jobs?

"Who's going to do this job, Jack? Are you in this time or is it just going to be me and Boles again?"

"Yeah, I'm in. It's going to be me, you, Boles and Larry."

"Hot damn," exclaimed George, rubbing his hands together as Jack turned and waved to Harriet.

"What can I get you?" she asked. "Another pitcher?"

"Bring us over a fresh bottle of Crown and three shot glasses," Jack said, grinning at his companions. "I think it's time to do a little celebrating."

Harriet returned in minutes with the bottle and glasses, and after placing a glass in front of each of the three men, she proceeded to fill them. As Jack and George lifted their glasses to offer a toast, Perkins waved his away.

"Not for me," he told her. "I got enough with all this beer. Thanks just the same."

Perk's aversion to alcohol had always been a source of amusement for Jack. Here was a guy who had done every crime in the book and probably some that hadn't even been catalogued, yet he couldn't bring himself to take a celebratory drink.

"Well, in that case," Harriet said, "I don't mind if I do." She picked up Perkins' glass. "I don't know what we're drinking to, but whatever it is, count me in," she said as she downed the contents with a single swallow.

Harriet returned to the bar and Perkins turned to George. "Looks like we got us a job, Georgie boy, and this time the boss is going to go with us just to make sure you don't screw it up again."

George took Perkins' needling good-naturedly, much to Jack's relief. Since there already seemed to be issues between Perkins and Larry, it wouldn't help matters to have George and Perk at odds with each other too.

"Nobody's going to get hurt if we do this right," Jack said. "We pull the guy over, relieve him of his money sack and we're on our way. I've worked this out a thousand times in my head and I don't see it any other way. It's clean as a whistle."

"Nobody gets hurt," George echoed. "I like it."

"Yeah," Perkins mumbled as they filed out the door into the bright sunlight. "Nobody gets hurt," then adding ominously to himself, "unless someone decides not to cooperate."

TWO

Plot

The year 1952 was a banner year for many reasons—some good, some not so good. America would elect war hero Dwight D. Eisenhower as its new president and in the same year across the pond in England, a young new queen was crowned.

Joseph Stalin was ruling the Soviet Union with an iron fist, Winston Churchill was England's prime minister, Eva *Evita* Peron died and Albert Schweitzer won a Nobel Peace Prize.

History's first hydrogen bomb was detonated in 1952 and though most Americans showed little interest before, during or since, America's fortunes of war in Korea had begun to improve; Joe DiMaggio had retired the previous year and yet the New York Yankees, for the fourth year in a row, won the World Series. For his masterful book *The Caine Mutiny,* Herman Wouk won a Pulitzer Prize; Rocky Marciano knocked out Jersey Joe Walcott to become the World's Heavyweight Champion; *Ozzie and Harriet* and *Howdy Doody* were the nation's favorite television fare, and in 1952 a loaf of bread cost sixteen cents. It was a time when a brand new, two-door Buick sedan would have set you back a cool $2280, regular gasoline was nineteen cents a gallon at the pump, men's sports shirts were selling at Sears & Roebuck for $3.66 and in 1952, nobody outside the state of Mississippi had ever heard of a truck driver by the name of Elvis Presley.

Thousands of young servicemen had returned from two debilitating wars to pick up their lives and to start new families or—thanks to the newly enacted GI Bill of Rights—complete their educations that had been so rudely interrupted by war.

Many would grab their share of the American Dream by purchasing a new home for "$99 down and $100 a month" and again, thanks to the GI Bill, that home would be a comfortable three bedroom, two bath dwelling and it would be located in the new American phenomenon they called *suburbia.*

But not all Americans were benefiting from the country's newfound euphoria. During those same post-war years, black Americans—*Negroes,* in the vernacular of the times—in some areas continued to be victims of virulent racism.

Devil's Tunes

Deer hunting season was that time of year when one could expect Jack Santo to show up in Chester to do a little business, but it was mainly a time to hunt and on these annual occasions he could always count on his good friends Larry and Lucille to act as hosts.

Jack Santo and Larry Shea had first met back in 1945 when, as hunting enthusiasts, they participated in the same goose-hunting expedition. Since that day their friendship, strengthened by mutual business interests, had become closer over the years. After Jack had become involved in a home-building business in and around his hometown of Auburn, he chose Larry Shea as his building contractor, reasoning that since Shea seemed to have the right business contacts, he would provide Jack with a much needed competitive advantage. At the end of the war, building materials such as plywood, nails and other manufactured goods, though not officially rationed, were very hard to come by. A builder or developer would go to extraordinary lengths to develop his business and personal relationships, most of which tended to ebb and flow according to the business climate of the moment. But be that as it may, Jack's friendship with Larry Shea seemed a little more genuine than that of his other acquaintances, most of whom he regarded as no more than useful idiots.

The unusual feature of this particular trip to Chester was its true purpose and the fact that Harriet would be there with him for the actual hit. Jack had always been slow to trust people—even someone as close to him as was Harriet—because he knew from bitter experience how fleeting these kinds of relationships could be and the

18

undying love that one may profess for you today, for the flimsiest of reasons, could turn to sheer hatred tomorrow.

While it was true that although Harriet would usually share in Jack's ill-gotten gains, Jack knew that without her active participation, she probably could never be charged with taking part in an actual job and that's what worried him.

He envisioned a morning when he might forget to put the seat down on the toilet and that would be the final affront. In Jack Santo's mind, there existed the real possibility that the day would come when Harriet would see herself as the proverbial woman scorned whose fury could be best vented by spilling her guts to the cops.

As a kind of insurance policy, he had decided that his best course of action would be to keep her involved just enough to guarantee her silence and to have her actually take an active role, similar to the Hansen job. The other guys might not like it, but Jack wanted Harriet in on the action because that would make her as guilty as the rest of them. Now all he needed to do is tell her.

It wasn't until Wednesday morning that he bothered to inform her that she would be accompanying him on this trip to Chester, meaning of course, that it would be up to her to find reliable fill-ins for both of them at the *Corner.* She was caught completely by surprise when he notified her that they would be spending the weekend with Larry and Lucille and they would be leaving early tomorrow morning.

His words, "Do what you have to do," to Harriet meant simply that she must not only attend to all the little operational details at the bar; she must make sure that all the necessary gear was packed, including an appropriate wardrobe not only for Jack but for herself as well. She would have to see that there was sufficient gas in the truck and of course he expected her, at every moment of the day or night, to be at his beck and call while seeing to his every creature comfort.

On Wednesday afternoon he called Harriet to remind her: "Grab two or three bottles of Crown Royal from behind the bar. Don't want to forget the really important stuff."

"My God," Harriet mumbled to herself. "Maybe he'd like me to stick a broom up my ass so I can sweep the floor while I walk around."

"What?" a customer, overhearing her remark, asked.

"Nothing, Marvin. Just thinking out loud."

Harriet Henson was the proud owner of two quarter-horses which Jack liked to take along when setting out on his hunting excursions. Hunting deer from the backs of horses was seen by most veteran huntsmen as the moral equivalent of shooting goldfish in a rain barrel. They would be quick to point out that anyone who engaged in such unsportsmanlike behavior belonged in an arcade shooting gallery; certainly not hunting wild game in a California forest.

But by Jack Santo's twisted reasoning, being able to keep up with the fast-moving deer by chasing them down and shooting them from his perch atop his horse was exactly the kind of an "edge" he had to have and he didn't give a rat's ass whether anybody else called it poor sportsmanship or not.

During the hunting season Harriet kept her horses stabled and pastured at a private ranch on the outskirts of Chester even though her two-horse trailer was garaged almost 150 miles away in Nevada City. Since this would probably be their final trip of the year to Chester, it would be their last opportunity to retrieve the horses and return them to their winter stables in Grass Valley. This meant that before hitting the road for Chester, they would have to stop off at the garage in Nevada City and pick up the trailer.

Still unaware of Jack's actual plans and that a hunting weekend was merely a pretext to mask its true purpose, Harriet made a mental note to herself to not forget the tags. She recalled how, on one of their previous hunting excursions, they had driven over a hundred miles before discovering his deer tags were out of date. The ensuing verbal abuse she had been forced to endure as a result was still fresh in her mind and she now prudently kept a checklist: Area maps, binoculars, rain gear, cold-weather clothes, extra ammunition, bug repellent, scent control soap, range finder, batteries, and of course, valid licenses and tags.

With the Nevada City detour, it would be at least a three hour drive to Chester and Jack wanted to arrive before dark. If this job was going to happen on Friday, there would be a lot to talk about and it would be better if they had that conversation earlier in the evening when, presumably, they would all be relatively sober. He would also need to find the right opportunity to bring Harriet in on the scheme.

"F'chrissakes, Harriet! Will you hurry up?" Jack shouted at her from the truck's front seat as she struggled to get the last piece of luggage onto the bed of the pick-up. Harriet had become used to his slave master persona, and how he enjoyed treating her as though she were one of the hired help. Even as far back as the beginning of their common-law relationship, Jack had always regarded her as little more than a piece of the furniture.

But those days were coming to an end she promised herself and there would soon come a day when, after filling herself with enough booze, she'd find the courage to tell him to shove it. That day would come—but not today.

Jack glanced at the gas gauge. "I hope you remembered to put gas in the tank," he said as Harriet climbed into the passenger seat.

"Yeah," she said, rolling her eyes. "I gassed up this morning before you got up." Harriet glared at him for a long moment. "Do you want me to wipe your ass, too?" She thought it but she didn't say it.

Harriet had been born in 1923 in Butte, Montana of devoutly religious fundamentalist parents. Her earliest childhood memories consisted mainly of how she, along with her four sisters and two brothers, had been forbidden to smoke, drink alcohol and utter the words "darn" or "heck." They were not permitted to attend school dances or even go to movies. It was a home in which a deck of cards was something to be shunned as the *devil's playthings* and the only kind of music they were allowed to enjoy was the raucous, hand-clapping, foot-stomping, *old-time-religion* variety which boomed in ear-splitting volume from the store-front church attended by her family every Sunday morning.

Harriet's parents at one time had seriously entertained dreams of their daughter becoming a Bible-pounding circus tent preacher, traveling from town-to-town on her God-ordained mission to save lost souls. They were convinced that Harriet was divinely destined to someday follow in the footsteps of that late, fire breathing radio preacher, Aimee Semple McPherson.

As preposterous as such an idea might sound now, there was no doubt in Harriet's mind that if the life of an itinerant fire-and-brimstone preacher had been her chosen profession, she would have been a damned good one.

She was married in 1943 to Calvin Henson, an alcoholic ne'er-do-well who had never been able to hang onto a job. About a year into the marriage, a pregnancy had ended in a miscarriage which then rendered her unable to have children; hence, the marriage produced no offspring and soon they divorced.

At one time—probably much longer ago than she'd be willing to admit—Harriet had been an attractive woman—a "hot number"—as Jack liked to brag to his friends. A tall, statuesque brunette, her soft, pleasant facial features would have appealed to any red-blooded male. But the years of hard living had taken their toll, causing her to appear years older than her actual age.

To Harriet, the day when she had first laid eyes on Jack Santo now seemed so long ago and far away. She often reflected on the train wreck her life had become since he had entered the picture. For some inexplicable reason for which she was at a complete loss to explain, he's been able to exert a powerful hold on her, making her do things that often are against her better judgment or even her will. Their relationship quickly became a real life reenactment of the classic DuMaurier novel, *Trilby* in which she plays the role of Trilby and Jack her Svengali.

Two hours after leaving Grass Valley, they exited the freeway at Chico and after successfully negotiating the rush-hour-traffic, they parked behind the Oasis Bar & Grill.

"Hey," he said, shaking Harriet's shoulder. "Wake up. Pit stop."

Harriet, visibly irritated at the rude awakening, stretched and looked around.

"Where are we?"

"This is Chico. I was thinking you could use a drink," he said.

"A drink?" she grumbled. "I don't need a drink. What I could use is some more sleep."

"C'mon. I need to talk to you. I figured it might just as well be over a drink."

Harriet continued to glower as Jack climbed out of the truck. She adjusted the rear-view mirror before completing a quick make-up repair while Jack was already heading out across the parking lot.

Without waiting for her to catch up, he started for the bar's rear entrance as she hurried to join him, and upon entering, even though there were two empty stools at the bar, he grabbed her arm and led her to a table in the farthest, darkest corner of the room.

The pounding blues strains of Lloyd Price's *Lawdy Miss Clawdy* wafted through the smoky room while a couple of loud-mouthed pool-playing cowboys whooped it up between missed shots. Jack was reasonably satisfied that the clatter and commotion would make it virtually impossible for anyone to eavesdrop. To put Harriet in a compliant mood, they'd first have a couple of drinks.

He went to the bar and returned to the table carrying a highball, a shot of whiskey and a mug of beer. Harriet always marveled at his ability to carry so many drinks without using a tray and yet not spill so much as a drop. As a waitress, it was a skill she had never been able to master.

After carefully placing the drinks in the center of the table, he pushed the high-ball over to Harriet, scooted his chair closer to the table and lit a cigarette.

After first clearing his throat, he began: "I've been wanting to talk to you about this hunting trip." Harriet had seen this act before. Jack doesn't consult with her about anything unless he wants something. She was more than sure that he wouldn't be asking for her opinion if he wasn't expecting to get something in return.

He motioned for her to lean in a little closer and warily, she complied.

"I haven't been completely honest with you about this hunting trip," he said.

"So what's new about that?" she answered, only half-jokingly.

"Well, what I mean is, I haven't told you everything about why we're going up to Chester."

He glanced around to be sure he wasn't being overheard before continuing. "We're not going to hunt deer," he said, then quickly added, "Although if we get the chance, we'll certainly do some of that, too."

Harriet squirmed in her chair, waiting for the other shoe to fall. "Get to the point, Jack. If there's something you want me to do, just come out with it."

"Let's have another drink." He rose and walked to the bar, again returning in a few minutes with a second round.

"Now where was I?" he asked, as he gathered his thoughts. "Okay," he said. "I'm going to level with you. We're going up to Chester to do a robbery." He paused, staring into her eyes while draining his glass. "There's a lot of money in this job and I may need your help."

He waited for a reaction and it wasn't long in coming but it wasn't what he'd expected.

"So what's the big deal? Did you think I'd be shocked to learn that you need my help?" She took a swig of her drink. "As long as you're not planning to kill someone." She looked at him uncertainly. "You're not, are you?" she ask with just a trace of apprehension in her voice.

"Nah," he assured her. "We're just going to jack this guy after he leaves the bank with a sack full of dough. We're just going to relieve him of it. Nobody's going to get hurt."

Harriet nodded. "Okay. Is that all you wanted to tell me? I don't know why you were so worried. You know I'd do just about anything for you." She thought for a moment. "That's the trouble with you and me, Jack. I'd do anything for you, but you . . ." The unfinished sentence dangled in the air.

Jack was confidently aware of his ability to con Harriet into doing just about anything he wanted her to do, but he failed to realize that, as much as he was using her to further his own agenda, she was using him for the financial benefits that in doing so would accrue to her. It was strictly a trade-off. She loved him, it was true, but her willingness to absorb the constant verbal abuse that always came with the perks would last only as long as the flow of cash continued.

"I what?" he asked, somewhat annoyed. "What were you going to say?"

"Never mind." She gathered up her cigarette pack from the table and swallowed the last few drops in her glass. "Maybe we ought to get going."

Jack stood up as Harriet headed for the door. Right behind her on his way out, he stopped at the bar, ordered another drink, chug-a-lugged it, and caught up with her in the parking lot.

Easing through what was left of the rush hour traffic, Jack found the on-ramp to Route 32 North and to the accompaniment of the squeaks and groans and metal-on-metal racket of the horse trailer being towed behind them, he pointed the truck in the direction of Chester, some fifty miles up the road.

A Sea of Troubles

Sometime around seven o'clock on the Thursday evening of October 8, 1952, residents of the tiny mountain village of Chester looked on with amused curiosity as a beat-up '49 International red pickup truck towing an empty two-horse trailer rumbled noisily through their otherwise quiet streets before parking in the driveway of the home of Lawrence *Larry* Shea. As they drove up, they could see Larry and Lucille clearing a large pile of firewood that had just been delivered that afternoon. His arms loaded with logs, Larry looked up as he seemed mildly surprised to see them. Walking over to the truck he exclaimed:

"Hey! It's good to see you guys. We weren't expecting you until tomorrow." Shea was a forty-six-year-old building contractor who had met Lucille during a visit to his home state of Iowa the previous year. She was an attractive, forty-one-year, old divorcee and it was not at all difficult for Jack to see why Larry had been immediately smitten.

After a brief courtship Larry had convinced her to relocate to Chester while they waited for her divorce to become finalized and although they were not yet legally married, she moved into his Chester home.

"We thought we'd get here tonight so we could get an early start in the morning." He said, sliding out of the cab as Harriet walked around from the other side.

"Looks like we're just in time to give you a hand with all that wood," Jack said to Lucille.

"Good idea," Lucille happily agreed.

With the aid of two wheelbarrows, the two couples hauled the wood to the lean-to shed at the rear of their ranch-style bungalow after which Larry ushered them inside through the kitchen door.

Larry led the way into the living room, and while Jack threw himself on the sofa, Larry stoked the smoldering fire and added another log. Lucille produced four glasses from the kitchen cupboard into which she poured four generous drinks. Jack immediately noticed that the bottle was now nearly empty. He called out to Harriet who had just made herself comfortable on the big living room easy chair.

"Go out there and get those two bottles of whiskey out of the truck," he barked. Harriet dutifully obeyed, grumbling quietly to herself as she headed for the door.

"Dumb broad," Jack mumbled. He drained his glass with a single swallow and waited impatiently for Harriet to return.

Harriet slammed the truck's door with a loud bang and with a bottle of Crown Royal in each hand, started back to the house. "One of these days," she muttered under her breath.

No woman she's ever known, she reflected—except maybe her mother—has ever had to tolerate such a degrading kind of emotional abuse from her husband. She couldn't help but notice the mutually respectful interaction that passed between Larry and Lucille. Their relationship was so different than hers and Jack's.

In a moment of wishful thinking she mused, maybe Jack notices it too. Maybe he'll take a cue from Larry. Maybe watching Larry and Lucille will make him see the error of his ways and maybe he'll try to emulate his friend and then maybe he'll start treating her with a little respect.

And maybe the tooth fairy will stop by tonight.

She placed both bottles on the table and returned to her easy chair while Jack poured the drinks. They sat around the crackling fire drinking and exchanging small talk but soon the conversation turned to more serious matters. Jack wanted to discuss Friday's job and after deciding that their target would be Frank Locatell, owner of one of the town's supermarkets, he turned to Larry.

"This guy we're going to hit, Larry—what can you tell me about him?"

"No need to sweat, Jack. Tomorrow we can go out on the road and I'll show you everything you need to know."

Jack couldn't quite put his finger on it but he noticed that Larry seemed to be preoccupied. Whatever was bugging him, he just wanted to make sure that it wasn't something that would end up throwing a monkey wrench into their plans.

"What the hell is bothering you?" Jack recalled how a few weeks ago, Larry said he was in some kind of trouble with the law; something about stolen guns and a robbery. "Is it that gun thing? Are you still answering questions about those hot guns?"

He looked at Lucille, not sure whether or not she had been brought into Larry's confidence.

"It's okay," Larry said. "We can talk. Lucille pretty much knows what's going on." He lit a cigarette.

"Yeah, the damn thing just won't go away. It's getting to be the talk of the town. People are starting to look at me now kind of funny. It's almost like they're afraid that if they're not careful, I'll steal the gold right out of their teeth."

Larry Shea, despite owning what, to all outward appearances, was a successful and legitimate contracting business, had nevertheless earned a reputation around town as a fast shuffle type; a guy not averse to cutting a shady deal if he thought it might enhance his bank account.

"I never did hear the full story on that, Larry. Maybe it's time you told me about it?" Jack prompted.

"Well," Larry said, "what happened was I bought a bunch of guns from some guy I didn't really know. He offered me a really good deal but the problem is, it turned out the guns were part of that Bremer Hardware Store robbery over in Yuba City a couple weeks ago."

Jack listened, but with more than a little bit of skepticism.

"C'mon, Larry. Are you trying to tell me that you didn't know those guns were hot?"

"Well," Larry hedged. "I kind of suspected they were, but I didn't know for sure."

Jack shook his head and frowned. "I don't think anyone's going to believe you. If you can't come up with a bill of sale, they could hit you with a 'receiving stolen property' charge. Hell, they could even try to pin an 'aiding and abetting in an armed robbery' on you too." He added, "That's a big time felony, Lar."

"What do you think I ought to do?" Larry was clearly worried.

"Hell, it's not the end of the world. I've beaten a lot of stolen property raps. All you have to do is phony up a bill of sale. Works every time."

"But it gets worse, Jack."

"What do you mean, 'it gets worse?'"

Larry refilled their glasses as Lucille prodded: "Tell him what's really bothering you, Larry." She looked at Jack. "Receiving stolen property isn't the half of it," she said.

"Yeah, okay," Larry said. "The worse part of it, Jack, is the guys who did that Bremer Hardware job held the people at gunpoint."

Jack shot a quizzical look at Lucille and then at Larry. "So what? That doesn't have anything to do with you. . . does it?"

Larry fidgeted and lit another cigarette. "Well, yeah, not really, except there was a witness there who identified me as the guy who was holding the gun."

Jack nearly choked on his drink. "Whoa . . . they're identifying you as the robber?" he asked. Incredulous, he repeated "You?" He sipped at his drink and chuckled, "Man, that's rich."

Jack was certain that Larry would never have the balls to pull off an armed robbery. Too many times, when given the opportunity to participate in one, he had weaseled out.

"It was you? You pulled that job?"

"No, Jack. Not me. You know me better than that. Old man Bremer knows me. If it was me that did that job, he would have said so but he didn't. But I ended up with some of the guns so that's why they're pointing the finger at me."

"Yeah," Jack scoffed. "I got a picture of that." For a moment, neither man spoke while Jack weighed the implications. Finally, he said, "If they pin an armed robbery on you, you could be looking at some serious time."

"I know," Larry nodded. "Man, I heard they got eight counties involved in this investigation." He ticked them off on his fingers. "Besides Plumas County, there's Lassen and Nevada counties, Butte, Placer and Shasta and Sutter counties." He thought for a moment. "That's only seven. I'm missing one. What am I missing, Lucille?"

"Glenn County," she added.

"Yeah, Glenn."

Jack went silent again as he considered Larry's predicament.

"I have to think about this awhile," he said. "Let's talk about it tomorrow."

Still, there were other issues. There was that messy little jewelry store business. Authorities wanted to know where Shea had gotten hold of a jeweler's tray full of diamond wedding ring sets—all stolen and again, according to witnesses, he had been trying to peddle.

With Larry's mention of the jewelry, Jack just smiled, shook his head and said reassuringly, "Don't worry about it. We'll find a way around it." He paused for a moment. "Weird, ain't it?" Jack chuckled. "I'm supposed to be the bad guy and you're Mr. Clean but now it looks like you're the guy who's up to his ass in shit and I'm lookin' like Joe Good Guy."

"Yeah." Larry thought about it before muttering wearily, "As long as it doesn't get any worse, I think I'll be able to handle it."

"It's not going to get any worse, Larry. You take care of your end tomorrow and I'll make sure you don't get in any more trouble with the law."

Over the years, Larry had become accustomed to Jack Santo's false bravado and his tendency to promise more than he could deliver. But right now, it was a small sliver of salvation and he hoped—even against his doubts—that this would not turn out to be just another one of Jack's broken promises.

A Walk in the Woods

It was mid-morning when the four conspirators piled into Larry Shea's car and drove east down Highway 36, on their way to a point just north of the Plumas - Lassen County line. After arriving at the intersection of the main highway and Old Malvich Road, Larry turned left onto the abandoned and now barely discernible logging road. After warily negotiating their way over potholes, rocks and tufted mounds of goose-grass, they reached a point set back a few yards from the road and about a quarter mile off the main highway.

After rolling the car into the small clearing, Larry exclaimed as he disembarked from the car. "This is the place I was telling you guys about, Jack."

"Look at this place, Jack," he exclaimed with a sweeping arm motion, pointing out the area's relative isolation and its close proximity to the main highway. Struggling to contain his excitement, he enthused, "It's absolutely perfect."

Jack, with Harriet and Lucille right behind, had exited the car and with rifles slung over the men's shoulders, they began the short walk that would take them deeper into the woods.

"Perfect for what, Larry?" Jack asked, surveying their surroundings, and only half kidding. "What did you have in mind?"

"It's just like I have been telling you, Jack. Frank Locatell owns one of the supermarkets in Chester. Twice a month he cashes payroll checks for the employees at Collins Pine Lumber."

Of course Jack knew full well what Larry was getting at but feigned ignorance trying to determine how far his friend had actually thought through this whole idea. "What are you saying—that we knock over his store and, do what—bring him out here?"

"No, Jack," Larry explained. "What I'm saying is, Chester doesn't have a bank of its own. You knew that, right?"

"Yeah. Okay. . . So what?" Jack asked, still pulling Larry's chain.

"Frank has to go to the bank in Westwood to get the cash for the paychecks. After he gets the cash, he'll be coming right by here."

For the first time that entire morning, Jack Santo broke into a wide grin. "How much cash we talking about?"

"Thousands, Jack . . . all there just for the taking." Now it was Larry's turn to grin. "After you stop him, it's a piece of cake. All you have to do is get him down this road."

"That shouldn't be too much of a problem," Jack agreed.

They walked a little further. The colors of summertime, save the evergreens, had already turned from a hundred shades of green to soft orange browns and the reddish rust color of autumn. The soft pine needles and twigs that had dropped to the ground a month ago were now dry and brittle, crackling under their feet as they meandered deeper into the forest's depths.

Traipsing about in the woods like this—even though not actually hunting—could still be an exhilarating experience for the men, but for Lucille and Harriet, it was getting to be a bit tiring.

"Can we take a break?" Lucille asked. Harriet welcomed her suggestion. Her feet were hurting and even Jack was starting to huff and puff. Larry gathered up a few dead logs and in a small clearing used them to form a circle of benches. They plunked themselves down on the logs and Larry passed around a fresh pack of Luckies.

The temperature had dropped into the '40s and Harriet, wearing only a light wool jacket, turned up the collar and rubbed her hands together.

"Let's build a fire," she said brightly, knowing that even before saying it that any kind of a fire in this dry timberland would be completely out of the question.

"We can't do that," Larry said, chuckling at her apparent naiveté, "but here's something almost as good." He reached into his knapsack from which he extracted a thermos of hot tea, some cups and a quart of whiskey.

There were nods and smiles all around as he poured the tea, being careful to leave room for a generous slug of whiskey.

"Nectar of the gods," quipped a shivering Harriet as she raised her cup before taking a deep swallow.

A light breeze had come up and as it blew through the trees, it made the already frigid air feel even colder. The four conspirators sat shivering in the morning chill, sipping whiskey-fortified tea and chain-smoking cigarettes.

"Hard to make a decent living these days," Jack remarked. "Been going through a rough patch lately. Seems like it's been chicken one day and feathers the next." Larry nodded in agreement.

"Let's talk some more about this job we're doing tomorrow," Jack said.

"Yeah, okay." Clearing his throat, Larry began: "Here's the deal, tomorrow . . ." He was suddenly interrupted in mid-sentence by a hunter appearing from out of the brush and as he approached the group, he was immediately recognized by Larry.

"It's Stan," Larry said. "Hey, Stan, how's it going? Any good hunting back there?"

The hunter looked up and recognizing who was speaking, responded: "Hey, Larry. Not too much goin' on back there," he said, rubbing his hands together. "I think there was a couple guys said they saw something about a half mile down the road." He sat down on one of the logs before adding, "But not me. I ain't seen or heard so much as a tree squirrel."

Larry did the introductions and after Stan had accepted and drained a cup of Larry's tea, he wished them all good luck, said his good-byes and they watched him plod off down the road until he was out of earshot.

"Know who that is?" Larry didn't wait for a response. "That's Stan Locatell, Frank Locatell's brother."

"Who's Frank Locatell?" Jack asked, somehow not remembering that Larry had already told him.

"Geez! Don't you listen to anything I say? I just got through telling you."

Larry lowered his voice to a near whisper. "Frank owns the Red and White supermarket in Chester," he said. "On the tenth and twenty-fifth of every month it's payday at Collins Pine Lumber. It's the biggest payroll in town. Hell, it's the biggest payroll in the county!"

Jack interrupted. "Tell me again. How much you figure that payroll's worth?"

"I figure we're looking at anywhere from five, six—maybe as much as ten grand." He waited for Jack to react. "Maybe even more," he added.

"I like it," Jack said, once more with a wide grin.

Good, Larry thought. Maybe now would be a good time to bring up another minor detail. "When you pull this off, I'm going to be somewhere else, right, Jack?"

"Yeah, that's right," Jack answered. "We have to keep those pretty hands clean. We don't want to soil that Mr. Good-Guy image, right, Lar?"

Larry ignored the dig. It didn't bother him because Jack Santo had a habit of insulting people and not be aware he was doing it. When he was called on it, instead of apologizing, he would simply grin and say, "It's just part of my charm."

"But for setting this whole thing up, Larry continued, I'm in for ten points, right? That's what we agreed on, right?"

"Yeah, Larry, that's right."

It was okay with Jack. Ten percent was a hell of a lot better than a full share. He did some fast figuring in his head. Ten percent of ten grand is a thousand dollars. If it turns out to actually be ten grand, that would leave nine to split with Perkins and Boles, meaning three apiece. Not a bad day's work, he mused. "All right, you got it. Ten points it is. If you're right about this and everything is like you say it is, it'll be worth it."

Jack returned to his somber demeanor and began to consider the mechanics of the job and how they were going to pull it off. He turned to Harriet.

"I think the three of us guys will be able to handle it," he said, backing off from his earlier intention of getting her involved in the action. "We won't need you, toots. I was thinking you'd be our driver, but now, that doesn't look like it'd be such a good idea. If there was any heavy lifting I'm afraid like always, you'd just be in the way."

It was the kind of dismissive remark that never failed to raise her ire. "Funny, you didn't think I'd be in the way in that Hansen disaster," Harriet shot back. "Quite a bit of 'heavy lifting' for that one, don't you think?"

Ignoring Harriet's jab, Jack turned back to Larry. "Now let's get specific."

Larry took it from there: "When Frank leaves the bank with the money, he'll be driving toward Chester in a light brown Ford pickup. When he reaches Malvich Road, all you gotta do is pull him over, bring him down this road so you can have a little privacy and then just help yourself to the cash. Nothing to it."

Jack frowned, weighing the pluses and minuses. "Yeah, right, he echoed, nothing to it." He added, "Maybe for you, there's nothing to it, because while this is all going down, you'll be sitting at home in front of a nice warm fire with a drink in your hand and not a care in the world. But for me and Perk, there's a lot more to it."

"Well okay," he said, to his now chastened cohort. "It does sound pretty good. I'm sure Perk will go for it."

They decided they'd had enough "hunting" for one day. The women were freezing and they were all getting hungry. They gathered up their gear, piled back into the car and headed for home.

In Chester, Thursday nights were pretty much like any other night. Visitors didn't come to Chester to partake of its glamorous nightlife. They might check out the relatively pricey Bear Club or, if that was a bit much, there was always Big Bob's Barbecue on Main Street. But that was about it.

So, instead of an evening out, the foursome chose to sit around the house and drink. Harriet and Lucille made roast beef sandwiches served with a big dollop of potato salad on the side and before the booze had a chance to take full effect, they discussed for the final time, tomorrow's impending job. By the morning's wee hours, more than enough whiskey had been consumed, and the four conspirators staggered down the hall to their respective bedrooms where they hoped to get a short night's sleep.

D-Day

Friday, October 10th in Chester was another sparkling autumn day. The previous night, for whatever reason, Jack, having had trouble sleeping, got up early, showered, dressed and after several minutes of fumbling with Shea's new-fangled electric percolator, finally figured it out well enough to brew a pot of coffee. After taking the first scowl-inducing sip, he made a bee-line to the liquor cabinet where he found a bottle of Crown Royal whiskey. He added a few generous shots to the pot and with a steaming cup of booze-laced brew in hand, Jack strolled out onto the back porch.

Inhaling the crisp morning air, he surveyed the picture postcard vista that stretched out before him. Dense forests teeming with wild game and sapphire like Lake Almanor, swimming with schools of trophy-size trout in the blue, crystalline water—clean and clear enough to drink. Looming in the distance, towering above it all, was majestic, snow-capped Mount Shasta.

But to Jack Santo, autumn in Chester meant only that it was deer season and because there were relatively few hunters who knew about this little paradise, it was his favorite time of year and Chester was his favorite place to be.

Anticipating the work that lay ahead, he began to feel that familiar tingle of excitement and the power surge that came with it. Sometimes he could actually smell the fear that would emanate from his victims, and in some weird way, he found that very comforting.

He was abruptly jarred from his reverie by Larry's sudden appearance, who, though still apparently groggy, and not yet fully awake, had poured himself a cup of Jack's coffee before joining him on the back porch.

"Well, well," Jack said, grinning broadly. "Look out, everybody. Jesse James is up and on the loose. Ready to go knock over a train, Jesse?"

"Very funny," Larry said and clearly not yet in a laughing mood, he growled, "Is there anything else about the plan that we need to talk about?"

"What's to talk about?" Jack said. "All you have to do is point the guy out to us and then get out of the way. We'll take care of the rest."

"Man, I really do hope that's the way it goes down," Larry said. "No fuss, no muss—no problem, Just a quick, easy hit and run, right?"

"Like I told you yesterday—as long as the guy cooperates, we should be home in time for lunch."

Larry took a deep breath. "Oh I forgot to tell you," he said as he lit a cigarette. "Me and Lucille have a trip to Reno planned for tonight. There's a big golf tournament Saturday and I want to see it." Against his better judgment since he wasn't sure how Lucille would accept the idea, he added, "You guys want to tag along?"

"Could be," Jack answered. "Check with me later."

"We're planning to have dinner and maybe see a couple shows," Larry said. "We'll probably leave here around seven or eight. It's a tad over a hundred miles so that should get us there in plenty of time and we can still get a good night's sleep."

Jack drained his cup, then paused. "You know I'm not that interested in golf, but if this grocery store guy is carrying as much cash as you say he is, we'll all have a few extra bucks to blow at the crap tables."

Larry changed the subject. "I've been thinking on what we were talking about last night," he said. "You know—that gun problem. It's starting to get to me."

"Tell me about the guns," Jack said.

"They were quality goods. Some Remington shotguns, a couple of 270 Winchesters, a Winchester 30-30 with a Ford scope; a 32 Smith and Wesson; a couple 9mm Rugers; there was a 336 Marlin—that's just the ones I can remember—and of course, they were all brand new."

"Well, the stolen property charge is really no big deal Larry, Like I told you. I got a buddy who can rig up a bill of sale for you, so I wouldn't worry too much about that," Jack said, but then adding ominously "But if they hit you with armed robbery, and they convict you, you could be looking at ten to twenty."

"Ten to twenty years—no shit?" Larry said nervously.

"Yeah, ask Perkins. He did two stretches on armed robbery. One at San Quentin, the other at Folsom. But he was a good boy and got himself paroled after a couple years, both times!" Jack chuckled. "Can you picture that? Perkins a good boy?"

"San Quentin? Folsom? Larry almost choked on his coffee. "Well, that certainly is encouraging. You really do know how to cheer a guy up," he said, his voice thick with sarcasm.

"Look, Larry. I think you can put it in the back of your mind," Jack said. "By the time they wade through all that red tape—you know most of these small town hick cops couldn't track an elephant in four feet of snow. Sheriffs are going to retire, evidence will disappear, people will forget, witnesses will die . . ."

"Yeah, maybe you're right. Maybe I should just quit worrying about it," Larry said trying hard—but without much success—to convince himself.

Larry looked at his watch. It was ten past nine. "I'd better get going. I want to stop at the jewelry store to pick up my trophy. They're engraving it and it's supposed to be ready today. Did I tell you I won a golf trophy?"

"What time does the bank open?" Jack asked.

"Ten o'clock," Larry said. "Look for me. I'll be waiting out in front."

Jack cautioned, "Perk and Boles should be showing up any time now. As soon as they get here we'll leave so we can get to Westwood before ten. Remember, we need you to already be there to point him out."

"Yeah, yeah, yeah. Just be careful and make sure you don't leave any tracks. When this is all over, you guys will be long gone, but me and Lucille are still going to have to live in this town and we sure wouldn't last very long if anybody thought we were involved in this job."

Larry was grateful that his personal responsibility would be limited to fingering the victim, But he was more than a little apprehensive when Jack informed him that George Boles would be riding shotgun. From all the stories Jack had told about Boles, he feared that by putting Boles and Perkins together again, there was a good chance that this whole thing could blow up like that Hansen disaster. Boles was unreliable and Jack knew it, so why, Larry wondered, would he bring such a loose cannon into the deal?

That was always the problem in playing with Jack. You just never knew what was going on in the guy's head. The first time the two had met, Larry asked him what he did for a living. "I'm the president of a corporation," Jack had told him. "Murder Incorporated!" And then he laughed. Only it wasn't a laugh that said he was just kidding. It was more like a laugh that said, "I'm *not* kidding!" It had taken a while for Larry to get over that one.

He knew Jack had done some time back in New York on an assault charge. But—murder? Did he actually kill people and then go around bragging about it? Well, it's possible, he reasoned. Anything's possible, especially when you're running around with scumbags like Emmett Perkins.

Larry arrived at the bank a few minutes before ten and hoping to pick up his newly engraved trophy, he walked across the street to the jewelry store, only to learn that the engraver hadn't yet shown up for work. Returning to his car he settled in to wait for Jack's arrival.

At around nine-fifty a dust-covered, tired looking blue Oldsmobile sedan came rolling down the street and parked a couple of spaces from Larry. Perkins was driving and Jack was his only passenger. There was no sign of Boles.

He walked over to the car and peered in nervously. "Where's Boles? Didn't you say Boles was coming?" he asked as Jack exited the car.

"Boles couldn't make it. The kid got himself nabbed on a bad check charge couple days ago," said Perkins, still sitting behind the wheel. "He's going to be a guest of the county for a while, so I guess he'll be MIA for the next few weeks."

Since Larry had already been harboring major reservations about Boles' participation, he accepted Perkins' report with a sense of welcome relief.

It was now ten a.m. and time for bank manager John Woods to open the doors and allow the people who had been milling about on the sidewalk to come inside. Larry noticed that Frank Locatell had joined the small circle of waiting bank customers and he quickly pointed him out to Jack.

"That's him," Larry said. "The tall guy with the hat."

Taking careful note of the man soon to be his intended prey, Jack returned to the car. Larry, after waiting for the small gathering to enter the bank, followed the last straggler in. He conducted his business and emerged fifteen minutes later and returned to the space where the blue Olds had been parked only to find that Jack, Perk and the car were gone. Again, he walked across the street to the jewelry store and tried one more time to pick up his golf trophy, but since the engraver still hadn't shown up, he went back to his car and started for home.

On Highway 36, he kept a watchful eye out for Perk's blue Olds or for Frank Locatell's brown pickup, both of which had left the bank a short while before he did. He looked for any sign of a robbery in progress but seeing none, he continued on directly to Chester where, turning off the main highway, he cruised leisurely down First Street, finally reaching his driveway and there—parked inconspicuously next to his house—sat Perk's blue Olds

It was now close to eleven o'clock and Larry, anxious to hear the good news, walked quickly into the house. Jack, Harriet, Perkins and Lucille, were sitting around the coffee table in the living room, each holding a drink.

"How'd it go?" Larry asked immediately as he poured himself a drink. "Did you get your business taken care of this morning?"

"No," Jack said. "We ran into a little snag."

"A little snag?" Larry stopped in the middle of taking a swig from his drink. "What kind of a little snag? Didn't you get the money?"

"No, I'm afraid we came up empty," Jack said. "We just couldn't catch him. He drove like a maniac," Jack explained, his voice heavy with frustration. "He had to be doing ninety." He paused, shaking his head. "What a lousy break. We'd all be in the chips right now but we just couldn't catch up with the sonofabitch!"

"Are you saying all this was for nothing?"

Jack, annoyed that Larry would ask the question and angry that he had to answer it, said, "Look, the bastard drove too fast! That's what happened! So sue me," adding, "If you think you could have done any better, maybe you should have been driving the car."

Harriet rose to pour herself another drink. "Maybe if you had a driver who knew what the hell she was doing, he wouldn't have got away."

"Like who?" Jack hissed. "You?"

Harriet returned to her chair with a fresh drink. "Yeah, Jack," she said with an undisguised smirk. "Like me."

Lucille said nothing but smiled at Harriet's audacity. Perkins and Jack looked at each other and laughed derisively at Harriet's suggestion. Larry just stared in shock and disappointment. "I was at the bank …right behind him. I saw him get eight thousand dollars in cash. I heard the teller count it out and I saw him stuff it into a bag. Shit!" he moaned. "What a fucking disaster."

They drank without another word being spoken and, after what seemed like several minutes, Larry brightened up. "Well, he said, finally breaking the awkward silence, "there's always plan B."

"Plan B?" the others asked in unison.

"If we're going to do this,
don't be too long. It's getting late."

THREE

Plan B

J ack sprang to his feet almost shouting. "Of course! How could we forget—the other grocery guy!"

Perkins looked puzzled. He vaguely recalled their conversation at Higgins Corner and the almost parenthetical mention of a second grocer.

"That's right, I almost forgot," Perkins grinned. "There's another guy. That means we're back in business, right?"

"Right, Perk! So, all is not lost," Larry said excitedly, to which Jack was all ears.

"Frank Locatell is not the only guy who cashes paychecks," Larry reminded them. "The other supermarket owner—his name's Guard Young—he'll be coming out of the bank with a bag full of cash too."

He paused momentarily. "But we're going to have to wait until this afternoon because he doesn't usually get to the bank until just before it closes, five or ten minutes to three."

"I guess that means you'll have to go with us, Larry," Jack suggested. "You're going to have to point him out to us."

Larry balked at Jack's suggestion. "Are you saying you want me to go back to the bank again this afternoon?" he asked. There was more than a little uneasiness in his voice. "That's going to look awfully suspicious. Look Jack . . . anybody who saw me hanging around the bank this morning and then sees me again this afternoon . . . I mean, they're going to start putting two and two together and Bang! I'm dead."

The notion of more personal exposure—no matter how necessary Jack thought it would be for this operation to succeed, for Larry, held little appeal. "I don't think that's a very good idea," he protested.

It was obvious to Perkins that Shea, as usual, was not eager to be involved in any of the dirty work and would go to almost any length in order to avoid being even close to the action. Instead of commenting, he decided to just sit back and enjoy watching Larry squirm.

Under Jack's withering stare-down, Larry was quick to add: "And think about this—we're only talking about ten percent. If I come in with you guys, you'd have to cut me in for a full share."

That was enough to persuade Jack, but Perkins didn't even try to conceal his contempt. His beady eyes glared at Larry.

"Yeah, I figured you'd duck out—a job like this takes real balls which is something you don't seem to have too much of."

Larry said nothing in response while Lucille shot Perkins a dagger-like look but which Perkins dismissively ignored.

Harriet spoke up. "I think I know him well enough to point him out. Lucille and I were in his store yesterday picking up a couple of bottles of liquor. We even chatted for a few minutes."

"Well, then," Jack said, relieved that he wouldn't have to referee a fight between Larry and Perkins. "I guess you're it."

It made sense, Jack reasoned, to use Harriet. He could cut her in for a full share, a large part of which, one way or another, would end up in his pocket anyway.

While Larry quietly seethed at Perk's barbs, Perkins snuffed out his cigarette in an already overflowing ashtray and as he looked at his watch he could almost hear the *ka-ching, ka-ching* of the cash register.

Perkins wanted to hear it one more time. "How much cash are we talking about with this Guard Young fella?"

"Young has a bigger store," Larry replied. "So he should have at least as much as Locatell, probably even more," Still bristling, he added, "Maybe you ought to try listening for a change."

The surge of exhilaration and sense of anticipation which—up until now—had been missing with all this talk of a second potential victim—had Jack reacting as though someone had pumped the room full of oxygen. The day was going to be salvaged after all. Jack studied his fellow conspirators, looking into their faces as he tried to determine whether their sense of anticipation equaled that of his own.

He waited—fully expecting to hear someone utter the dreaded "yeah but"— when cold logic and hard reason tells you why something *can't* or *shouldn't* be done. He wondered and waited but there were no negative comments.

"I didn't think we'd need an alternate plan," Larry said. "I thought Locatell would be an easy mark."

"He must have seen us coming up fast in his rear view mirror and got spooked," Jack opined. "That's the only thing I can figure why he took off like a bat outta hell. But, I don't give a damn how fast this one drives—this time we'll catch him."

"He's a big guy. You wouldn't want to get in any kind of a physical tussle with him," Larry cautioned. "But he's a family guy. Very religious. A law abider. He'll probably stay inside the speed limit," Shea guessed, "at least until he sees that he's being chased."

"To Plan B, then." Jack exclaimed, grinning broadly as he lifted his glass. "Let's drink a toast, boys and girls, to a successful and profitable afternoon."

Perkins, not normally a big drinker, grimaced as he closed his eyes and swallowed his shot in a single gulp.

Larry drained his glass to the last drop and slammed it down on the table. He looked at his watch. It was almost two o'clock.

"You still got an hour until the bank closes," he said as he lifted himself from his chair, "—but you don't want to wait until the last minute. Give yourself some extra time 'cause you don't want to miss him. You only got one chance so you better make it good." Larry stood up, stretched and yawned.

"I'm done," he said. "You guys wear me out." He started for the hallway. "When you figure out what you want me to do, let me know."

He lurched unsteadily toward the bedroom, mumbling unintelligibly to himself.

Watching Larry disappear down the hall, Perkins couldn't conceal his visceral dislike for the man despite his knowing that he was Jack's friend. Maybe it was a matter of trustworthiness. Larry Shea was just a smooth talking con artist as far as Perkins was concerned.

Picking up on Perkins' thinly veiled animosity, Lucille looked at Jack. "You and Larry have been friends for a lot of years, haven't you, Jack?" Although her question had been posed in an idle conversational tone, what she really wanted was for Perkins to understand that if Jack Santo liked Larry, then by God, Perkins better like him, too.

"Yeah," Jack said, "a lot of years."

He looked away from Lucille, shifting his eyes directly toward Perkins. "A lot of years, Perk," he said pointedly. Harriet nodded, helping to reinforce Jack's unmistakable drift.

Just to be certain that the message had been received by Perkins, after pouring another drink and polishing off the bottle, Jack began to expound on everything from the illegal gold trade to buying and selling stolen guns and how Larry Shea had always been such a good partner over the years.

Perkins, seemingly untouched by Jack's walk down memory lane, rose from the chair. "I'm going out to the car, Jack. If we're going to do this, don't be too long. It's getting late."

Perkins went out through the back door, while the others, one by one, emptied their glasses. Jack motioned to Harriet.

"C'mon toots, get your butt in gear." Harriet stood and feeling the effects of the booze, wavered noticeably as Lucille escorted them to the car.

They piled into the Oldsmobile sedan, Jack sliding behind the wheel, Perkins in the passenger seat and Harriet in the back. He swerved the car onto Main Street before steering toward the east end of town.

Jack was trying to think ahead now, hoping he'd be able to anticipate whatever unforeseen problems they might encounter by having changed targets.

For one thing, had they been able to overtake and stop Frank Locatell, there would have been little danger of being recognized since Locatell didn't know any of them. But Guard Young presented a different potential problem. If he gets a good look at Harriet, he's almost certain to recognize her. Somehow, Jack concluded, he'd have to keep her out of sight.

"Jack," Harriet broke in. "Do you remember the time you traded that lug of tomatoes at Young's market?"

Jack was annoyed that out of nowhere, she'd bring up a seemingly unrelated incident that had occurred months ago. "I traded a box of tomatoes I got somewhere for a box of apples. Yeah, I remember it," he frowned. "So what? What the hell's that got to do with anything?"

"Well," Harriet explained, "that was Guard Young."

"That was Young?" Jack repeated, obviously surprised. Perkins was listening intently but said nothing. "Yeah, I remember now. The bastard tried to Jew me down. We haggled over those damn tomatoes." After a pensive moment, he finally had to admit, "You're right. He'd be sure to recognize us both."

"Hey, Perk, I'm going to need a mask," he said. "Maybe we should stop at a store."

"Yeah," Perkins agreed. He thought for a moment. "Hey, wait, how about that mask we used in the Hansen gig?" Perk said. "I think it's still in the trunk. I figured we might need it again sometime," he bragged. "Lucky for y'all I did."

"Yeah, good thinking," Jack said, sarcastically. "You're a fucking genius. Let's stop and make sure it's there, because if it's not, we'll have to get one in town."

Jack pulled the car to the side of the road and Perkins walked around to the trunk, lifted the lid and began rummaging through the litter of wrinkled clothes, yellowed newspapers and other assorted trash. A garish Halloween mask stared at him from beneath a pile of old girlie magazines, dirty socks, and one shoe missing a shoelace. When he lifted the mask he spotted a skein of sash cord which he recalled purchasing months ago, although he couldn't remember why. He grabbed that too, just in case. As he jumped back into the front seat, he held up the mask.

"This should be a big improvement on your ugly mug, Jack," he said with a loud chuckle. Harriet stifled a giggle while Jack, unamused, glowered.

"You're not only a genius—you're a comedian too."

It wasn't until they were approaching the town of Westwood that the three conspirators began to hurriedly put their slap-dash plan together. Jack explained again for Harriet's benefit how, first, they would stop Young's Chrysler just before he reached the spot they had scouted out the previous day. The old abandoned logging road, with the surrounding dense underbrush would allow them to conceal their activities from passing traffic. Combined with the fact that there would be no cops around, this made it the perfect place to do what they had to do.

Perkins turned to Harriet. "You should try to stay out of sight." Harriet nodded as she began to rummage around the back seat clutter. She came up with a man's wide brim straw hat that had been squeezed and crushed between the seat and backrest.

Trying it on and hoping to elicit even the tiniest of compliments, she said to Jack, "How do I look?"

"Big improvement," he smirked.

"Thanks, Jack. You really know how to make a girl feel good."

Perkins was also harboring misgivings about being identified. He wasn't concerned about being recognized by Young since the two had never met, but there was still that slimmest of chance: somewhere, sometime—weeks, even months from now—it was entirely possible that Guard Young would pick him out of a police photo lineup. Or maybe, after spotting him in a newspaper photograph, he'd be able to make the identification. It was a long shot, to be sure, but still, the possibility remained.

"We only got one mask," Jack reminded him. "But don't sweat it. Just make sure you stay in the background. If I have to, I'll tie him up and cover his eyes with a blindfold."

And that would be the total extent of the "careful planning" that went into the commission of a crime which, come the next morning, would create banner headlines across the nation.

In the tiny village of Westwood, even on a Friday at the peak of hunting season and while many of its citizens were busily preparing for their weekend activities, one would not expect to have much difficulty in finding a place to park a car. In Jack Santo's case, however, not only would he have to find a parking place, it would have to be in a location where they could keep an eye on Guard Young as he entered and exited the bank but without attracting undue attention.

"Good Lord," Jack grumbled. "You'd think that in a two-bit burg like this a man would be able find a place to park. I swear, there are more cars in this town than there are in downtown L.A.!"

After circling the block at least three times, he discovered a spot opposite the bank just a short distance down the street. "Perfect!" he said as he backed in and shut off the engine.

Payday in Chester

At the supermarket, Guard Young gave his watch a quick glance as he surveyed the short checkout line of customers, most of whom he recognized as housewives picking up a few last minute items for the evening's supper.

After a long, hard week at the mill, Friday was the day when the family men of Chester could always count on something special cooking on the kitchen stove when they arrived home. Even here in Chester, where supper usually means plain old meat and potatoes, once in a while a taste of something "cook-book" special was always a welcome change of pace.

This particular Friday, since it falls on the tenth of the month, means that it's payday at the Collins Pine Lumber Company. Given the fact that it was one of only two of the town's businesses where mill workers and loggers, as well as other working people, could get their paychecks cashed, things could become pretty hectic at Young's Supermarket.

In the late 1940s and early '50s, due to the nationwide post-war building boom, Chester had been enjoying steady growth, its permanent population now pushing two thousand and counting. But despite this promising future, large banking establishments such as Wells Fargo and Bank of America had not given the town fathers much hope that either bank would be adding a branch in Chester anytime soon. It meant that Chester's merchants, as well as its private citizens, would still have to make the thirteen mile drive to Westwood in order to conduct their banking business. For merchants who dealt almost exclusively in cash, this short run between the two towns was always a risky endeavor. The lack of a local bank forced these merchants to transport their cash to and from the bank in Westwood, usually without the protection of an armored car or even a security guard.

To replenish the town's cash coffers, it fell to the proprietors of Chester's only two grocery stores—Young's Supermarket and the Red and White Market—to make the bi-weekly bank run to Westwood. Both owners Guard Young and Frank Locatell, in spite of the obvious risks, considered the regular bank trips as just another cost of doing business. As responsible merchants, they were aware that in a town like Chester, cash was the oil that kept the retail machinery humming.

* * * *

Guard Young was a handsome, fiercely religious forty-three-year-old father of three daughters, two of them adopted, and an infant son. Both he and his wife Christal were devout members of the Church of Jesus Christ of Latter-day Saints. In fact, Guard was a great-grandson of Lorenzo Dow Young, brother of Mormon founder, Brigham Young.

It was those same deeply held religious convictions that had at one time nurtured aspirations in both Guard and Christal to enter the life of Mormon missionaries. The Youngs had agreed early in their marriage that at some point there would come a time when they would sell their material goods and travel the country as missionaries in response to that calling. But until then, Guard and Christal had settled in the tiny mountain community of Chester seven years earlier. Occasionally, he would only half-jokingly remark that by making their home in Chester, they would be that much closer to God. Some of the town's less spiritually motivated though, would take pains to point out that even in a "God blessed Utopia" such as Chester, the devil could always be lurking. There was a real concern among many that in the absence of an armored car or police escort, individuals traveling between Chester and Westwood while carrying large sums of money would be easy prey for bandits who could be lying in wait along that thirteen mile stretch of largely deserted highway.

On State Route 36 between Chester and Westwood, town fathers had placed a series of historic markers along the road every three or four miles apart. These markers were there to serve as mute reminders of where 49er gold miners had been ambushed by highway bandits and relieved of their gold and why, even now, a hundred years later, it wasn't a good idea to dilly-dally while driving on this section of highway. Graphic stories were told of mountain pirates lying in wait for prospectors to come down from the hills, their saddlebags heavy with the gold ore that had been dug from improvised mines or panned from the hundreds of placers that had once dotted these mountainsides.

Guard Young was widely respected and well-liked, but a man who found it difficult to accept the fact that evil could exist in an Eden-like setting such as Chester. Those familiar with his payday routine were understandably concerned for his safety, feeling that because of his deeply held faith and what some characterized as a trusting naiveté—his unspoken belief in an intrinsic goodness that resides in all God's creatures—he did not fully appreciate his vulnerability. His friends would argue that thousands of dollars—in those days an enormous sum of money—was far too much for anyone to be carrying around without protection. Some of those warnings had come directly from Sheriff Mel Schooler's office.

A large part of Melvin Schooler's responsibilities as Plumas County Sheriff consisted of policing the county's more than three thousand square miles of rugged mountain forests and its twenty thousand permanent residents. With his severely limited resources, he found that dealing with crime by using a pro-active, rather than re-active approach, particularly during deer season, was just not feasible. On those occasions when a crime was committed, Sheriff Schooler's office could respond only after the fact. Of particular concern to Sheriff Schooler were Guard Young and Frank Locatell's biweekly errands to and from the bank in Westwood. There was little doubt in the sheriff's mind that those regular bank runs had by now become common knowledge among the area's small—but no less real—criminal element.

On October 10, 1952, at two-thirty in the afternoon, Guard realized that if he expected to get to the bank before it closed, he'd have to get a move on. He had just walked out of his office carrying a pouch containing the checks the store had accumulated over the past couple of weeks.

"You'd better get cracking," cashier Dorothy Elliott reminded him. "Won't kill you to get there early for a change."

The Final Errand

Guard, Christal, and their four children lived in a small apartment above the market. On this particular afternoon, in a departure from her usual routine, Christal had picked up their two older daughters from school. Jean, seven and Judy, six, along with three and a half-year-old Sondra Gay would be accompanying their dad to the bank today where, after he had attended to his banking routine, they knew that soda fountain treats for all would follow.

It would be a few more years before Wayne Robert, their infant brother, would be able to join his big sisters on these special occasions. In his stead, four-year-old neighbor boy Michael Saile had been invited to join them and this otherwise ordinary drive into Westwood had now taken on the festive aura of a party for the kids.

Sondra Gay ducked her head into the store's doorway just in time to see her father remove his store apron. She spun and ran back to the car to excitedly report to the other children that he had taken off his apron and was about to come through the door.

Judy, Jean and Michael clambered into the back seat while Sondra Gay jumped into the front. Christal peered out through the big store window and chuckled as she watched the four children scurry into the car. Guard would certainly have his hands full with this rowdy quartet, but she knew he wouldn't have it any other way. His girls, and now little Wayne Robert, were his pride and his joy. Michael, whose parents had divorced when Michael was still an infant, had begun to look to Guard as a kind of fatherly role model and Guard, of course, was only too happy to oblige. In the relatively short time that Michael and his mother Rosemary had been neighbors and friends, Guard showered as much love and fatherly affection on Michael as if the little boy had been one of his own.

"Okay, Dottie," Guard said with a smile to his cashier, "try not to steal too much while I'm gone. I should be back in an hour or so."

"Nah," she joked back. "I'll wait until you get back with all that cash. Then I'll make my big move."

He looked around and said to Dottie, "Where are the kids? They were here just a few minutes ago."

"They've been waiting in the car for you," Dottie replied without missing a stroke on the cash register.

"Well, alright. I guess I'd better get going." Guard picked up the bag containing the checks and pushed open the door.

"I'll be back in a flash with the cash."

He stepped through the doorway and headed for his car, now commandeered by four squealing, rollicking children. Wearing a broad grin he eased himself into the driver's seat, admonished the kids to simmer down and started the engine.

Swinging the powerful Chrysler down Main Street, he circled past the northern tip of the lake and turned eastward onto the smooth, recently paved Route 36 Chester-Westwood connector.

While the kids were whooping it up in the back seat, Guard took another quick look at his watch. Two-forty he noted. In another ten minutes, they'd be at the bank—plenty of time before it closed. He'd finish up his bank business, stop at the Variety Store's soda fountain to buy the kids something and be home before four o'clock.

Approaching the outskirts of Westwood, Guard made a conscious effort to keep his speed below sixty. He still had a full fifteen minutes so there was no need to take a chance on another speeding ticket. Christal would have a fit. He thought it was almost comical how she used to worry about him when he made these runs to the bank. It may have taken a while, but eventually she got used to it. She rarely mentioned it now, even on those special occasions when the kids went along. In fact, he reasoned, his wife probably assumed that any robber, on seeing a car full of kids, would think twice about causing them harm.

Guard marveled at how far he and Christal had come since those early days of their marriage when they had been so disheartened by their inability to start a family. His heart warmed as he recalled the joy that filled their tiny apartment—their "castle in the clouds," as Christal had named it—on receiving the news from the adoption agency: After eight long years of waiting and praying—after eight childless years—their prayers had been answered. Baby daughter Jean would soon be joining the family. And in just a few short months after Jean's arrival, in another miracle—literally—a second call came from the agency bringing the wonderful news that Jean would be getting a little sister. Judy was now ready to make her entrance.

Guard glanced quickly back at the frolicking kids and it brought a smile to his face as he thought back to the day when, through the miracle of natural childbirth, Sondra Gay had first made her appearance. Within another year, Christal had given birth to Gardner Lee, only to see her happiness turn to bitter sorrow when their first son died just two days later. "The Lord giveth and the Lord taketh away," the heartbroken Christal had remarked at the time. But six months ago, their anguish turned to deep gratitude when Wayne Robert was born and they now had added a baby boy to their growing family.

The irresistible smile on Sondra Gay's face, as she looked up at him once again, reminded Guard that all the waiting and all the disappointments had been well worth it.

"Look at them, Perk. Look how small they are."

FOUR

Prey

It was 2:50 p.m. when the green Chrysler Windsor sedan pulled into the parking space that had just opened up almost directly in front of the Bank of America. Jack and his two passengers, Perkins and Harriet, stared intently as the door swung open and the driver began to exit the car.

"Is that him?" Perkins asked Harriet.

"Yeah, that's him," Harriet replied.

Squinting through the bright sunlight, Jack noticed another figure—a very small figure—come tumbling out of the car. He readjusted his glasses. "But who's that with him?"

They strained to get a better view. Harriet, her mouth agape, was stunned to see a little girl hop out.

"Oh my God!" Harriet cried out. "A kid! He's got a dammed kid with him!"

Guard Young stood beside the car while leaning in through the open window, apparently talking to someone and making it suddenly all too apparent that there were three other children romping in the back seat.

Harriet screamed, "Holy mother of God—he's got a whole car full of kids!"

"Holy shit!" Jack muttered, visibly shaken.

But no emotional outburst came from Perkins—no outward reaction. Instead, he remained stoically silent, already thinking about how they were going to deal with this unexpected hitch in their plans.

Jack kept shaking his head. "Larry didn't say anything about kids. How the hell could he have overlooked something like that?" There was dead silence in the car until Perkins finally added his thoughts.

"Not a big deal," he said. "In fact, those kids could make the whole thing go down a lot easier. Think about it. He's not going to try to be a hero and take a chance on those kids getting hurt." Without waiting for a response he added, "See what I mean? He'll be a regular pussycat."

Harriet was skeptical. "I'm not so sure. Are you saying you can do this and control those kids? Did you count them? I saw four of them. Have you ever tried to control four wild little kids?" She looked at Perk for an answer but his only response was an ominous smirk.

"Look at them, Perk," Harriet persisted. "Look how small they are. And what if something goes wrong? Those kids would probably be right in the way. What happens then, Perk?"

Perkins shrugged off Harriet's sudden concern. "It's all the same to me," he said. "They won't get hurt because you're going to keep them out of the way. That's all you have to do. Just make sure they stay out of the way.

"I don't like it Jack," Harriet argued. "This has disaster written all over it. Let's get out of here. Let's just forget the whole damn thing."

"No chance, Harriet," Jack said. His thoughts were focused on the ten thousand dollar score he was sure was within their reach and he refused to allow this little speed bump to derail their plans.

"Just don't worry about it. Perk's right. Just make sure you keep those kids under control and everything's going to be fine."

Harriet wasn't convinced. When there are kids involved, everything becomes unpredictable. Too many things can happen and all of them are bad. What if Young decided to put up a fight? What would they do then, and how would the kids react? Knowing Perk and how emotionally unbalanced he could be sometimes . . . She shook her head in dismay.

"How the hell can I herd a bunch of kids around and still stay out of sight? Tell me that." She looked pleadingly at Jack. "This is just too much, Jack. It's a bad idea."

Jack patted her on the arm. "Don't you worry about it, toots. We'll handle it. Just make sure you do your job."

She hated that "toots" crap. It was his condescending way of almost admitting that she was probably right but not enough to make him change his mind.

What's the use, she thought. There's no convincing him. Come hell or high water, no matter what—children or no children—his mind was made up and her protest be dammed. For a fleeting moment she considered just chucking the whole thing. It wasn't too late. All she had to do was get out of the car and walk away.

They continued to watch in silence as the man appeared to leave a few parting words for his back seat passengers. After a final admonition, he stepped away from the car and the little girl clung tightly to his outstretched hand as she ran at his heels, struggling mightily to keep pace with the man's giant strides. To Harriet, she appeared to be about three or four years of age.

It was 2:56 p.m. as Harriet stopped to consider that in just a few more minutes her window of opportunity was going to close and it would be too late to back out. The downward spiral her life had taken since hooking up with Jack would continue. There was a time when she had fantasized of a better life and maybe a small horse farm in the country. Whatever happened to that dream she wondered? What the hell was wrong with her? Why was she so weak that she found it impossible to say *no* to Jack Santo? Jack's almost nonchalant demeanor clearly signaled that, like Perkins, he was determined to see this thing through, kids or no kids. It was the money. It was always the money, and Harriet had to admit—if only to herself—that she was just as motivated by it as were the men. She decided to say nothing more.

Carjacked

Ten minutes after entering the bank, Guard, with his three and a half year-old daughter still in tow, left the building and returned to his car. As Guard pulled away from the curb, Jack Santo sat behind the wheel of the blue Olds, his cold steely eyes fixed on the green Chrysler. As Guard entered the traffic lane, Jack fell in behind him and began to follow.

"Looks like we're in business," he said.

"Yep," Perkins drawled as he fondled with exaggerated tenderness the nickel-plated revolver he had just removed from the glove compartment.

Guard rounded the corner and to Jack's puzzlement, after driving just a couple of blocks, he pulled over to the curb and parked in front of Bennight's Variety Store.

"What the hell is he doing now?" Jack spat out the words as he quickly scanned the street in a frantic search for another parking spot.

"Don't get your ass in an uproar, Jack. He must have a little more business to take care of," Perkins said. "I don't reckon he's going to be too long, what with all them kids."

Clearly annoyed at having to circle the block one more time, Jack finally eased into a spot across the street where he resigned himself to yet another unexpected snag.

"We'll just wait here," he groaned.

Harriet, however, was watching in bemused admiration as Guard Young opened his car's rear door, spilling its exuberant occupants out onto the sidewalk where they scurried excitedly into the store. Guard followed closely and the whole scene, she mused, reminded her of a Norman Rockwell painting.

In less than fifteen minutes they were back out on the sidewalk, each child clutching a bright red popsicle. The moment passed quickly but Harriet was deeply touched by its warmth; images that would remain in her mind to replay again and again.

The big Chrysler roared to life with its carload of squealing passengers and a driver anxious to get back to the store where he could finish out the day, lock it up and get home for a big family dinner.

Approaching the small rise about four miles past the town limits, Guard began to be mildly concerned about the blue Oldsmobile on his tail. He had first noticed it as they were leaving Westwood. Were they being followed, he wondered, albeit at a far enough distance so as not to cause undue alarm? Just coincidence, he told himself, but he'd keep an eye on it just to be safe. If it started to look like a threat, he'd step on the gas and just out-speed whoever it was.

In the Olds, still smarting from their earlier failure to overtake Frank Locatell, Jack remarked to Perkins, "At least he's driving at a sensible speed."

Perkins nodded. "Yeah, not like that Locatell maniac. You ought to be able to get in front of him and slow him down without much of a problem. But you got to do it fast before he has a chance to react."

Jack slipped on the mask that had been resting beside him and yelled to Harriet, "Put that hat on now," he said, and make sure you keep the brim pulled down over your face. Try to stay back out of sight so no one sees you. We'll try to make it quick."

Guard, who had been holding his speed down to a moderate fifty-five, was beginning to feel a growing uneasiness as he continued to watch the blue car that now loomed threateningly in his rear-view mirror. The distance between the two cars had noticeably shortened, making him even more uncomfortable.

His attention was momentarily diverted by the kids who had now polished off their popsicles and had begun to rough-house in the back seat

Before he could react, the blue Olds had moved out and to his left as if attempting to pass. When he looked up, to his horror, he found himself staring into the barrel of a shiny .32 caliber revolver. His first instinct was to hit the gas and get the car up to eighty as fast as possible, but the realization that the kids were with him and there was a gun being pointed at them convinced him to do otherwise. The man holding the gun was screaming unintelligibly as he motioned for Guard to pull off the road.

Guard lifted his foot from the accelerator and began to ease the car toward the road's right shoulder, assuming, that the man wanted him to pull over and stop. But instead of turning onto the logging road as Perk had wanted him to do, he pulled onto the dirt shoulder and came to a full stop short of the road's entrance.

"Damn!" Perkins exclaimed as Jack positioned the Olds partly off of the road and slightly in front of Young's car. "He didn't hear me. Now it looks like we're going to have to work out here on the highway."

Jack was concerned that should Young decide to bolt, he'd have to do it while he still had complete control of the kids. Even though he'd be partially blocked by the Olds, it was still possible for him to squeeze through and then he'd only have to make it a couple of miles before he'd be in the clear. It would be the whole Locatell thing all over again because being so close to town, there'd be no way they could catch up to him, get the money and get away. The only way they could prevent that from happening would be to take control of the kids immediately.

Jack turned to Harriet. "I want you to bring those kids over to this car."

Harriet sighed, but nodded.

Inside the Chrysler, Guard cursed to himself. He should have paid more attention to the warnings. This was the very scenario that Sheriff Schooler and Christal had warned him about. He fought off the temptation to just back up, tromp on the accelerator and make a run for it. Had he been alone, without the children, he would have done so without a moment's hesitation but as it was—discretion being the better part of valor—he had to consider other alternatives.

The three tots in the back seat, not fully realizing what was actually happening, had not yet reacted, but Sondra Gay was visibly frightened and confused. She looked up anxiously at her father, her eyes welling with tears, and as he looked back into that tiny fear-stricken face, Guard realized there were no alternatives. Without argument or hesitation—he would hand over the money and very quickly they'd be on their way. The only thing that mattered now was that the children remain safe and unharmed. The important thing now was to get them all safely home. The money was replaceable; his kids were not.

To Guard the man appeared small. Almost bald with little beady eyes and big ears, and without the gun, he would have been about as threatening as one of the seven dwarfs. But that gun turned him into a giant.

"Out of the car," Perkins snapped. "Keep your hands where I can see 'em."

Must be an out-of-towner, Guard thought since he knew of no one around Chester who spoke with such a pronounced drawl. Guard got out of the car and the little man with the gun swung open his door and stepped out.

As he had been instructed, Guard stood between the two cars, motionless and helpless; his thoughts a jumble of emotions as he tried to clear them long enough to assess his situation. His eyes darted from side to side, anxiously searching for a way out of this mess and as he glanced into the thieves' car, he couldn't help but notice the driver was wearing some kind of a mask. He also noticed a woman in the back seat, but when she saw that he was looking at her, she quickly pulled the brim of the hat down over her eyes in an obvious effort to hide her face. The mask and the woman's odd behavior caused Guard to wonder: were they both afraid of being recognized? Is it possible that he could know them?

Perkins continued to point the gun at Guard's chest and while they stood face to face between the two cars, the woman, after exiting the Olds, walked over to the Chrysler, opened the rear door, leaned in, and appeared to be saying something to the obviously now terrified children.

Guard, at well over six feet tall, towered over his diminutive adversary. To any casual passersby, the scene was nothing more than that of two men engaged in some kind of a roadside discussion.

Perkins had been keeping his eye out in either direction for oncoming cars, but as he looked southward, because his view was being obstructed by a small rise in the road, he wasn't able to see the car that was fast approaching from that direction.

"I want all that money you just got from the bank," he said. "Where's it at?"

It was a jarring indication to Guard that during all the time that he and the children were going about their business, they were completely unaware that these people had been monitoring their every move.

"I'll give you the money," he said. "You can take it. I don't want any trouble. I just don't want the kids to get hurt."

"We got no intention of hurting those kids," Perkins said. "As long as you don't give us a problem, there won't be any trouble."

Even as Perkins spoke, the thought of leaving witnesses behind to testify against them had already entered his mind.

"Where's the dough?" Perkins demanded.

Harriet meanwhile, had ushered Jean and Judy into the rear seat of the Oldsmobile, but before she could return to the Chrysler for Michael and Sondra, Jack, who had been watching the road through the rear-view mirror, stopped her.

"Hold it Harriet, Here comes a car. Get back inside."

She returned to the Olds to take a seat next to the two girls, but in her haste to get out of sight, she had inadvertently left the Chrysler's door hanging ajar. Michael, thinking that the strange lady wanted him to follow the girls, slipped out through the open door, but since the

Oldsmobile's doors were shut and unsure of where he was supposed to go, he began to wander aimlessly between the two cars.

The oncoming car crested at the top of the grade and as the driver, upon seeing the two men standing beside the parked cars and assuming that one of them was probably having car trouble, began to decelerate.

"Just act natural," Perkins warned. "Do something stupid and you can say goodbye to your kids."

The car crept closer and although he couldn't be absolutely certain, Guard thought he recognized Calvin Bacalla, a local horse rancher and an occasional customer, and judging from the way he stared at them as he drove past, Guard was sure that he had been recognized as well.

The Slaughter

While Harriet waited for the car to pass, Jack was unleashing a stream of invectives aimed at her for allowing Michael to wander away.

"Damn it, Harriet," he screamed. "You're supposed to be watching those kids!"

"Get into this car, boy," he yelled out to Michael.

But instead of obeying, Michael, now completely disoriented and frightened even more by Jack's threatening tone, turned away and in his confusion, began to run in the opposite direction which only made matters worse. Mistaking Michael's bewilderment for defiance, Jack bellowed again, "Boy, I told you to get into this car!" His rage succeeded only in driving the terror-stricken child even further away, his cries becoming louder and more agitated.

"I'll get him, Jack," Harriet said, fearing the worst. But before she could get out of the car, Perkins shouted, "Here, take the gun, Jack. I'm going to teach the little bastard a lesson."

Jack, making sure the passing car had driven out of sight, was already preparing to exit by sliding across the front seat. He stepped out of the car and took possession of the gun.

Guard, now seeing that Michael, rather than being defiant was simply confused, shouted to Perkins.

"Wait! No! Let me talk to him. You're just scaring him."

Like an enraged animal, Perkins chased after the terrified boy, overtaking him by the Chrysler's right rear fender and after grasping him by one tiny arm, he violently lifted the thirty-five-pound Michael two feet off the ground.

"I'm going to show you what I do to kids who don't do what they're told," he roared, showers of spittle spraying from his mouth. He spun Michael around, and still holding his arm, he brought his fist crashing down against the boy's face. Michael screamed and blood flew from the impact of the vicious blow.

Because Guard's view was being blocked by the car, he couldn't see the anguish and the stark terror in Michael's eyes as he pled for mercy while blow after blow rained down on his face. His screams, amplified by the forest's stillness, resonated as if emanating from some giant echo chamber, and were more than enough to tell Guard what was taking place.

Instinctively, and with little regard for the gun that was aimed directly at his heart, Guard lunged, taking two steps before being brought to an abrupt halt as Jack turned and pointed the gun directly at Sondra Gay's head.

"Take one more step—I swear—I'll put a bullet right through her skull," he shouted.

Guard stopped in his tracks and turning, he stared at the barrel of the gun now barely three feet from his daughter's head. His shoulders slumped in abject despair. Never before had he felt so completely and totally helpless—and useless.

How, he kept asking himself, could it have come to this? How could he have been so stupid as to put these vulnerable children in such a perilous situation and he, not able to help them?

The enraged Perkins, still holding Michael by his arm, used his free hand to slam the boy's head against the car's fender, continuing until the sound of his loud crying gradually changed to a baleful whimper. Finally, it stopped forever. He released the boy's arm and the lifeless body dropped to the ground.

Heartsick at being unable to lift a finger while being forced to stand helplessly by as Michael's life was being pounded away, Guard quietly wept as he whispered a silent prayer.

Like Guard, Jack had not been in a position to actually see the extreme brutality of Perkins' assault on the helpless boy. He continued to hold Guard at gunpoint and when Michael's crying stopped, he had assumed it was only because the beating had stopped. But Harriet had been in position to witness the entire spectacle.

"Perk!" she screamed in horror. "For Christ's sakes! Have you lost your mind? What in the name of God do you think you're doing?"

Perkins did not respond as Jack, still holding the pistol on Guard, walked to the back of the car where he could better view Perkins' handiwork.

He was shocked at what he could now see. "Jesus, Perk," he said, "Did you have to hit him so hard?"

Perkins stared at the little body as it lay silent and motionless on the gravel. Even he appeared to be shaken by his own savagery. He reached out with his foot as he attempted to roll the small, inert form to its side and speaking in a now moderated tone, as he gasped for breath, he said, "C'mon now kid, get up." But Michael could no longer hear; he was no longer able to get up.

"He's not getting up Jack," Perkins said after a quiet minute. "I think he's dead. I must have hit him a little too hard."

After watching the brutal attack from their back seat vantage point, Judy and Jean stood up, craning their necks in a vain effort to see their little friend. Struck by the grim realization that they had just watched Michael being beaten to death, their almost inaudible whimpers grew into primal screams. Their ear-piercing shrieks stabbed into Harriet's eardrums like needles, pushing her to the very limits of her endurance.

"Shut up! Just shut up!" she screeched. "That's what will happen to you if you don't shut up!" But their cries grew even louder.

She buried her face in her hands and moaned, "Oh, Jesus, I can't take this!" Never before had she felt so utterly trapped. "What in God's name is going on here?" she asked herself over and over again. "What the hell are we doing?"

Guard watched with utter revulsion the glowering little man with the big ears and beady eyes who, after his savage assault on the four-year-old boy, much like the conquering hero after slaying the dragon, standing straddled over the tiny lifeless body as it lay on the ground.

He was almost overwhelmed by a visceral urge to grab this monster by the throat and twist him into the ground like a giant corkscrew but that impulse was quickly tempered at the sight of Jack ominously pointing the gun at Sondra's head, her eyes tightly shut as she cowered in fear.

Motioning with his gun hand, Jack ordered Guard behind the wheel but not before Guard and Perkins had made eye contact. When Perkins noticed Guard's undisguised expression of disgust, his gaunt face twisted into a demonic smirk. To Guard, it was like staring into the eyes of the devil himself.

Guard could only shake his head in disbelief. What are we dealing with here? He asked himself. What kind of heartless monsters could do this to innocent children?

"Get in the car," Jack snarled at Guard as he opened the Chrysler's driver's side door. Sondra Gay was still standing in the front seat, quietly sobbing.

"It's okay, Daddy's here," Guard said as he got into the car and slid behind the wheel, taking a quick moment to wrap an arm around her tiny shoulders. Jack walked around to the rear of the car where Perkins stood over Michael's body.

"What should we do with him?" Perkins asked.

"Throw him in here," Jack said, lifting the trunk's lid. "And do it fast." He glanced nervously up and down the highway. They had been extremely lucky so far—traffic had been unusually light—but he knew that their luck would not hold indefinitely.

As dispassionately as if he were picking up a pile of roadside litter, Perkins gathered up Michael's body and heaved it into the trunk.

"We got to get these cars out of here before someone else comes along," Jack said. "I'll have Young drive and you can follow with Harriet and the kids."

Now realizing that Sondra Gay was still in the front seat, he yelled at Perkins, "Get this kid out of here! Put her in the other car with Harriet."

As Perkins reached out to pick her up, she recoiled, her blue, tear-filled eyes looking at her father, pleading with him to help her. Her gut-wrenching sobs pounded in Guard's ears like hammers, tearing his insides out.

"It'll be okay, honey," he managed to choke it out as reassuringly as this nightmare situation would permit.

"We're going to be alright," he said to her. "Just do as the man tells you."

To the children Guard may have appeared calm but the seething cauldron of rage boiling inside him had to be kept under control. It would be rational thinking, not emotional reaction, that would get them out of this.

Guard turned to watch as Perkins carried Sondra Gay to the Olds, placing her—not too gently—alongside Jean, Judy and the figure in the back seat. It gave him an opportunity to study the mysterious woman, and as he held his gaze in order to catch a better look at her, their eyes locked and before she could avert his stare by looking away, he recognized her as someone who had recently been in the store.

Jack came around the front of the car and climbed into the passenger seat, drawing Guard's attention away from Harriet.

"Why don't you just take the money and go?" Guard asked. "You can have it. Just take it. You don't have to hurt the kids."

Without answering, Jack, still wearing the mask and menacingly waving the gun in Guard's face, told him to start driving.

"Take it down that road there," he said, pointing to the entrance to the logging road that they now had identified as Malvich Road.

Guard slowly edged the big Chrysler onto the abandoned road, carefully negotiating the deep potholes and scattered natural debris while Perkins, with Harriet and the children in the Olds, followed closely behind. In the few minutes it would take to negotiate the quarter mile, and even as Jack continued to threaten him with the gun, Guard began to wonder—why? If all they wanted was the money, why not just take it and go? It would have taken no more than two minutes for them to have asked for the money, which he would have gladly handed over. Two minutes! What then, could be the purpose of leading them all down this isolated path to do what they could have done so easily and so quickly back there beside the highway? It kept coming back to the one logical answer: they must be afraid that the woman in the back seat had been recognized as one of his customers and so they planned to kill him to prevent him from identifying her. But if that were true, what have they planned for his children? His stomach churned with a quiet sickening fury. If their intentions were to kill him as well as the children, he swore silently to himself that he would not allow that to happen—and if in the process, it cost him his own life—then so be it.

Guard weighed his alternatives. Whatever he decided to do would have to be done with split-second suddenness before Jack had time to react by pulling the trigger. His best opportunity, he calculated, would come when Jack went for the bag of cash in the glove compartment. If there was to be an opening—one fleeting moment when Jack's attention would be apt to stray—that would be it. He'd have to act swiftly and decisively; get the gun and if it became necessary, shoot him, all before he had a chance to react. In the end, the whole thing boiled down to a single proposition: he needed to get possession of that gun.

They arrived at the clearing and once again, as he had done yesterday, Jack surveyed their surroundings. He still liked what he saw.

"Here! Stop right here," he ordered.

Set back several feet off the road, the small clearing was bordered on three sides by clumps of stumpy bushes, scraggly trees and tall dried out grasses, all serving to block the view from the surrounding landscape and screening them from wandering hunters whose presence in the area would be a constant but unavoidable risk.

Guard tapped the brake pedal and the big Chrysler squeaked to a stop. He turned off the ignition as Perkins, driving the Olds, pulled up alongside. An eerie quiet fell over the scene as the girls' crying had subsided and for a brief moment, their soft sobs mingled with the gentle sound of rustling leaves; creating, illogically, an aura of serene beauty mixed somehow with a sense of impending horror.

He noticed a scattering of discarded paper bags, broken bottles, cans and other trash that had been gathered into a small pile, a clear indication that at one time, the area been a hunter's rest stop. This accumulation of trash and debris, although no one knew it at the time, was to play a major role in the terrible events that were soon to follow.

With his right hand, Jack continued to level the gun at Guard's stomach while twisting his body so as to bring the two men face to face. Jack's smug—almost arrogant—demeanor gave Guard reason to suspect that this man was not fully aware of his own vulnerability or the awkward position in which such tight quarters put him should he need to react quickly.

"Alright—enough of the bullshit. Where's the money?" Jack demanded, and just in case Guard was harboring thoughts of resisting, he added, "And be very careful how you move. Your kids' lives depend on it."

Guard wasn't listening. He stared down at the weapon, his mind racing. Here it comes, he was thinking. This, most likely, was going to be his moment of maximum distraction. He reasoned that when Jack reached for the money he'd probably use his right hand—the one holding the gun—and his attention will almost certainly shift as he switched gun hands. For just those few seconds—maybe when he starts to count the money—that would be the moment when Guard would have his one and only chance to grab the gun.

For just a moment he considered Perkins: where was he and what was he doing? Apparently, he had left Harriet with the kids and was now walking about the clearing, using a stick to poke through the brush. He seemed to be looking for something, but where, exactly, was he? Was he far enough away to give Guard enough time to snatch the gun from Jack's grasp before either could react? Life itself, Guard had always told himself, is a series of gambles, and if it's God's will that you win, then you will win. The gamble that Guard was about to take would be the most consequential of his life.

"It's in the glove compartment," Guard said, bracing himself.

"Get it," Jack commanded.

Here it comes, Guard thought. He opened the small compartment and reaching in, grasped the moneybag before slamming it shut. As he turned to face Jack and while holding out the moneybag, he caught a break. Jack's left arm was pressed against the seat's back-rest, preventing him from reaching out for the bag. To free his right hand so he could accept the money, he instinctively started to switch the gun from his right to his left hand. His motion was interrupted as he stopped to adjust the mask which had started to slip. It was in that instant—that split second when Jack's vision was impaired by the mask covering his eyes—Guard struck.

Seizing Jack's wrist with his own strong right hand, he wrapped his left arm around Jack's neck, squeezing it in a powerful head-lock. Jack reacted with such force his horn-rimmed glasses were sent flying through the car's interior, together with a flurry of twenty-dollar bills as they poured from the bag. In the life or death struggle for possession of the gun, the mask, now having been ripped from Jack's face, also went flying. As they grappled in the confined quarters of the car's front seat, neither could get the leverage needed to gain an advantage. The two big men wrestled against the passenger side door, the force of their combined weight tripping the door latch and when the door swung open, the two men tumbled out onto the ground. In the melee, Guard was able to deliver a crushing blow flush to Jack's jaw, causing him to release his grip on the gun. It slipped from his hand and dropped to the ground. Guard pounced on it, picked it up and pointed it at Jack's heart. Now, he thought, thankfully, the shoe is on the other foot.

Guard, while not taking his eyes off his adversary, and with the gun still firmly leveled at Jack's heart, lifted himself to a kneeling position while Jack, on one knee, remained on the ground.

Unbeknownst to Guard, while he had been scuffling with Jack, Perkins had found a short length of lead pipe in that small pile of debris and now brandishing it menacingly above his head and either unaware or unconcerned about the gun that was now pointed at Jack, he began to advance on the two struggling figures.

Guard turned the barrel of the gun to face the threat now presented by the pipe-wielding Perkins while Jack, obviously relieved that the gun was no longer pointed at him, looked on in bemused astonishment.

"Hold it right there," Guard said, bringing the gun into a firing position, "and drop the pipe."

Perkins either didn't hear Guard's warning or didn't care because he kept coming, and even though it would be contrary to one of his most deeply held beliefs—that of taking another's life—Guard had already made up his mind that in these circumstances where his children's lives were at stake and with one already dead, he would—without so much as a second's hesitation—shoot to kill.

He attempted to lift himself into some kind of a firing position as Perkins ignored Guard's repeated warnings and continued to advance.

Perkins had once again taken on the look of an enraged beast as he raised the pipe above his head but before he could strike, Guard squeezed the trigger. To his horror, the gun would not fire. He squeezed it again and—nothing. In one violent motion, Perkins brought the pipe down, slamming it against Guard's forehead. Stunned by the blow and with blood gushing from the wound, Guard relaxed his grip on the gun and even as he felt it slipping from his hand, he instinctively struggled to rise to his feet.

Jack knew, despite Young's being badly hurt—even on the verge of unconsciousness—that he would continue to fight back with the ferocity of any father protecting his children from imminent mortal danger. To Jack, even in his condition, Guard represented—if not an actual threat—certainly a complication that needed to be taken care of.

With Guard now lying motionless on the ground, Jack began to bark out orders. "We need to tie this guy up," he said. "If we don't, he's going to be a problem because, believe me, he's a load and I don't want to have to deal with him again."

Perkins walked back to his car and retrieved the skein of clothesline he had pulled from the trunk earlier.

"This ought to work," he said, handing it to Jack. "I'll hold him down and you can tie his hands behind his back."

He rolled the half-conscious Guard over on his stomach, placing a knee into the small of his back while Jack grasped Guard's hands and with Guard able to offer only a minimum of resistance, he tied them together.

When Perkins had been digging through the junk pile, he came up with a piece of cloth which he now put to use as a blindfold. Once Guard, still badly dazed from the ferocious blow to his head, had been rendered immobile, Jack began to gather up the money that had spilled from the bank bag and now was strewn about the car. Meanwhile, Perkins' attention was being drawn to Harriet and the three children whose piercing cries, he feared, could be heard across the entire surrounding area.

"Jesus, Perk, these kids are driving me crazy," Harriet wailed. "Can't we just get the money and get the hell out of here?"

"I think we got other problems, Harriet," Perkins said. "I think the guy might have recognized Jack."

"Yeah, well, so what?" Harriet said. "He can't identify Jack by name because he doesn't know who he is. Besides, I'm sure he recognized me, too, when he looked into the car, but so what? It doesn't mean he can identify me."

"This ain't good," Perkins said, pondering their next move. He walked back to Jack who was still gathering up the twenty-dollar bills.

"How much did we get?" he asked.

"I don't know for sure," Jack replied. "I'm guessing that it's a little over seven. Nothing like ten grand, but still a pretty nice haul. We can count it after we get out of this jungle."

"We have to do something with these kids," Jack said ominously. "They could pick us all out of a lineup if we let them go."

"I think you're right, Jack. You and me have so many mug shots on file it would take them about five seconds—even the kids—to find us."

"We have to kill them, Perk," Jack said matter-of-factly, his voice as cold as death itself. "We have to kill them all."

"Kill them all?" Perk said. "That's pretty drastic, isn't it?"

"I'm sure the sonofabitch made me and probably Harriet too," Jack said. "Besides, you already killed one of them, so what's a few more?"

"Yeah, but one murder isn't like five," Perkins countered.

"What's the difference, Perk?" Jack grinned, "They'll fry you for one murder just as well as for five. My daddy always taught me—if you're in for a dime, you might as well be in for a dollar."

"Alright," Perkins said. "I'll take care of it. Help me get them out of the car and I'll do the rest."

As Jack and Perkins talked, they made little effort to lower their voices, unaware that Guard, though his mind was still befogged by Perkins' blow, was able to overhear the entire dialogue. Stunned by its sheer barbarity, he strained at his bindings, not thinking clearly but still, instinctively trying to free himself so he could get to the children.

Perkins glared down at his struggling adversary on the ground and decided it was time to bring this part of the problem to an end. As if swatting a fly, he raised the pipe over his head and brought it crashing down on Guard's skull. The violent blow and the one that immediately followed sent a cloud of blood spatter mixed with bits of flesh and bone flying through the air. Before he was done, Perkins would deliver a total of seven blows, any one of which could have been fatal.

For the Young girls it was like watching a horror movie as they were being forced to witness the ghastly tableau playing out before their eyes. Seeing their father being beaten to death, watching Perkins' merciless attack on Michael, not yet fully realizing that their friend was already dead, and terrified that they would be next, the girls, understandably had become completely unmanageable for Harriet. Although she tried everything she could think of to placate them, her lack of experience in dealing with small children now had her on the brink of panic.

"You kids get out of the car!" Perkins shouted as he approached the car where the petrified girls sat shivering and huddled together.

"Help them out," he barked to Harriet.

Had she been aware of his intentions, it's doubtful that she would have been so compliant; however, not having been privy to the exchange between Jack and Perkins just moments ago, she slid over to one side so the girls could get out of the car. Their angelic faces streaked with tears, shaking and trembling in the cold autumn air, they stumbled in single file through the open door.

"Stay right here," he ordered the girls before calling out to Harriet, "Give me a hand out here."

Harriet climbed out from the back seat. "What do you want me to do?" she asked warily as she stood next to the three girls.

Grabbing Jean's arm with a violent jerk, Perkins started toward the car's opposite side. "Hang on to those two," he growled over his shoulder.

Things were starting to become clear to Harriet. Her voice rose in uncertain concern. "What are you going to do, Perk?"

But she knew. She turned to Jack whose jaw was still throbbing from the blow he had taken from Guard.

"Jack, you have to stop him! Please, Jack. Don't let him do this!"

Jack was still fuming and Harriet's appeal for mercy fell on deaf ears. "Don't worry about it," he said ominously. "We'll do what we have to do."

Wielding that same weapon with which he had ended Guard's life, Perkins slammed it down against the skull of the innocent child and suddenly the stillness of the autumn afternoon was pierced by the shrill screams of seven-year-old Jean Young. Amidst a crimson gusher of blood and tissue, the violent succession of blow after blow brought an abrupt end to her anguished screams.

Perkins lifted the limp sixty-pound body from the ground with the same care and concern of a highway worker picking up the weekend's road kill, casually tossing it into the trunk beside the body of little Michael. The savage orgy was about to gather momentum.

"Oh, my God, Jack!" What the hell are we doing?" Harriet was coming close to her breaking point. "Jack, this is absolutely insane!" She screamed in wild-eyed horror. "He's gone crazy! You've got to make him stop!"

When Perkins emerged from behind the car his face was contorted into a malevolent grin. Breathing heavily with beads of sweat rolling down his brow, he advanced on the terror-stricken girls as they shivered and cowered, clinging desperately to Harriet. She made a feeble attempt to shield them, but ignoring her efforts, Perkins reached out and grabbed Judy by her tiny arm. Oblivious to the little girl's shrieks, he dragged the golden-haired, six-year-old to her painful death.

"One more to go," Perkins mumbled to himself as he picked up Judy's body, again callously depositing it in the trunk alongside those of Jean and Michael.

It was now Sondra Gay's turn. Harriet gazed down at the wistful three-year-old who, with her father, her friend and both sisters all now dead, was all alone. She looked into the innocent eyes, and as she considered the awful fate that she was certain awaited this little girl, never before in her lifetime had she felt so utterly helpless.

Why wouldn't Jack put a stop to this? His lack of compassion, Harriet thought, had always been one of his major shortcomings, but never did she ever imagine it could go this far.

At this moment, Jack's attention was drawn to Guard as he lay in the dirt amidst the fallen pine needles. Harriet couldn't tell if he was still alive. Jack bent down and rolled Guard onto his back, placed an ear against his chest and, satisfied at the absence of a heartbeat, stood up and matter-of-factly pronounced, "He's dead."

It would take only minutes for Perkins to complete his grisly work, dealing out the same bloody punishment to Sondra Gay as he had to Jean and Judy. When the frenzy had at last run its course, the glowering Perkins reappeared for the final time, panting, sweating and drenched in blood. In his wake was a trail of battered, broken tiny bodies, their small heads smashed like melons, hair matted with blood and piled in the trunk like so much unwanted trash.

Aftermath

"We're done, Jack," Perkins said.

"Hurry up and let's get this place cleaned up so we can get the hell out of here," Jack snapped, wanting to put as much distance between this scene and someplace else—*any* place else.

"It'll be a miracle if we can get away clean on this one," he said as he studied Harriet's speechless reaction. What she had just witnessed would probably haunt her every minute of every day for the rest of her life.

But at that point Jack's only comment was, "What a mess!" he said, shaking his head.

Harriet, even though she hadn't actually been hands-on involved—not very much, anyway—was now a part of it. But what could she have possibly done to prevent it? Surely, she rationalized, her own life would have been in serious jeopardy had she attempted to put herself between the kids and Perkins in the midst of his maniacal rage.

As echoes of the children's wails continued to ring in her ears, she was suddenly jolted from her zombie-like trance by Jack's shouts.

"F'chrissakes, woman!" Jack barked, "don't just stand there. Give me a hand here!"

"What do you want me to do?" she asked, still in a daze.

Jack walked over to Guard's blood-saturated corpse and began to rifle through his pockets. Finding Guard's wallet and without inspecting its contents, he stuffed it into his own pocket.

"Help me get this guy into the trunk."

Harriet was dumbstruck. This, she thought, was just too much. Simply too much.

"Do I have to, Jack?" she pleaded. "I mean ... he's dead ... I can't..."

"What do you mean, 'you can't'? You can sure as hell help spend the money, can't you?"

Fearing that he was about to launch into one of his hallmark rants, Harriet reluctantly bent down and grasped Guard's battered form as she attempted to help Jack carry it to the car. Struggling under the two-hundred-forty pound weight, she exhaled an audible groan The futility of her effort triggered another profanity laced tirade from Jack, his booming voice had risen to decibel levels loud enough to draw the attention of hunters a half-mile away.

"Jesus, Jack!" Perkins said. "Keep your voice down. What are you trying to do—wake up the whole dammed county?" He hurried to the Chrysler and after pushing Harriet aside, he helped Jack, carry Guard's body the ten feet to the rear of the car, flinging it into the trunk where it landed with a dull thud atop the bodies of the slain children. When Perkins tried to close the lid, he found that Guard's hands, which had been tied behind his back, were protruding beyond the trunk, making it impossible to close. After several unsuccessful attempts to readjust Guard's body, in frustration he turned to Jack.

"His hands are in the way. Give me a knife."

Assuming that, after committing the brutal murders, Perkins was now about to start mutilating the bodies, a horrified Harriet couldn't contain herself. "Knife?" she screamed, "What the hell are you going to do with a knife?"

"Shut up, woman, I'm just going to cut this cord," Perkins said with a grin, "so I can move his arms out of the way." He quickly severed the sash cord binding on Guard's hands and threw his now freed left arm over Judy's body. When Harriet next looked at the grisly scene, what she saw was a father, even in death, embracing his sleeping daughter.

"What do you want me to do now?" she asked.

Like an angry teacher reproaching a dull-witted schoolgirl, Jack growled, "Make yourself useful. Get behind that wheel and drive this car into that brush. Do you think you can do that?" he snapped. "And bring me the keys when you're done."

Positioning herself behind the wheel, she slipped the gearshift lever into drive and gently eased the Chrysler into the thick undergrowth as far as it would go. She turned off the ignition, pushed open the door and after having to inch her way out by fighting through the prickly scrub branches, finally emerged into the clearing.

Jack looked approvingly at the car's new location and even though it was only partially concealed, it was now out of view and so, he calculated, would not be quickly spotted.

"Give me the keys," he said. "I have to lock the trunk."

Harriet, with trembling hands gave Jack the small key chain on which, he noticed, held but one key which he assumed was the ignition key.

"Damn," he said. "There's no trunk key here. I guess we're going to have to leave the trunk unlocked."

On discovering that Perkins' rearrangement of the bodies had gone for naught, Jack closed the lid as far as it would go and after a feeble attempt to cover the top of the car with a few branches and twigs, he tossed the key chain into the grass at the side of the clearing.

"Let's get the hell out of here," he snapped.

Harriet was in tears. "Those kids? Why the kids?" she mumbled to herself.

Jack had heard enough. With a powerful back-handed swing, his hand smashed against the side of her head, causing her to lose her balance. Harriet staggered backward and started to go down and had the car not been there to break her fall, she would have dropped to the ground.

"Shut up!" he snarled. "That's enough! Don't talk about this again—to anyone—ever! Do you understand?"

Jack was as agitated as anyone had ever seen him since he was only partially confident that Harriet, even as disturbed over the killings as she appeared to be, would not dare open her mouth because, as an accomplice to multiple murders, she'd be just as dirty as he or Perkins.

She picked herself up and after pulling herself together, she opened the car door and crawled into the back seat. Jack and Perkins returned to the front and after first carefully wiping the murder weapon clean of blood and fingerprints, Perkins heaved it into the underbrush.

"Wouldn't look too good if we happened to get stopped," he remarked dryly. "Someone might get the wrong idea."

The blood spatter that had covered most of Perkins exposed skin had also been wiped clean by using a piece of the material he had found in the debris—the same material from which Guard's blindfold had been fashioned.

It was almost four in the afternoon when they started for home. With Jack behind the wheel it took them only seconds to reach the main road. He glanced to his left and after momentarily waiting for an approaching truck to pass, veered onto the highway. Only the hum of the engine could be heard as they rode in silence, reflecting on the events of the past half-hour and the part each of them had played.

"Perk," Jack said, breaking the silence. "You have to get out of town. This car could have been spotted back there beside the highway. As soon as they find those bodies they're going to be putting up road blocks and the first thing they're going to be looking for is a dark blue Oldsmobile sedan."

"Yeah, you're right," Perkins said. "If I leave right away, I can be back in L.A. before they ever start looking. I can just take my share now and you won't have to worry about getting it to me later."

Jack considered for a moment. "Take your cut and take Harriet's too," he said. "She's going with you. Drop her off in Auburn."

Handing Harriet the wallet he had taken from Guard Young's pocket, Jack instructed her, "Get rid of this. Burn it so there's nothing left."

He slid the gun from under his belt and gave that to her as well. "Get rid of this worthless piece of junk too," he said with disgust. "Throw it in the Truckee River. Nothing worse than trying to pull a robbery with a gun that don't work. If I need a gun, I still have that .38 that you guys used in the Hansen job."

Harriet was surprised but grateful that Jack wanted her gone. Anything that would get her far away from this nightmare would be welcome.

She'd go home and take a long, long shower. If she could just wash away the grime, the dirt and yes—even the blood—especially the blood—maybe she wouldn't have to think any more about what they had done. Fat chance, she thought.

Jack reminded Perkins, "We have to take the ten percent off the top for Larry. The bank receipt says there's seventy-one hundred there so ten percent of seventy-one hundred is seven ten . . ." Figuring quickly in his head, "One full share would be . . . let's see . . . seven ten from seventy-one hundred would leave . . . sixty-three ninety. Divide that by three and you get . . . twenty-one and change," he said, obviously proud of his ability to come up with the answer without the aid of pencil and paper.

"Leave the rest in the bag and I'll straighten up with Shea later," Jack said.

Perkins counted out forty-two hundred dollars and then stuffed the rest back in the bag as they rolled up in front of the Shea home. Jack shut off the ignition and exited from the car allowing Perkins to slide behind the wheel. Harriet, without speaking, moved into the front seat vacated by Perkins. There were no goodbyes or promises to call later. He stood and watched as the blue Oldsmobile rumbled slowly down the street until it disappeared around the corner.

As Jack walked up the driveway his thoughts were turning to other matters. What was he going to tell Larry and Lucille? What will they say when they find out that they are now accomplices in five murders? Would they go running to the cops? Probably not, he supposed. And if push should come to shove and they were hauled in for questioning, would they be able to maintain their cool?

As he approached the side door leading into the kitchen, he met Larry coming out of the house.

"What did you do with the cowboy?" Larry asked after seeing that Jack was alone. "And where's Harriet?"

"Perk went back to L.A. and he's dropping her off in Auburn on the way," Jack told him.

"That's too bad," Larry said. "Lucille will miss her. She went into town awhile ago to get a few things. Let's go in and have a drink."

"Man, I'm beat," Jack said. "I could sure use a drink. It's been a shitty day so make it a good one."

Larry held the door open as Jack walked through the kitchen into the living room where he plunked himself down on the sofa.

Grabbing the nearly full bottle of whiskey and a couple of glasses, Larry spread them out on the coffee table. "Are you going to tell me what happened, Jack? What do you mean it's been a shitty day? Don't tell me you didn't get the money again."

When Jack failed to reply, he asked warily, "did you get the money?"

"Yeah," Jack said. "We got the money. Your cut is seven hundred." He hesitated. ". . . but we had some trouble. It didn't quite go the way we planned."

Jack handed Larry seven hundred dollars in twenty dollar bills. Larry's smile slowly turned into a puzzled frown.

"Trouble? What kind of trouble?"

This is going to be difficult, Jack thought. Unsure as to when and how much he should tell him and worried as to how he would react, Jack waved him off.

"I'll tell you about it later," he said. "Right now, I just want to clean up a little."

"Yeah," Larry said, somewhat relieved that he wasn't going to have to listen to any bad news—not at this moment, anyway.

"You look like you could use a little cleaning up. Is that blood on you?"

"Yeah, it might be. I'll tell you all about it later, alright?" Jack took a deep swallow of his drink.

"Are we still going to Reno tonight?"

"Yeah—we're going but . . ." Larry hesitated again. "Are you still planning on going? I mean since Harriet's not here now, I was kind of thinking you might want to, you know, pass."

"Don't you worry about ol' Jack, Larry boy. I don't need Harriet around to have a good time," Jack said as he rose from the couch and headed for the bathroom.

Larry was still wondering what Jack meant when he said "trouble." Was something going on with Harriet? And what about Perkins? Could Perkins have done something stupid? Wouldn't put it past him, Larry thought. And that blood. What was that all about? Did someone get hurt?

Minutes later, cleaned up and reinvigorated, Jack came out of the bathroom and as if today had never happened, appeared to be in good spirits and looking forward to a night out on the town.

"I need to use your phone. I think I'll call Bernadine to see if we can hook up tonight." Then he stopped to think. "You think Lucille will mind if I bring Bernadine?"

"Nah," Larry said. "Why would she mind? She already knows you for what you are which is a lousy, two-timing asshole."

Ignoring Larry's good-natured jibe, Jack began to rummage through his wallet until he found what he was looking for. Using the kitchen wall phone, he dialed Bernadine Pearney's number. Bernie was one of Jack's former dalliances currently employed as a civilian secretary at Beale Air Force Base, a sprawling military facility located on the outskirts of Marysville about a hundred miles southwest of Chester.

Jack's phone conversation with Bernadine was another indication that, as it was with most of his ex-girlfriends—even after having dumped her in favor of Harriet—he still managed to exert that same manipulative hold on her.

"Been a good girl?" he asked. "Or the same ol' Bernie we all know and love?"

"Of course. I'm always good. No one should know that better than you," she replied warily. "Why—what's up?" and then recalling that not that long ago Jack had hit her up for a "loan" of fifteen dollars, she cautioned him, "I don't have any more money I can lend you, Jack. I'm tapped out."

"Nah," Jack cut her off. "I don't want your money, Bernie. In fact, I'm flush and I want to show my appreciation for your generosity."

"Yeah?" she asked, even more guardedly. "What do you have in mind?"

"I'll tell you what I'm going to do, little girl," he said, sounding more like a used car salesman than a man angling for a date. "If you would like to be wined, dined, see some great floor shows and maybe even get yourself a brand new wardrobe, then you need to get in your car and get that pretty little ass up here to Chester because I'm going to take you to Reno and show you the time of your life."

Bernadine was hooked. "How about my fifteen bucks?"

"That too."

She explained that her car wasn't running well enough to chance the drive to Chester. "I'll have to catch a bus," she said. "Give me your number there and I'll call you back after I find out about the bus schedule."

A smug Jack was grinning as he cradled the phone and joined Larry in the living room where he poured himself another drink.

While Larry was hoping that he might now get some answers, Jack instead plopped himself on the couch and started to talk about Reno and what he was going to do tonight. Finally, Larry brought the subject back to the robbery.

"You going to tell me what happened today?" Larry said.

Jack hesitated before answering. "You know, Larry, sometimes things happen that you don't intend to happen," he began clumsily. "Sometimes things just get out of control."

"Sure, Jack," Larry said. "Is that what happened today? Things got out of control?"

"Yeah, real bad out of control." Jack lit a cigarette and while he poured himself another drink. Larry waited—not sure he wanted to hear it.

"Is that what all the blood was about? Things got out of control and someone ended up getting hurt, or even killed?" he persisted. "Is that what happened?"

Jack sat silently, groping for the words that would minimize what they had done; words that would somehow sugarcoat the killing of five human beings. Not surprisingly, those words wouldn't come. He snuffed out his cigarette.

"Can we talk about this later?"

Larry had been prepared to bore in with more questions but was stopped short when the phone rang.

It was Bernadine calling back to inform Jack that there was no bus service between Marysville and Chester. They agreed that she would instead take a bus to Reno where he would meet her at the Reno Greyhound bus terminal at around ten-thirty. For Jack Santo, the events of the past few hours were now the farthest thing from his mind.

Lucille called shortly after five o'clock and Larry told her to hurry on home so they could leave for Reno.

"Larry, did Jack and Perk get back yet?" she wanted to know.

"Jack's here but Harriet caught a ride home to Auburn with Perk. He's headed back to L.A., thank God, so we won't have to put up with his horseshit for awhile."

Lucille seemed to be a little out of breath as she gasped, "There's a big hubbub going on down here around Young's Supermarket. I asked someone what all the fuss was about and they told me that the store's owner was missing and so were the four little kids he had with him. They're talking about getting a search party together to go out looking for them."

Immediately the recollection of Jack's bloodstained hands and clothes which he hadn't even tried to conceal, began to form in Larry's mind.

"Do you think Jack and Perk could have anything to do with that?" Lucille asked.

"Don't know, Lou. Just get home so we can leave for Reno. If Jack had anything to do with Young being missing we need to get our asses a long way from Chester before these Keystone Kops get wind that he's been staying with us. Please—get home now!" he urged as he hung up the phone.

This was starting to look like anything but good, especially when Larry stopped to consider the fact that Jack's lowlife buddy, Emmett Perkins, had been involved. And was Harriet really on her way home? Maybe she was missing too. Larry was getting an uneasy sense that he and Lucille were in this a lot deeper than either of them had bargained for. He resolved to himself that he wasn't going to take any more of Jack's pussyfooting around the issue. On the drive up to Reno, Jack would have to come clean with the whole story and that's all there was to it.

FIVE

Premonitions

As the late Friday afternoon wore on, a pervasive sense of anxiety was beginning to spread throughout the Young Supermarket. The emotional stress that had been growing in Christal, although she was doing her best not to show it, was becoming obvious to the growing lines of anxious customers, several of whom had tried to cash their paychecks but had been turned away and told to come back in half an hour.

Highly unusual thought Dottie, the store's manager. Guard, especially when he has the kids with him, would always have been back by now. Of course it was quite possible that he had gotten himself hung up at the variety store, but even so . . .

"What in the world could have happened to them, Christal?" Dottie asked. "I swear, this ain't like him," she said. "He always calls if there's a problem."

"I'm sure we'll hear something pretty soon," Christal said. It was an attempt to convince herself as much as it was to reassure Dottie. She glanced at the clock for at least the tenth time and noticed that the hour had now crept past five o'clock. But she knew Dottie was right. Guard would know how anxious they all would be waiting for him to get back with the cash. He would never leave them hanging like this. Christal fought off the uneasy feeling that had been gnawing at the pit of her stomach.

"I'm calling the bank," she suddenly announced.

Dottie interrupted. "The bank closed at three, Christal."

"Yes, I know, Dottie, but on Fridays people usually stay a little later. Besides," Christal said hopefully, "I know that the staff works from nine to six even though the front doors are locked."

She found Bank Manager John Woods' business card and dialed the number. When the male voice on the other end answered, her words were clear and concise: "Hello, Mr. Woods. I'm so glad you're still there. This is Christal Young at Young's Supermarket in Chester."

"Yes, Mrs. Young," his voice was irritatingly cheerful. "How can I help you?"

She came directly to the point. "My husband Guard left the store here in Chester over two hours ago to go to your bank and no one's seen nor heard from him since."

Before Woods could respond, Christal quickly added, "He has our three girls with him as well as their little neighbor friend. We're starting to worry, Mr. Woods; he doesn't usually do this." Christal paused momentarily before asking the question, the answer to which she wasn't sure she wanted to hear. "Have you seen them, Mr. Woods? Have they been there?"

"Yes, Mrs. Young. They were here. It was shortly before closing time. I remember because I locked up behind them as they walked out."

"Did you notice anything unusual? I mean, did everything seem normal?"

"Normal? Yes. I'd say so. Nothing seemed to be amiss. He had seven thousand dollars and change in the pouch when he left. It was a perfectly normal transaction—nothing at all out of the ordinary— except he had one of his little girls with him," he added.

"That sure is some cute little lady you've got there, Mrs. Young. She's a real charmer." Christal smiled at his words but her heart sank when she considered the implications of what she had just heard. She thanked him, hung up the phone and rejoined Dottie at the checkout counter.

"Maybe he had a flat tire," one shopper suggested. Bill Watson, a Collins mill-worker who had come in over an hour earlier with his wife Lydia, walked over to Christal. The Watsons had been expecting to purchase a week's groceries, cash his paycheck and then head home for supper.

"Maybe we should get in the car and go out on 36 to see if we can find them," Watson offered. "What kind of shape are the tires in, Christal? Does he have a good spare?"

"I know one of those tires had been showing wear," she recalled, before suddenly brightening at this new possibility. "I've been telling

Guard that he should get it taken care of. And I remember his complaining about the jack. I think he said there was something wrong with it and he was going to take it back to the dealer for a replacement."

"Well, a flat tire and a busted jack would definitely be a problem," Watson said. "He's probably stuck out there and has been trying to wave somebody down for help. Not too many cars out there, y'know."

Christal felt herself relax ever so slightly. A flat tire would be a far more welcome alternative to any of the other scenarios that had been bouncing around in her over-imaginative mind.

When Michael Saile's mother Rosemary arrived home from work a little past five o'clock, she was puzzled by the unusual amount of customer activity in front of the store. Rosemary and four-year-old Michael lived in an apartment above the Young Supermarket directly adjacent to the apartment occupied by the Young family.

Recently divorced, Rosemary and her little boy had arrived in Chester from Chicago five weeks ago. At age twenty-eight, a bitter divorce had left Rosemary disillusioned and wistfully imagining a better life for herself and her son.

Through a friend she learned about a small town lumber mill in Northern California that had been advertising for a private secretary, a position for which she was well qualified. She sent her resumé to the company's personnel manager and while waiting for a response, spent a rainy Chicago afternoon at the public library in an effort to learn something about this little town in California called Chester. She poured over articles and travelogues, and much to her pleasant surprise, she discovered that the citizens of Chester were enjoying the very kind of idyllic lifestyle which she had imagined for her and little Michael. The colorful photos of redwood forests, azure lakes and snow-capped mountains all seemed to be beckoning.

So when Rosemary received a phone call from The Collins Pine Lumber Company inviting her to come in for an interview she didn't hesitate. She immediately flew to Sacramento and from there embarked on a long, six-hour Greyhound bus ride to Chester.

Her interview at Collins went better than well and a week after returning to Chicago, Rosemary was informed that she had the job. If she could start right away, the company would be willing to pick up her travel and moving expenses.

When they arrived in Chester, she found that although the apartment above the supermarket was small, it was comfortable and convenient to her new workplace. Added to that, she was thrilled that the neighboring Young children had taken an immediate liking to Michael. They had all become instant friends.

On this evening, Rosemary pulled onto the gravel driveway that ran along the right side of the building, and upon seeing the small crowd of people milling about the front door, she assumed the store was having some kind of a sales promotion. But if that were the case, then why, she wondered, were most of the people not carrying grocery bags? Instead of smiles, she noticed that the expressions on their faces were sober and uncharacteristically grim.

Curious as to what all the commotion was about, she elbowed her way through the crowd and upon entering the store, her eyes began to search for a familiar face. Quickly discovering Christal standing behind the check-out counter, she whispered, "Hey—what's going on? What's with all these people?"

Christal hesitated, but from the anxious expression on her face, it was clear to Rosemary that she was about to receive some bad news.

"Guard and the kids left the bank at three o'clock this afternoon and no one has seen them since," Christal said, trying to keep her voice steady and calm.

"The kids? Do you mean Michael, too?"

"Yes," Christal said. "I'm afraid so."

Rosemary felt herself flush as a sense of dread washed over her.

"Oh dear, Christal. What do you think happened to them? That was more than two hours ago. Is anyone out looking for them?"

Christal did her best to answer Rosemary's questions, except, of course, the big one—the one that burned the most: Where are they?

Christal, by far the less emotionally fragile of the two women, was bearing up remarkably well under the circumstances, exhibiting little, if any, outward turmoil. Rosemary, on the other hand, despite a brave effort to keep her emotions in check, was not. Her son—her only child—was out there somewhere and nobody could tell her where or with whom. The evening was beginning to turn cold—some were even predicting snow for that night. The awful realities slowly started to sink in: without a coat, Michael was probably freezing out there and more than likely, he was scared and crying for his mother.

In the five short weeks they had lived in Chester, Michael Saile and his mother Rosemary—a devout Roman Catholic whose circle of acquaintances had for the most part, revolved around her church activities—had become almost surrogate members of the Young family. Despite their differences in religious beliefs, Rosemary and Christal had developed between them a sister-like relationship.

Dottie had been watching the clock and had noted that it was now closing in on five-thirty. "It's getting dark—if someone doesn't go pretty soon, they won't be able to see nothing."

She turned to her husband Howard who had stopped by on hearing that Guard and the kids were missing.

"Howie, why don't you drive down 36 to see if you can spot them? Make sure you've got our jack with you."

"We're going with you," Christal said, nodding at Rosemary. It would soon be closing time and neither mother was willing to sit around the store or wait at home while others were out searching for their missing loved ones.

"Do you think you could stick around a while longer?" Christal asked Dottie. "I'd hate to close up and leave all these people stranded without their groceries," she said. "I'm sure we'll get all this straightened out soon and Guard and the kids will be back and we'll all have a good laugh about it." There was very little conviction in her voice.

"Of course, Christal," Dottie replied. "You go ahead with Howie and find them and don't you worry about the store."

Growing numbers of apprehensive customers were now all wondering what could have happened to Guard and the children—some voicing opinions, others complaining about the wait, most of them with un-cashed paychecks in hand. By the time five-thirty had come and gone and still no sign of Guard and the children, up and down the aisles, the suggestion of forming a search party began to circulate to which there were more than a few volunteers.

Some of the more impatient in the crowd were beginning to straggle through the exits, heading for Locatell's Red and White Market.

Taking Dottie aside, Christal said, "Dottie, I think we should let these people—at least the ones we know—go through the line, check out their groceries, keeping track of their purchases and then we can let them settle up tomorrow."

Dottie, obviously, wasn't so sure. "Well, it sounds like a good idea, Christal, but how on earth will I ever keep track of who owes what?"

"Just have them sign the register tape," Christal said.

"Great idea," Dottie said. "For a minute I was afraid you were trying to turn me into a bookkeeper."

It was another illustration of why the Young family had become such a beloved and integral part of the tightly knit Chester community.

"One more thing," Christal said to Dottie. "I'll get Wayne's bassinette and set it up here by the cash register. He's a sound sleeper so I don't think you'll have to worry about him fussing. He'll probably just sleep through the commotion."

Dottie would have gladly volunteered to keep an eye on the baby while she checked groceries although she was relieved when Ada Johnson, one of the LDS church ladies, came to the rescue.

The Search

Tires squealing as they made contact with the pavement, Howard Elliott's big red pickup carrying the two anxious mothers shot out of the gravel driveway and zoomed down Main Street. Their hastily devised plan was to proceed rapidly toward Westwood on Highway 36, scanning both sides of the road as they drove, and if Young wasn't spotted on the way in, they would turn around in Westwood and come back toward Chester—only this time, at a slower, more deliberate pace.

Rosemary studied the shoulders on both sides of the road looking for anything that might be out of order, logically assuming that whatever happened to their missing loved ones had to have happened during the short ten or fifteen minutes it would have taken them to drive back to Chester. She couldn't help but wonder how it could be possible for five people to completely vanish in such a short space of time and distance.

In Westwood, having arrived at Bennight's Variety Store scarcely a minute before closing time, they learned from the clerk that Guard and the four children had been there at a little past three o'clock, purchased popsicles for himself and the kids and, as best as she could remember, had all piled back into the car and headed off down Ash Street toward Chester.

Christal was now energized by the fact that instead of just sitting around waiting for someone else to do something, she had become actively involved in the search. It gave her a sense of hope and encouragement, if only for the moment.

Before starting the return trip to Chester, they would first stop at the Lassen County Sheriff's office in Westwood to alert them that five people were missing, a serious crime may have been committed in their jurisdiction and hopefully, they would help with the search.

They were greeted warmly by Deputy Arthur Bates, the officer in charge

When they sat down to face the deputy in his office he immediately noticed their troubled demeanor.

"How can I help you?" he asked. Christal leaned forward to describe in a clear yet anxious voice, the events of the previous three hours.

On learning of the large amount of cash that Guard had in his possession, Bates became concerned.

"Could he be having car trouble?"

"No," Christal answered firmly. "We just drove up the highway looking for them. There was no sign of anybody on either side of the road. Besides, it's almost a new car. I can't see how he'd be having car trouble."

"How about visiting someone?" Bates suggested. "Could he have stopped off to see a friend or maybe a business associate?"

Again, Christal shook her head dismissively. "No, he would have told someone," she said as both Rosemary and Howie nodded in agreement.

"Art, he had the kids with him," Christal continued, "and he had all that money—he wouldn't have just gone off someplace else—he knew we were waiting for him to return with the money because we needed it to cash payroll checks. He just wouldn't have done that."

Bates' tone grew more serious. He lifted a small notebook from his shirt pocket and a pencil from his desk drawer and began to write as he continued to ask questions.

"Is that the new Chrysler Windsor he's driving?" he asked, taking special care to keep his questions in the present tense. "That light green one?"

"Yes."

"That's a four door, isn't it?"

"Yes."

"Remember the plate number?"

"No, I'm sorry," Christal said.

"It's okay. Do you remember what Guard is wearing?"

Christal looked at Rosemary as Howie linked an arm under hers to steady her. She had to think for a moment.

"A blue shirt, I think. He has on gray slacks. I remember because I had to press them this morning. I don't think—no, I'm sure—he's not wearing his jacket."

Bates scribbled and the questions got tougher. "Now can you tell me how the kids are dressed?" He hesitated when he got to the word "are," once again resisting the temptation to say "were."

Christal recognized and appreciated his thoughtfulness but it didn't make it any easier. "Oh, Art, is that really necessary? I mean . . . do you think . . ." at which point Bates interrupted. "I'm afraid so, Christal. Now just take your time."

"Well," Christal began, "Jean—she's the oldest—she's wearing a white blouse with a blue skirt." Her eyes closed as she tried to form a mental image of the kids as they piled into the car that afternoon. "She was carrying her green sweater which I think she put on in the car," she said, her anguish more apparent with each question.

"Okay," Bates said gently.

Christal continued. "Judy's wearing a white dress with little colored square-like figures on it. Sondra Gay is wearing a striped green sunsuit."

Bates interrupted, "A sunsuit?" he asked. "Are you sure? Isn't it a little cool out there for a sunsuit?"

"You're right, she had a yellow sweater with her."

"And Michael..." Christal said as she looked at Rosemary.

Tears began to well in Rosemary's eyes at the mention of Michael. Taking Rosemary's hand in hers, Christal said, "Little Michael's wearing blue overalls and a red plaid flannel shirt. He had no coat or jacket."

Bates sensed that the strain was starting to get to Christal as they all began to imagine the worst.

"Now after you left Chester on your drive into Westwood, did you see or hear anything—anything—on either side of the road that looked to be out of the ordinary? Did you hear any strange noises—or see any fire or smoke—anything at all?" Deputy Bates asked, strictly as a matter of routine.

Howie assured him that they had not. "But it was getting on six o'clock and starting to get dark, Art. There wasn't a whole lot that we could see," he said. "Before we left the store a bunch of the folks were talking about getting up a search party to go out looking for them. Maybe they'll get some flash lights so they'll be able to see."

"Okay, Howie. I think that might be a good plan," Bates said, rising to shake Howie's hand. "I'll alert the Plumas sheriff's office in Quincy and then see about rounding up some folks here in Westwood."

He turned to Christal and Rosemary. "You ladies go on home now and try not to worry," he said as he walked them out the door. Nodding to Howie, "We'll get on this right away and we'll be keeping you all updated."

At six thirty-five p.m. the threesome was on their way back to Chester and Bates was on the phone to Bill Abernathy, his Chester counterpart.

"Bill, maybe it's nothing, but we just might have a problem. Have you heard anything about Guard Young and his kids?"

He had not.

"Well, his wife Christal was just here, and she's worried sick. Guard left the bank this afternoon around three o'clock with seven thousand dollars in cash on him—that was over three hours ago and no one's seen him since. And Bill, he's got his three little girls and his little neighbor boy with him."

Abernathy, though at a loss to offer a plausible explanation for the Youngs' mysterious disappearance, downplayed its gravity.

"Well, I wouldn't get too excited, Art. There's probably a million reasons why he hasn't shown up yet. Maybe he's broke down somewhere out on 36. Maybe he stopped off to see a friend. If I didn't know better, I'd think he might even have a girlfriend stashed away somewhere."

"We're talking about Guard Young, Bill, so you can cross that possibility off your list," Art replied and Bill concurred. "But I don't like it, Bill. His wife, Christal says it's not like Guard to be gone like that without telling someone."

Deputy Abernathy said that it might be a good idea to put in a call to his boss, Plumas County Sheriff Mel Schooler in Quincy. Maybe he could offer some input.

Meanwhile, Lassen County Sheriff Olin Johnson, on being advised by Bates of the developing situation, placed the entire staff of the Lassen County Sheriff's department on alert. He delegated the responsibility of coordinating the search party groups to his deputy, Roland Gillespie who immediately got on the phone and by seven o'clock, had been able to recruit a small army of volunteers.

After setting up a command station alongside the highway at the county line, Deputy Gillespie looked on as men and women began to gather; many carrying lanterns and flashlights; some packing rifles and a few with machetes.

Two trucks equipped with two-way radios would soon be on their way to the scene. The hope was that these trucks would be able to push through the dense overgrown terrain while remaining in communication with each other, as well as with the command station. However, they would discover to their disappointment that, having not been outfitted with searchlights, for all practical purposes on this moonless, inky black night, the trucks would prove to be ineffective.

At around mid-point on the drive back to Chester, their progress was slowed by the unusual amount of activity that was taking place alongside the highway, forcing them to slow to a near standstill. Howie leaned his head out of the window to engage the three men approaching the idling truck and on recognizing one of them as a fellow mill worker, he asked, "What's going on, Ed?"

"Guard Young and his kids have been missing for over four hours and we're forming a posse to go look for them." Not able to see or maybe because he failed to recognize either Christal or Rosemary, he added gratuitously, "Probably going to be dead when we find them." he said.

Rosemary gasped audibly and Howie moved quickly to roll up the window and as he stepped on the gas, floods of mixed emotions welled up inside Christal. No, she thought—he's wrong. There's another explanation. She didn't know what it was, but there had to be another explanation. But as reality intruded, she was forced to admit, if only to herself—yes, it's possible. Not probable, she could argue, but certainly possible.

It was after seven o'clock by the time Christal and Rosemary had returned to the store and after dropping them off, Howie turned around and drove back toward Westwood to join the search party.

News traveled fast in Chester and all across town it wasn't long before the ominous clouds of foreboding had started to gather. As they waited, townsfolk braced themselves for the worst, plunging the store into an almost funereal atmosphere. When Christal and Rosemary had to report to the anxious crowd that on their drive down the highway they had seen no sign of Guard and the kids, the mood turned even darker. Those lingering few who, for whatever reason, had decided earlier not to volunteer in the search effort now gave their wives a quick peck on the cheek and hurried out the door to join up with the group that was now assembling on Route 36.

Every scenario imaginable had been thoroughly considered, weighed and examined before being discarded—every scenario that is, except for one: Viola.

It made absolutely no sense but there was a slim though highly unlikely possibility that instead of returning directly to Chester after leaving the bank, Guard for some inexplicable reason, might have taken a last minute detour and headed in the opposite direction down 36 to visit Viola, who, beside being Christal's younger sister, happened to also be her closest and dearest friend.

Viola Hardy lived with husband Joe in a small enclave on the outskirts of Susanville, some twenty miles on the other side of Westwood. It was the longest of shots, but there was nothing else. Christal had run out of options.

She dialed the number and when Viola answered, without a preliminary hello or the slightest effort to conceal her anxiety, she asked, "Vi, by any chance have you seen Guard?" The obvious angst in her voice immediately brought Viola to attention.

"No, Christal," she said. "Is there trouble? Is something wrong?"

"Well, it's hard to say," Christal explained. "He took the kids and went to the bank this afternoon. They left the bank with seven thousand dollars in cash and now they're all missing. They've vanished. No one's seen them since about three o'clock. That was five hours ago."

"Oh, no," Viola said. "I guess you've considered all the possibilities, right? I mean like a flat tire, or some kind of a breakdown?"

"Nothing makes sense, Vi. I'm just worried sick. We've looked everywhere. They're even forming a posse out on 36. I just can't imagine."

"Try not to worry, Christal. I'm sure there'll be a perfectly reasonable explanation when they finally do show up." Viola wanted so much to help.

"I think we had better come up," she said.

"You may have trouble getting through," Christal warned. "They've got a posse out there and there's a lot of heavy traffic."

"Well, I'm sure Joe will want to join them," Viola said. "But in any case, I'll see you as soon as we can. Is there anything you need—food or anything?"

"No, Vi," and for the first time in many hours, there was the faintest trace of a smile in Christal's voice. "If I need food, I can just go downstairs and get it. We live over a supermarket, remember?"

"Oh, yeah, right," and Viola had to chuckle, too. "I guess I wasn't thinking."

They said good-bye and as Christal hung up the phone, she was resigning herself to the fact that with every passing hour the list of plausible possibilities continued to shrink and as of now that list was just about down to zero.

Reno Bound

Darkness had fallen and although Larry had been hoping for an earlier start, it wasn't until a little past seven that Larry and Lucille, along with Jack Santo, their newly energized passenger now sprawled out in the back seat, finally drove out of Chester.

After skirting the northern tip of Lake Almanor, they turned eastward on Route 36 and had just begun to pick up speed when suddenly they found themselves caught up in a cluster of slow-moving vehicles. Coming up on an array of flashing and blinking red brake lights, they were forced to join the double line of bumper-to-bumper traffic.

"Uh oh, this doesn't look good," Larry remarked. A traffic jam in Chester was almost unheard of unless a serious accident had occurred somewhere up the road. But they suspected that this particular hold-up at this time and place was not due to any accident.

They ground to a dead stop and Larry rolled down his window. He leaned out and called out to one of the pedestrians walking alongside the road.

"Hey man, what's going on?"

"You're probably going to find it like this all the way to the county line," the man answered while pointing down the road. "They're putting together a search party. Must be a hundred cars all looking for a place to park. It's a real mess."

"What are they searching for?" Larry asked.

"Seems a guy and a bunch of kids disappeared somewhere out here this afternoon so we're going to try and find them. They say he had a lot of money on him and they think he might've been robbed or something."

"Thanks," Larry said, a sickening feeling starting to form in the pit of his stomach. He rolled up his window. Lucille looked back at Jack as if waiting for him to say something. But he said nothing.

The two eastbound lanes on 36 backed up in a stop-and-go stalemate; the traffic coming from the opposite direction had also been brought to a near standstill. Larry continued to inch along, the headlights of the cars behind them clearly illuminating the westbound lane and in it, a slow moving red pickup. In the cab sat two female passengers next to the driver. Lucille immediately recognized one of the women.

"Hey Larry!" she exclaimed. "That's Mrs. Young, the grocery store owner's wife. She was at the store this afternoon when I called you."

Traffic had begun to open up a bit and Jack, who had up until now been quietly watching the commotion without comment, finally spoke up.

"Let's get the hell out of here, Larry!" he said and Larry hit the gas.

Ever since he had asked Jack about the bloody clothing, Larry had been having difficulty trying to shake the uneasiness over the feeling that more than a robbery had occurred that afternoon. Jack's evasive manner and his cryptic behavior in response to being asked what he had meant when he used the term "out of control," was more than a little troubling. Jack's eagerness to avoid conversation about the Youngs only added to his trepidation.

Of course none of this would have been nearly so worrisome, Larry reckoned, had not he and Lucille themselves been so deeply involved.

After making one quick stop in Susanville to pick up a couple of bottles of whiskey and with the big green sign above the roadway reading "Junction I-395: Reno," Larry steered the car to his right and after exiting 36, roared onto the southbound freeway. He figured he would have about two hours and a hundred miles—give or take—to find out just what in the hell those two lunatics did to the Young family back there in Chester and whatever it was, come up with a story that would put him and Lucille miles away.

Aside from that bit of commotion outside of Chester caused by the gathering search party, the first ten to fifteen miles had flown by uneventfully. The steady drone of the car's engine and the twang of guitars wafting from the radio had lulled Lucille into a fitful half-slumber while in the back seat, contentedly nursing his bottle of Crown Royal, Jack, atypically, had been quietly keeping his own counsel.

When the silence and his own burning need for answers had finally reached their demolition points, Larry reached over and turned off the radio.

"Are you going to tell me what happened out there Jack or am I going to have to guess?" he asked. "I'm not good at guessing," he said. "I need to hear it from you, Jack. At some point you're going to have to cut us in on what happened. It might just as well be now as later."

The abruptness of the question caught Jack off guard. Although startled, he recovered quickly.

"Yeah," he said with a tone of reluctant resignation. "I guess there is no getting around it. I'm going to have to tell you guys the whole screwed up story." He looked ahead about a quarter-mile down the road where against the pitch-dark mountain background, a neon sign blinked its garish message: *Food and Bar.*

"Pull into that joint up there, and we'll have a couple drinks and maybe grab a bite to eat. You're not going to like hearing it but I figure it'll be best to clear the air."

Instead of waiting for a response, he quickly added, "And then we can go out and have us some real fun. See a few shows, do a little gambling, some fancy eats maybe. What d'ya say, Larry boy?"

Larry boy? A precursor to bad news, Larry had no doubt. Grease the knife so it'll slide in a little easier.

Larry swung the car into the parking lot as he shot a quick, apprehensive glance at Lucille who could only mumble a muted "Oh shit!"

Another noisy place, Jack noted appreciatively, so it wasn't likely their conversation would be overheard and after taking a small cocktail table as far away from the bar as possible, Jack volunteered to fetch the drinks. As soon as he was out of earshot, Lucille couldn't wait to ask, "What do you think he's going to tell us, Larry? Doesn't this all sound so... so..." she searched for the right word, "so ominous?"

"It's not sounding good, Lou. You know, I smelled a rat right from the get-go—right from the time he got back from wherever he was this afternoon. All that blood and stuff."

Jack reappeared with three bourbons in hand. "All right," he said, "Drink up because you are not going like what I'm about to tell you."

"Does this have anything to do with the missing Young family?" Lucille asked, knowing, that it absolutely did. They braced for impact.

"We ran into some unexpected trouble," Jack said. "Mr. Young, it seems, decided to bring his kids along today." His hands trembled noticeably as he lit a cigarette.

"When I saw those kids, I wanted to call the whole thing off," he continued. "But Perk—he didn't see any problem. He said we could do the job anyway."

"What about Harriet?" Lucille interrupted. "What did she say when she saw the kids? She must have been horrified."

"Well, you know Harriet—she likes money. She thought we should go ahead with it," he lied.

"So what happened, Jack?" Larry asked.

"Well, everything seemed to be going along as planned and all of a sudden—"

He hesitated as he emptied his glass.

"What? All of a sudden *what*?" Lucille demanded, even though she dreaded what she knew had to be coming.

"This one little kid—the boy—he darts out of the car and starts to make a run for it," Jack stammered, not altogether accurately.

"So Perk chases the kid down—and you know Perk when he loses his temper—he catches him, beats him to a pulp and he accidentally kills him." The matter-of-fact tenor in Jack's voice could easily have been mistaken for someone who was describing an afternoon at the beach.

They stared at Jack in appalled silence, trying to make some kind of sense from his words. Lucille thought that maybe she didn't hear him correctly. "Wait a minute, Jack," she broke in. "Perk killed the little boy? You're not saying Perk killed that little boy, are you?"

"Yeah, that's what I'm saying, Lou," Jack gesticulated with his fist, emulating Perkins' brutal pounding of little Michael. "It was over so fast I couldn't do anything to stop him," he said, lying again.

Their glasses had long since been drained, but at that moment there were no thoughts of refills—not even by Jack. He seemed to be as anxious to get this story out as were both Larry and Lucille to hear it.

"But you ain't heard the worst of it, guys," Jack said, and while Larry had already begun to conjure up schemes that might allow him and Lucille to wiggle out of this mess unscathed, Lucille couldn't help but dread what she feared was still to come.

In his typical remorseless monotone and in chillingly graphic detail, Jack proceeded to describe how Guard Young and the three little girls had met their gruesome deaths at the hands of—according to Jack, of course—Emmett Perkins. Every skull-shattering blow; every child's heart-wrenching cry; every pitiful whimper and every stomach-churning drop of blood seemed to come to life as he completed his verbal portrayal of the slaughter of five innocent human beings.

To Larry and Lucille, after what had seemed like an eternity of listening to his self-serving rationalizations and buck-passing, Jack finally wrapped it up without showing even the slightest trace of remorse or compassion for their victims but instead, only a pathetic attempt to shift the entire blame onto Emmett Perkins.

"It wasn't me, I swear. I didn't have anything to do with those murders. It was that crazy maniac Perkins." He did the killings and once he got started, well, he just couldn't stop."

While Larry was having trouble digesting all that Jack was telling them, Lucille's stomach had started to churn uncontrollably. How, she wondered, could a man they considered a friend—a man whom they had welcomed into their home—be a party to acts so unspeakably cruel and then talk about it as though he were describing the plot of a movie?

But Jack seemed relatively unmoved and even relieved that he had finally unburdened himself; it was now out in the open.

"Now, how about we all grab a bite to eat?" He cheerily suggested.

The thought of food made Larry want to gag and Lucille was becoming more nauseous by the minute. They agreed to forego dinner and Jack, his monologue now finished, rose to excuse himself. Before heading off toward the restroom, he wanted to leave them with one lingering, though chilling thought.

"I know you two are going to be discussing this while I'm gone but when you do, you need to keep one thing in mind." He glared menacingly at Larry and after pausing a moment for effect, he continued. "I always expect my partners on any of my jobs to keep their mouths shut. If I ever thought for a minute that I had a partner who couldn't be trusted, that partner would soon disappear."

Larry and Lucille exchanged knowing looks. Larry knew Jack Santo well enough to know that he was not in the habit of throwing out empty threats and it was not until that moment that he realized that he and Lucille were in a lot more trouble than anything they had originally bargained for.

When they returned to their car, and after Larry had pulled onto the highway, Jack resumed the self-serving portion of his ghastly narrative.

"You can't blame me," he whined. "Blame that crazy Perkins! He's the guy that did it," and then added, "I think the guy has serious mental problems."

It wasn't obvious to Jack that Larry, pondering his next move, had other concerns.

"But don't you worry none, Larry boy. No one knows you're involved. If they ever question me, I'll keep you out of it."

"Keep me out of it?" Larry sputtered, elevating his pitch by at least a full octave. "How the hell are you going to keep me out of it? Everybody in town knows you're staying at my house," He screamed. "How the hell are you going to keep me out of it?"

While Larry shrieked at Jack, Lucille, despite a growing urge to vomit, couldn't help thinking about that day back in Iowa when she had let Larry talk her into trading the quiet small town life of county fairs, Fourth of July parades and Sunday picnics for the promise of glamour and excitement in faraway California. That was only three months ago and now that dream of living the good life had turned into her worst nightmare. Killing children? The mere idea brought on a violent shudder.

"Kids? You killed kids?" she finally said incredulously. "I can't believe you killed kids!"

"What are you, deaf?" Jack exclaimed, his voice rising in anger. "I told you it was Perk who killed the kids. Or are you just too stupid to understand that?"

Under normal circumstances Larry's first impulse in response to an insult directed at Lucille would have been an immediate fist to the jaw. But these, he knew, were not normal circumstances. Jack Santo, among many other character flaws, possessed the most volatile and most unpredictably explosive temper of any man Larry had ever known. He looked at Lucille and seeing that she had taken Jack's crude affront in stride, thought it best to let the matter slide. She nodded and Larry decided that he would just let it rest since Jack now seemed to have gotten a grip on himself.

"Don't worry about it," Jack said. "If anybody asks, what you need to do is tell them that all you know is I went out this afternoon and you have no idea where I went or what I was doing."

Larry considered the possibilities. He wasn't there. He didn't even know about the actual robbery and he certainly didn't know anything about anyone being killed. The most he could be charged with would be helping to plan the robbery, nothing more.

"Come on, Larry, lighten up a little. I'm planning on having a little fun tonight. I don't want you guys to be thinking about what happened today."

For now, that ended the discussion. As far as Jack Santo was concerned, the subject was closed.

The Long Night

After dropping Viola off at Christal's, Joe U-turned back down the highway toward the county line where he would join the gathering search party while Viola, with her hugs and optimistic words of encouragement to both distraught mothers, was gratefully welcomed into Christal's apartment.

The grim mood was suddenly interrupted when, wakened by the sudden commotion, baby Wayne started to cry. Christal lifted the infant from his crib and placed him in Viola's outstretched arms before heading into the kitchen to make sandwiches.

Most of the people who knew Christal Young would tell you that by nature, she was the most totally composed, self-assured woman, less given to emotional outbursts, than anyone they had ever known. It was this inner strength of Christal's that bolstered Rosemary's dimming hopes as the three women ate their sandwiches in uncertain silence waiting for news of their missing loved ones.

While maintaining an almost detached equanimity, Christal listened as Rosemary contemplated the dire possibilities of what awful fate might have befallen the Young family and that of her own son.

The minutes turned to hours as Christal gazed wistfully out of her living room window, hoping against hope that any second now, Guard's big green Chrysler would come racing down Main Street. It was taking every ounce of that vaunted inner fortitude to fight off a creeping, totally uncharacteristic sense of despair. Never in all her thirty-nine years—thirteen of them married to Guard— had she been forced to deal with anything that even approached this kind of emotional trauma.

Seven years earlier she and Guard had made a life-changing decision to gamble everything they owned by selling their small Susanville grocery business and move to Chester. They would purchase a large lot on Main Street's downtown strip and erected what would become Chester's most imposing structure and after trucking in load after load of inventory, they began to do business as Young's Supermarket.

Despite the never-ending demands on her personal life; the many sacrifices, and the often back-breaking work that the realization of their dream would require; with much love and passion, Christal and

Guard had been able to build a thriving business, always believing that with God's help, there was no adversity they would not be able to overcome; their faith would see them through no matter the obstacle.

"Oh, Christal," Rosemary said, jarring Christal back to reality. Her eyes pooled with tears, "why won't they tell us? Surely by now they must have learned something."

The cruel waiting had started to take its inexorable toll on both mothers. "I'm sure they're doing the best they can do," Christal offered. "Eventually they'll come walking through that door, and when they do, just wait 'til I get my hands on that man!" she said, but with little conviction.

"But," Rosemary softly sobbed as she dabbed at her eyes, "where on earth could they possibly be? Where haven't they looked?"

"I wish I knew, Rosemary," Christal sighed. "All we can do is pray."

"Well, I can't imagine where they could be," Viola said in an attempt to ease Rosemary's fears. "But one thing you can be sure of, Rosemary; there's no one you'd rather have looking after your son than Guard Young."

Rosemary, grateful for Viola's thoughtful remark, seemed to brighten, if only for a few brief moments.

In another mood-lightening gesture, Viola nodded to Christal as a signal that Wayne had dropped off to sleep and after handing the baby over to Christal, she rose from the big easy chair and walked across the room, pulling back the curtain to peer out the window.

"Yes, you're probably right, Christal. We're getting ourselves all worked up over nothing," Viola said, and seeing no activity on the street, returned to her chair. "Let's just hold that thought."

The three women sat in silence while the minutes ticked away. Rosemary looked at Christal as if a question had been preying on her mind but was afraid to ask. Finally, she said, "Christal, do you believe that God would have allowed something bad to happen to them? Wouldn't you think that God would protect them?"

Christal had been fighting off her own doubts. Was this a test of her own faith? Is that what was going on? Could God be testing them the same way he tested Job or Abraham?

"We know that sometimes God does things that sometimes we don't understand, Rosemary. We just have to be strong." And in the same breath she added, "This is not God's doing."

Over and over again Christal's mind replayed the day's events searching for something they might have overlooked—something that might have been forgotten that could give them some small clue. She could think of nothing.

Twilight had long since faded into night and still there were no reports of anyone seeing Guard's green Chrysler. Not a trace; nor had there been the slightest indication of anyone having roadside car trouble. Christal was slowly coming to the harsh realization that something much more sinister, much more terrible had happened.

The Search Suspended… a Knock on the Door

The number of search party members continued to grow until it now approached two hundred and fifty men and women. For Deputy Gillespie, attempting to control such a large mob of unruly citizens, many with loaded weapons and primed with alcohol was starting to become a real concern; in fact it was a sure-fire recipe for disaster.

Plumas County Sheriff Mel Schooler would be arriving at dawn to head up the search effort. At first light, citizen pilot John Masson will be doing a fly over in his private Cessna in which he'll be able to scout the entire area in a fraction of the time it would take two hundred and fifty searchers on the ground. To Gillespie, it just didn't make sense to continue the search under these conditions.

Praying that Guard and the children—wherever they were and in whatever circumstances—would somehow be able to make it through the night unharmed—at around eleven o'clock, Gillespie called off the search.

* * *

When the knock at the door came, the three women looked at each other, apprehension, anxiety and a trace of hope covering their faces.

With Rosemary standing at her side, Christal slowly opened the door.

"Evening, ma'am," said the nervous young man standing on the other side of the doorway. He told them he had been sent by Deputy Gillespie to deliver a message to the mothers.

"Is it good news?" Christal asked excitedly. "Have they found them?"

"No, I'm sorry, ma'am. Deputy Gillespie wanted me to let you know that they have suspended the search operation until morning."

It may not have been terrible news but it certainly wasn't the news for which they'd been hoping. Christal wanted to know how they could suspend the search knowing that somewhere out there a father and four small children were waiting to be rescued. Didn't they know that up here in these mountains it was not unusual for October temperatures to drop by as much as thirty degrees after the sun goes down?

"Oh no," Rosemary groaned. "Please don't quit now. You can't leave them out there all night—they'll freeze to death. Michael probably doesn't even have a coat." She looked beseechingly at Christal as if by her saying something—anything—she could make everything right.

"There must be some way" Christal added her own anguished plea. "They don't even have blankets. They could be hurt and in need of medical attention. Isn't there something you could . . .?" Her voice trailed off.

"I'm sorry, ma'am," the deputy interrupted. "There's just no light out there and you know how rugged that terrain is. But don't worry. We'll get started again tomorrow as soon as it's light."

When the deputy had delivered his message he bid the women a hasty good night. Now resigned to the fact that there would be no further news until at least daylight, they all settled in to wait out the night.

Fifteen minutes later, after having dropped off one of the searchers who were in need of a lift back to Chester, Joe returned to Christal's apartment.

"I guess you guys heard," he said as he removed his coat and hung it on the back of a kitchen chair. "They shut down the search until morning."

"Yes, we heard, Joe," Viola said. "And we're not happy about it."

"It's a real mess down there, Vi," Joe explained. "Guys stumbling around in the dark with loaded guns. Lucky no one got shot. Couple times I heard a gun go off—Lord only knows what they were shooting at."

Rosemary curled up on the couch where she dozed fitfully. Christal, after insisting that Viola and Joe take her bed, took up her own vigil at the window where she gazed out onto the quiet and empty street. Maybe, she pondered, through some miracle, Guard and the kids really will come walking through the door. Or if she just goes to sleep, maybe she'll wake up to find this whole horrible scenario had been a dream—a bad, bad dream.

The Split

The one-hundred-fifty mile drive from Chester to Auburn should normally take no more than three hours, but because of Perkins' unfamiliarity with the area's geography, plus a couple of beer and restroom stops, he and Harriet had been on the road for more than seven hours. For Harriet, it had been a harrowing day like none she could ever imagine. Try as she might, she couldn't make herself fall asleep. Images of children with blood-streaked faces clouded her troubled semi-consciousness. They were simply too awful and too vivid to allow any respite from reliving the horror she had witnessed.

Emmett Perkins, seemingly a man without a conscience, was untroubled by the day's gruesome events.

"Well, after all's said and done," he remarked over the steady drone of the car's engine, "that was a pretty good haul."

Rubbing the back of his neck and speaking as dispassionately as if he had been talking about mowing the backyard grass he added, "But man, that kind of work always gets me tired out. Guess I'm getting too old for this business."

Overcome by a strong sense of revulsion brought on by just being in the same space with this man, Harriet slowly and imperceptibly inched toward the passenger door. Breathing the same air and sharing the same thoughts with a man she now regarded as a deranged animal had become almost intolerable.

But Perkins, disregarding her anxiety and oblivious to her growing sense of loathing, continued to remind her, "You can buy yourself a lot of pretty things with two thousand bucks."

Thinking about the money and the way it had been obtained was already tugging at Harriet's conscience. But even though she was filled with misgivings, she was sure—at least she hoped—that, as it usually did in these circumstances, those qualms would eventually dissipate with the passage of a little time.

"I don't want to talk about the money now, Perk," she said and, turning away, Harriet curled up in a ball, shut her eyes and hoped that if she could just doze off for a while, she'd wake up and before she knew it she'd be home.

It was a little past eleven when Perkins turned off I-80. Jarred by the car's sudden deceleration, Harriet was shaken out of a fitful sleep and on opening her eyes, she was grateful to see the familiar Auburn landmarks. She shook the sleep from her eyes as the realities of the day's activities started to come back into focus. It had been the worst day of her life. It would be a long, long time—if ever—before she'd be able to expunge the memory of those innocent faces and the look of a crazed monster grabbing them by their little arms and dragging them off to their deaths.

It was far too late now, Harriet rued, but the tears came anyway. She brushed them back and tried hard to think of other things while the town's few bright neon lights flashed by the windows. But those dreadful images just wouldn't go away. Shortly before midnight they pulled into the driveway of Harriet's house.

Before Perkins hit the road again to head for Los Angeles, which was a good four-hundred miles south of Auburn, he reached into his jacket pocket and extracted the roll of bills.

"Let's go inside and take care of this," Perkins said. "Then I have to get going. I want to get to El Monte and get a little sleep so I can get over to the club."

"The club" was a reference to the underground twenty-four hour high stakes poker game he was operating in the grimy Los Angeles suburb of El Monte. Perkins explained, "I want to check in to see how much money I'm making."

Few people—especially the suckers who play in these *home games*—realized how brazenly they were being fleeced, not by cheats or hustlers, although God knows, there was no shortage of those, but by their up-front concurrence given before they even sat down to play. The premise on which these games were promoted was that the house would "rake" a predetermined percentage from each pot, sometimes as much as ten percent, ostensibly to pay for such overhead expenses as rent, food and liquor. The truth is, no one ever took the trouble to do the math. The house hired experienced dealers, proficient in moving the game with such rapidity that it would not be unusual for a good dealer to crank out as many as sixty hands an hour.

With pots in a heavy action game averaging five to six-hundred dollars, house revenues could reach an astounding three-hundred-sixty dollars an hour. In a twenty-four hour, seven days a week home game with two tables going full bore, Perkins' income potential could have been enormous, especially when talking about 1952 dollars.

Unfortunately for Emmett Perkins, due largely to a scarcity of well-heeled suckers coupled with his extremely poor management skills, instead of operating the games on a steady 24/7 schedule, they were held only if or when sufficient numbers of cash-rich players could be rounded up and steered to the tables.

Perkins maintained a small stable of hookers and hustlers whose only job would be to hang out in upscale bars and restaurants where, acting as bait and for a percentage of the sucker's losses, the *hook* would steer the well-heeled *fish* in the direction of his El Monte poker game.

Perkins grinned creepily at Harriet. "You know, toots, maybe you ought to think about coming to L.A. and going to work for me. With your kind of moxie and looks, you could make yourself a pretty nice living." Harriet didn't know whether to be flattered, insulted or disgusted.

In Harriet's living room, Perkins sat on the couch as he cleared a space on the coffee table onto which he arranged the twenty dollar bills in neat piles. When Harriet emerged from the bathroom, she went straight for the kitchen, calling out, "I could use a drink. How about you?"

"I'd rather have a cup of coffee," Perkins replied. "Long drive to L.A. I got a couple bennies in my pocket and with a little coffee, they will keep me awake until I get home." "Bennies" were Benzedrine tablets, an over-the-counter stimulant commonly used by long-haul truck drivers to help them stay awake during their two or three day non-stop cross-country runs.

Constructing two stacks of bundled bills, each stack containing two thousand dollars, he sat back and admired his work.

"This one's yours and this one's mine," he said pushing one of the stacks across the table. "Jack already got his cut. And he held out numb-nut's share, too."

"Whose share?" Harriet asked.

"Shea's ten percent," he said. "I think his cut came to around seven hundred, maybe a little more." Realizing that Harriet was no idiot and his numbers weren't adding up, Perkins explained, "The other three hundred is for miscellaneous expenses," to which Harriet merely nodded.

"Sure, Perk," she said. She wanted him out of her house and out of her life as quickly as possible.

He quickly swallowed two cups of coffee, and after cramming the remaining stack of bills in his jacket pocket, he rose from the couch. "If you should change your mind about moving to L.A., let me know. You could probably get this kind of a payday every week."

Harriet hoped her reply would leave no doubt about what she thought of this idea. "Not bloody likely," she said as she opened the front door.

Perkins shrugged as he returned to his car, switched on the headlights, backed out of the driveway and pointed the car toward Los Angeles.

Rendezvous in Reno

At around the same time Emmett Perkins and Harriet were arriving in Auburn, Larry and Lucille Shea, along with their passenger Jack Santo, were rolling through downtown Reno, finally bringing their car to a stop in front of the Greyhound Bus depot where Bernadine Pearney had been waiting for the past thirty minutes.

Oddly enough, one of Jack's earlier encounters with Bernadine had come in the aftermath of another murder in which he had been involved—that of Edmund Hansen. While Jack had waited at Higgins Corner Bar for the trio to return from the Hansen home with the cash and gold, who should come walking through the door but old friend and bed pal, Bernadine Pearney. In addition to her reliable utility as one of Jack's once-in-a-while shack-up playmates, Bernadine, from time to time, could be counted on to hang a little paper for him. That was back in the days when he was running a small-time ring of bad check artists.

The attractive thirty-year-old party girl had come in to celebrate her divorce which had become final on that very day and this chance meeting gave them an opportunity to reminisce about old times. For Bernadine at least, it was a chance to rekindle an old flame, the embers of which had been smoldering beneath the surface ever since the last time they had seen each other. But before any sparks had a chance to burst into flame, Harriet had walked in to join them and that, to Bernadine's dismay, was that.

Of course the first thing Jack had wanted to know from Harriet was where the hell were Perkins and Boles? He listened in stone-faced silence as Harriet gave him the rundown of Hansen's shooting (at that point she didn't know whether or not Hansen had died) and details of the botched robbery, explaining that she had dropped Perkins and Boles off in Grass Valley before coming to the bar.

Bernadine had been taking in every word as the three huddled over a small cocktail table. She remembered listening in rapt fascination as the discussion had taken a somewhat angry turn.

"Where the hell is the gold? Didn't they get anything?" Jack had asked, more than a little agitated.

"Forget the gold—forget the money," Harriet had told him in disgust. "There isn't any. The whole damned thing was for nothing!"

Jack frowned. He was not pleased. "Well, did they tell you what happened?"

"Yeah, Jack," Harriet said. "They thought it was funny. They laughed about it. I think it was George who said he didn't see how anyone could still walk with so much lead in him."

"Fucking idiots!" had been Jack's reaction.

Party Time

Jack beamed with pride when he caught sight of Bernadine's flashy blond hair and that svelte slender body because there's nothing Jack

Santo enjoys more than strutting around town with a piece of arm-candy like Bernadine.

Jeez, he mused, she's still looking good. Looks like we're gonna have a good time tonight.

They embraced warmly while Jack whispered something in her ear. She blushed and Jack looked over at Larry and Lucille, who had remained in the car. He smiled and winked.

"I think we could all use a drink," Jack suggested. "Let's park this pile of crap somewhere and then I'll buy you guys dinner."

"Pile of crap?" Larry asked in mock indignation. "Did you forget? I bought this car from you."

"Oh yeah," Jack replied. "I forgot. Sorry about that."

"Next time, try to steal better cars and then maybe you'll be able to ride around in style," Larry said.

As Lucille listened to their exchange of light-hearted banter, she wondered how in God's name—in view of what had just been done to those five people back there in Chester—how either of them could be in such a festive mood. How, she also wondered, would she even be able to stand the smell of food—let alone try to eat it?

They checked in at the South Virginia Hotel where Larry and Lucille had already been pre-registered. Jack and Bernadine were able to snag the room directly across the hall and after dropping off their bags in their respective rooms, they went to dinner.

Reno, Nevada at this time was known as the nation's gambling capital and The Golden Phoenix, shortened by locals to "The Golden," was one of Reno's finest and most luxurious nightclub-restaurant-casinos. With its upscale accoutrements such as white-linen dining room service, a cellar stocked with rare vintage wines—even a glamorous floor show—the Golden, was not a place in which you'd expect to find a group such as this unholy quartet. Oblivious to how under-dressed or out of place they may have appeared to other diners, Jack bragged loudly that his money was as good as anybody else's in the joint; that he was the kind of guy who would spend it if he had it, and on that night, by God, he most assuredly had it.

Although Lucille had spent a good portion of her evening hanging out in the ladies' powder room, while Jack and Larry, not having eaten for at least the past twelve hours, tore into their dinner as though they were being fed their last meal. Jack paid for four filet mignon dinners and since Lucille could do little more than look at hers, she left her entire meal for Larry and Jack to split. The steaks were served beside a lavish tray of appetizers; baked potatoes with loads of butter and sour cream. Dessert was a spectacular flambé presentation of Cherries Jubilee, all accompanied by a chilled magnum of vintage champagne—Dom Perignon, of course.

The separate bar tab was also taken care of by Jack—who made sure that everyone within earshot was aware he had left a generous tip—and the foursome moved on.

Jack was having the time of his life as he flashed his over-sized wad of twenty-dollar bills at every opportunity. His celebratory mood seemed to be gathering steam as they reeled from club to club.

The drinks got stronger, Jack got drunker and the tips got bigger as they bar hopped their way through the six block downtown neon area. At Harrah's they caught the Guy Mitchell floorshow and from there, they had more drinks at the Mapes Hotel. They staggered into the Riverside for yet more drinks and even, perhaps, a little gambling with Jack footing the bill at every stop. Eventually, Lucille was able to prevail on Larry to call a halt to Jack's impromptu bacchanal—at least as far as they were concerned.

Using the early morning golf tournament as an excuse, and at Lucille's urging, Larry decided to pack it in for the night. Of course he was fully aware of Jack's proclivity to go off like a stick of dynamite whenever a drinking partner would express a desire to call it quits before Jack was ready to stop. But with Lucille fretfully tugging at his sleeve, this time he finally found the gumption to stand up to Jack. To his surprise, Jack meekly acquiesced.

After expressing his deep regrets, Larry, with Lucille now feeling worse with every passing minute, bid Jack and Bernadine goodnight and staggered out through the hotel lobby before disappearing into the cold Reno night.

"What a couple a' candy asses," Jack sneered. "The night's just getting started," He ordered another drink. "Not me. I have a whole lot of gas left in the tank. How about you, baby?"

By now, he was noticeably slurring his words and his behavior was beginning to make Bernadine uncomfortable. She couldn't remember ever seeing him in this kind of shape before. He'd consumed an enormous amount of alcohol and for the past hour or so, it had been showing—not just in his speech, which seemed to be getting more garbled by the minute, but even more so in his physical movements. He was starting to get sloppy; dropping money on the floor, spilling drinks, and when he excused himself before heading out for the restroom, it was obvious that he was having trouble just walking.

As he fumbled through his pockets while trying to find the appropriate denominations to pay for another round of drinks, a cascade of twenty dollar bills came tumbling out of his pocket, dropping onto the floor and eliciting a loud gasp from Bernadine.

Eyeing the scattering of bills strewn about the floor under the table and noting that every one of Jack's pockets seemed to be stuffed with more of the same, she asked in shocked amazement, "My God, Jack, you're spending money like a drunken sailor. Where the hell is all that money coming from?"

For as long as Bernadine had known Jack Santo, she had never seen him when he wasn't short of money and it was rarer still to see him order drinks around and then volunteer to pay for everything.

"I'll tell you later," he said, his words now becoming almost unintelligible.

"Why can't you tell me now? Is it so bad you don't want to talk about it?"

It was not that Bernadine wasn't aware of the life Jack led. He was an out-and-out gangster. She knew it and so what? How bad could it be? A few years back when she had become involved with him in a bad check gig and she was headed for at least a year in the big house, good ol' Jack stepped in. If it hadn't been for one of his high priced shylocks and a five-hundred-dollar bill, she would have had to do the time. So there was no act—short of murder—that was beyond the bounds of her imagination.

"Let's have one more drink before we hit the sack," Jack suggested "You know, to kinda get me in the mood."

Bernadine laughed. "Honey, after all you've had to drink tonight, if you need another drink to get in the mood, we're both in trouble."

Jack looked hurt. "What do you mean by that? Are you saying you don't think I'm the man I used to be?"

"Yeah, something like that," she said.

Bernadine stared wistfully at her drink. "That seems like such a long time ago. I can't even remember that far back."

But she did remember. Jack was different now and so was she, and now she was just another one of his one-night-stands. But there was a time—she was sure—a time when to Jack, she had been something special.

The downtown streets of Reno, even though it was now almost 3:00 a.m., were still bustling with gamblers, drunks and late night partiers. Jack held onto Bernadine's arm as they half-walked, half-stumbled the one block to the South Virginia Hotel. Bernadine was hoping that the man with whom she was about to crawl into bed would be shocked into relative sobriety by a few sharp blasts of the night's cold wind.

Once in bed, after a few minutes of groping and making excuses, Jack rolled over and before Bernadine could fluff her pillow, he began to snore. Bernadine leaned over and sighed quietly in his ear, "My, my, lover boy, you must have had a very busy day." She curled up next to him and drifted off to sleep.

* * * *

Across the hallway the mood had taken an entirely different turn. While Larry showered, Lucille sat on the edge of the bed and chain-smoked. She was in near panic mode thinking that if Larry didn't come out of that bathroom soon, she would start to have a nervous breakdown.

"Larry, will you please get your ass out here!" Lucille pleaded until, with a towel wrapped around his mid-section, he finally stepped from the bathroom and parked himself on the edge of the bed next to Lucille. Her hands were trembling as she lit another cigarette.

"We need to talk about this, Do you realize what this means?"

Larry nodded. "Lou, take it easy. . ."

"Can you believe what those lunatics did?" she exhaled a cloud of smoke before taking another puff. "Five people, for God's sake Larry! Four of them children!" Larry nodded again. He looked utterly miserable.

"Perk!" she hissed, as if spitting a fly from her mouth. She had always had a creepy feeling just being in the same room with him. Now she knew why.

"Larry, we've got to call the police. We've got to report this!" she said.

"Report it?" Larry resisted the urge to scream. "Are you nuts? Report it? We can't report this. We're in it as deep as they are, Lou. We are what the cops call 'accessories' Lou. You do know what that means don't you?"

Lucille had begun to shake uncontrollably. "Accessories" to five murders! "Oh dear Lord," she sobbed, "What in the hell are we going to do, Larry?"

"Alright, Lou, please get hold of yourself. It's not so bad. I'm thinking there's a way out for us. I got an idea." Larry's thoughts were a whirling jumble of excuses, alibis and lies—any and every kind of story that could be concocted to help get them out of the mess in which they now found themselves.

Between sobs, Lucille thought she could see the wheels turning inside Larry's head. "What, Larry? What are you thinking? You're thinking something, aren't you?"

"Yeah, Lou," he shot back. "I got a way. It'll work and I want you to quit crying okay? You just lie back and leave it to me." He took her hand. "Will you do that?"

"Can't you tell me what it is, Larry?" Lucille asked.

"I'm going to tell you, Lou. I'm going to tell you but just trust me for now. I need to get it worked out in my brain—but it's good. It'll work. Now just lie down and go to sleep. You can quit worrying."

Lucille wanted so much to believe him. She had to believe him. It's bad enough that she'll carry this around for the rest of her life, but the thought of their being charged as accessories to five murders was almost too much to bear.

Whatever it was that Larry had in mind, is it possible that it would not only get them off the hook with the cops, but somehow, assuage her conscience and even more importantly, involve Perkins' being held accountable for this monstrous crime?

"There's nothing to see. They're all dead."

SIX

Pandemonium

As the Saturday morning sun begun to show its face above the foothill rim of the Sierra Nevada Mountains, private pilot and Collins Pine executive John Masson took off from Chester's tiny landing strip in his company's new twin engine Cessna. On the ground, the search party had been re-organized to accommodate the growing number of volunteers. The group had swelled from the two hundred who had first shown up the previous evening to at least two hundred and fifty by the time operations were suspended. Everyone in the search party was fiercely determined to find Guard Young and the four small children who had mysteriously disappeared over sixteen hours ago.

The Lassen County Sheriff was there along with his two deputies and since it was not yet known what had happened to the missing family or exactly on which side of the Lassen-Plumas county line it had happened, it was decided, for jurisdictional purposes, that Sheriff Melvin Schooler of Plumas County would take charge of the search.

It was about that same time on Saturday morning when Jeff Cooley, California Highway Patrol officer and himself a Chester resident, was startled by a loud pounding on his front door. Twenty-nine-year-old Cooley, still recovering from a bout with the flu, had crawled out of his sick bed the previous evening and braving the cold mountain air, together with Collins executive George Gerbing, formed a two-man posse. They spent the entire night—dusk to dawn—walking the highway between Chester and Westwood, combing both sides of the road as they searched for any trace or indication of what had become of Guard Young and the four children. While Cooley walked, he shone his powerful flashlight into every nook and cranny along the way while Gerbing, driving a borrowed pick-up truck, crept along at his side. They covered the entire twelve miles—first in one direction and, after alternating roles, the other. When they had finally ended their search and after failing to generate a single clue, both men— especially the flu-weakened Cooley—were more than ready for a few hours of well-earned sleep.

Wondering what all of the ruckus was, a weary Cooley rose from his bed to answer the loud knocking at the door. He was confronted by a breathless, wide-eyed Jerry Bridges and his wife, Helen. Jerry was a local Collins mill worker whose imposing build, silhouetted against the bright morning sunlight, seemed to fill the entire door frame.

"Morning, Jerry, what's up?" Cooley asked, clutching at the lapel of his robe. It very quickly became apparent to Cooley that the Bridges couple were extremely agitated about something.

"Have they found the Young car?" Cooley asked

"Jeff," Bridges said, his words coming in gasps, "we just remembered something that I think you ought to know. We know where that car is—you know, the one they're looking for—I think we seen it yesterday."

He turned to Helen even though she was every bit as tightly wound "You tell him, honey," he said. "I don't think I'll be able to make any sense."

Helen, who had been waiting impatiently for a chance to speak, jumped in.

"We were down by old Malvich Road yesterday. We were hunting with Charlie Marshall and we seen a car parked back in the brush. It was a big ol' light green sedan but we just thought it was another hunting party, so we didn't pay it no mind."

Cooley, suddenly oblivious to the fatigue that had been brought on by his struggle with the flu, snapped to attention.

"Keep talking," he said as he motioned for them to come inside. He listened as the words tumbled out of her mouth.

Standing in the small foyer, Helen's sense of excitement escalated. "The freaky thing is, Jeff—God help me—I swear I could hear the sound of children coming from that car; like they were you know . . . crying, kinda."

"We just thought it was a bunch of deer hunters—with kids maybe," Jerry broke in. "You know, getting spanked for doing something." His voice wavered. "Honest to God, Jeff, we didn't know about Guard and them kids until we heard it on the news this morning." Helen glanced nervously at her husband and nodded.

"I need you to show me where you saw that car," Cooley's tone sounded more like a command. "Give me just a minute while I put on some clothes." He turned and quickly disappeared into his bedroom, emerging two minutes later in full uniform, still buckling his belt. He grabbed his hat and like a Marine drill sergeant barking out his orders, snapped, "Let's move!" ushering them out the front door and down the walk to the curb where Cooley's black and white patrol car sat.

"I want you to lead me to the spot where you saw that Chrysler," he said as he literally pushed them into the back seat before hurrying around to the driver's side, sliding nimbly behind the wheel.

"Talk to me while I drive," he said, as the powerful cruiser roared away from the curb, leaving a huge dust filled rooster tail in its wake. "I'm familiar with Malvich Road," he said. "It's on the north side of the main highway, right? How far off 36 would you say you saw it?"

"Not far," Helen answered. "Maybe a quarter mile."

"Oops!" Cooley said, cursing to himself. "Almost missed it." Within minutes, he had skidded to a stop alongside Route 36 near the spot where the old logging road ended. The faded letters—*Malvich Road*—had been painted on the weather-beaten wooden sign a half-century ago and now had become virtually unreadable. He backed up, made a hard left and very carefully guided the car over the potholes and debris that littered the now almost indistinguishable logging road. Six eyes peered out from each side of the vehicle, squinting as they attempted to penetrate the thicket of trees and dense underbrush as they searched for any sign of a light green car.

"There!" Helen shouted as she pointed to a clearing not fifty feet from where Cooley had brought the cruiser to a stop. "Right over there—can you see it?"

At about the same time that Cooley and the Bridges couple were scrambling from the patrol car, citizen-pilot John Masson, who had been flying over the area in his twin Cessna, was now crackling out a radio message informing searchers on the ground that he had spotted Young's car. Sheriff Schooler, using his two-way wireless while leading his brigade of volunteers, was being directed by Masson to the partially hidden Chrysler. They began to converge on the site while

114

Cooley, with Helen and Jerry Bridges leading the way, approached from the opposite direction.

The car's trunk, protruding rudely out of the undergrowth, was clearly visible from their vantage point, but to Cooley it was obvious that in order to get a peek inside, he would first have to fight his way through the thick tangle of briar-like underbrush.

The thorny barbs and prickly broken branches felt like saw teeth digging into his bare arms as he cautiously approached the car and once there, he peered through the dust-coated rear window. An eerie quiet descended on the scene as Jerry and Helen waited for Cooley to tell them what he was seeing. Finally, it was Helen who broke the silence.

"What do you see? Are they in there or not?" she asked, not sure exactly which answer she would have preferred.

"Nope. It's empty," Cooley replied, and after looking closer, "and I don't see the key. It's not in the ignition." He squeezed back out— scratches, scrapes and all—and proceeded to the back end of the car to make sure the trunk was locked.

Although the lid, as seen from a short distance away appeared to be closed and probably locked, on closer examination, it became immediately obvious to Cooley that it was actually slightly ajar. With heart pounding and hands trembling, he wrapped his fingers around the handle and with Helen and Jerry's eyes riveted on the trunk, he slowly lifted the lid.

For the next five seconds they stood mute—motionless with mouths agape— staring incredulously into the now sun-lighted trunk with its ghastly contents. Ordinary forest sounds—the rustling of leaves, blustery winds and twittering of birds—all seemed to fall suddenly and eerily silent as the three stunned onlookers, overcome by a spectacle of unmitigated horror, gasped in unison.

"Merciful heavens!" Cooley choked, his gaze fixed firmly on the trunk's grisly contents. "My God! No! Oh, no!"

The five bodies were stacked like piled cordwood and to all appearances, completely lifeless. Guard Young's battered figure lay atop a tangle of tiny arms and legs; Cooley could see a matted mass of blond curly hair resting in a puddle of dried blood.

Other nearby searchers by now had arrived at the scene. They elbowed and jostled one another for a better look but were quickly repelled by what they were able to see.

Most were totally unprepared for the scene that now lay before them—the sight, the smell and the sheer horror—and they turned away in utter revulsion. One police officer, so sickened by the sight of the broken bodies, remarked "I've seen about all I can take," before jumping into his car and, accompanied by Jerry and Helen Bridges, drove quickly away.

Cooley was finally able to speak. "They're dead. They're all dead!" He stopped abruptly as his eye caught sight of a tiny movement behind the pile of bodies. Against the back wall of the trunk's farthest reaches, three-and-a-half year-old Sondra Gay Young, youngest of the three girls, whimpered softly as she squinted in the bright sunlight. Covered in dried blood from head to toe, she struggled to sit upright while reaching out with one tiny, blood-streaked arm for Jeff Cooley. To the incredulous onlookers, it appeared as though she had just risen from the grave.

"Look, that one's alive! She's alive!" another voice shouted. Cooley leaned in and gathered the obviously terrified child into his beefy arms. It was apparent that little Sondra Gay had suffered a massive head wound, and now the re-agitated open gash above her right ear had started to ooze blood.

"This little girl's in real bad shape," he said. "She's got to get to a doctor, pronto!"

Upon arriving and taking control of the crime scene, Sheriff Schooler barked to his deputies "Move these people out of here." A path was cleared for Cooley who, after having lifted the dazed tot from the trunk's blood-soaked floor, moved quickly through the gathering crowd.

Cradling the battered little body firmly against his chest, Cooley raced to his patrol car parked at the edge of the clearing. After securing her in the front passenger seat, he slid his six-foot frame behind the steering wheel, switched on the ignition and the powerful engine roared to life. He mashed on the accelerator creating a flurry of dust, leaves and other debris as his patrol car's tires spun their way out of the forest and onto State Route 36 heading for Chester, some eight miles up the road.

With red lights flashing and the whine of his blaring siren piercing the cold morning air, Cooley streaked down the highway, his precious passenger lying semi-conscious in the seat beside him. Time was of the essence, Cooley told himself, if she were to have any chance of coming through this ordeal alive.

After entering Chester's outskirts, they roared down Main Street before hanging a tire-screeching left turn onto First Street, finally skidding to a stop in front of an office building and a door on which were inscribed the gold leafed letters, *R.A. Greenman, MD, Medical Examiner, Plumas County.*

Alerted by the ear-splitting siren's wail as the patrol car approached their offices, the doctor and his wife had come out to the curb and were waiting as Cooley pulled up. Mrs. Greenman, who also happened to be the doctor's head nurse, on seeing Sondra Gay in such obvious distress, quickly hurried to the passenger side of the car, pulled the door open and immediately began to tend to the stricken child's wounds.

"My God, Jeff," the doctor exclaimed as he took a closer look at Sondra Gay, curled up in a fetal position and covered in blood. "What in the world. . .?"

"She's been worked over pretty bad, doc." Cooley said, and thinking that seconds mattered, didn't want to take the time to explain. "I can give you the full story—at least as much as I know—while you're working on her."

But after a cursory examination, the doctor noted, "This little girl is much too badly injured to be properly treated here."

"We need to get her to the hospital," Mrs. Greenman urged.

"Oh no," Cooley moaned. The hospital was in Westwood, thirteen miles away.

"You did the right thing," Dr. Greenman said. "There was no way you could have known."

The doctor's movements were as purposeful as they were decisive. "Quickly now," he said as he stepped toward the garage where his station wagon was parked, calling out over his shoulder, "Let's get her to the hospital."

As he turned on his engine, Cooley watched as Dr. Greenman brought his car directly in line behind him.

He glanced over at Sondra Gay and, grateful that she was now being safely held in Nurse Greenman's arms, he jammed down on the accelerator and the big cruiser literally leapt from the curb.

"Hang on, little girl," he said, as much to himself as to Sondra Gay. "We're going to make it! I promise you, we're going to make it!"

Sondra Gay stirred and groaned as Mrs. Greenman dabbed lightly at a freshly formed stream of tears. "I know it hurts, honey, but the nice doctor is going to make it better," she whispered soothingly in Sondra Gay's ear, ". . . and then it won't hurt anymore."

With the speedometer needle nudging ninety, Cooley's CHP cruiser rocketed down the highway, its red and white lights flashing and shrieking siren's wail cutting through the cold autumn's stillness.

Normal Saturday morning traffic edged to the side of the road and straggling onlookers scattered as the streaking two-car convoy approached the spot where this frantic errand of mercy had begun. The crowds of searchers milling about the side of the road gaped in shocked curiosity as the black and white Highway Patrol cruiser zoomed past, the doctor's car following closely behind.

Another Knock at the Door

The four worried people sitting around the kitchen table looked up in startled unison as somewhere off in the distance the mournful wail of a police siren shattered the outside morning's quietude. There was, of course, no way Christal could have known that what they were actually hearing was Cooley's car tearing down Route 36 in a desperate race to save the life of Sondra Gay, who was now Christal's only living daughter.

No one could remember the last time any of them had eaten anything so they sat at the kitchen table nibbling on sandwiches which Christal had made earlier, struggling to get a few bites down despite their lack of appetite. Even Viola's husband Joe, who ordinarily would have had little trouble with whatever amount of food Viola placed in front of him, had no appetite.

"You should try to eat something," Viola said, addressing all three. "Lord knows when you'll have another chance."

They had passed much of the long night reminiscing about days gone by—they made small talk and prattled on, trying to calm their nerves with mindless chatter.

Throughout the night Christal fussed obsessively over baby Wayne, subconsciously fearing perhaps, that if she didn't hold him close, someone would take him, as she was beginning to believe they had taken her other children.

At the sound of a knock on the door Christal and Rosemary exchanged glances. Did they dare hope? Had Guard and the kids been found unharmed? Had it all been some kind of a crazy misunderstanding or will they finally succumb to the undercurrent of dread that, with every passing hour, had been eating away at their insides?

Christal cracked open the door to confront the same deputy who had come last evening to tell them the search had been called off. That was bad news, but this morning the news would be worse—much worse. It was written all across the deputy's face—almost as if she didn't have to ask.

"Ma'am—Mrs. Saile," he said with a nod to both women. Hesitating and twisting his cap in his hands, he chose his words carefully. "Sheriff Schooler asked me to come by and tell you that they have found your husband's car."

Neither mother said a word; instead steeling themselves for the painful story that they were sure was about to follow. "I . . . uh . . ." the young deputy stammered as he clumsily groped for the right words. "He said to tell you . . ."

"Now try to calm down." Christal, ever the comforter, always the rock, even at times like these, said to him. "Relax now, and just let it come out. It's going to be alright," all the time feeling as though her insides were on the verge of exploding.

"Now," she asked, struggling to control her own emotions, "what else? What about my husband? What about the kids?"

Rosemary, fearing that at any moment her legs would give way, steadied herself against the arm of the sofa as she clung tightly to Christal's arm for support.

"What about my son?" she cried out. "Michael—what about Michael?" and then realizing how such an outburst must have appeared to the others, begged an apology.

"Oh, I'm so sorry, Christal. That must have sounded terrible."

"Don't fret about it, Rosemary. Don't you think I know how you feel?"

Viola wrapped an arm around Rosemary's shoulder while offering the weeping young mother a handkerchief.

"Isn't there something else you can tell us?" Joe asked of the deputy. "Were they robbed? Were they hurt? C'mon, man. There must be something—"

"Please," Christal's eyes clouded in dread as if she already knew. "Please tell us."

The deputy, becoming more uncomfortable by the second, shuffled his feet, squeezed and wrung his cap.

"I'm sorry, ma'am, but that's about all I'm authorized to say. I can't tell you any more. The sheriff himself will be along directly to fill you in."

Exchanging looks with Viola, each as if to say it looked hopeless, Christal, using a more modulated but much firmer tone asked, "Would you at least tell us where the car is?"

"Ma'am, I really don't know how they are. I didn't see them 'cause I left the site before anyone told me," the deputy said, "but I can tell you that they found the car down on old Malvich Road, not very far off the highway." His eyes looked away in an obvious attempt to avert Christal's dagger-like stare.

"Malvich Road?" Christal repeated. "I know exactly where that is."

"Sheriff Schooler said to tell you that if you could just wait, he'll be coming here real soon to tell you everything you want to know." The words had not completely left his mouth before he turned on his heels and scurried down the hallway. With a crushing sense of foreboding, Christal watched him as he rounded the corner and quickly disappeared down the staircase.

Closing the door behind her, Christal snapped into action. At the same time she was reaching for her coat, she announced, "Get your coat, Rosemary. The sheriff won't have to come here," she said. "We'll go there!"

She looked at Viola and Joe. "Will you drive us, Joe?"

Joe was already halfway into his coat. "Of course," he said.

"Something terrible has happened," Rosemary said, mostly to herself. "I just know it. Oh Lord, please let them be, alright," Rosemary prayed as she clutched a string of rosary beads tightly against her chest. But of course she didn't *know* it. The deputy's refusal to give them even the scantiest of details had left them all fearing the worst.

In a matter of minutes, with Joe at the wheel and Christal barking out directions, they were racing down Route 36 toward Malvich Road. Rosemary was chanting *Hail Marys* and *Our Fathers*, and using the beads to keep count, pausing abruptly to ask, "Why is it so hard for them to tell us what happened?"

"I don't know, Rosemary," Christal said. "I guess because he didn't know anything about their condition, he couldn't tell us anything. Maybe we're thinking it's worse than it really is." But the words rang as hollow to her as they did to the others. It was obvious that she had just about run out of anything hopeful to say.

They had negotiated a quarter mile of the debris strewn trail when they were confronted by a growing assembly of police and curious onlookers. Several yards off the road sat the Chrysler, its back end plainly visible. It was positioned at a distance close enough from their vantage point to be able to make out its outline but not close enough to see what or who was in it.

Joe parked the car and as they started to walk toward the Chrysler, they were stopped by a guard and a barrier rope stretched across the road. Christal ignored the guard by stepping around the tree to which the rope was tied but she found herself blocked again by a second guard.

"Sorry, folks," the first guard said, obviously failing to recognize either of the two mothers. "I can't let you get any closer."

"Why won't you let us see it?" Rosemary asked. "What is it that we're not allowed to see?"

"There's nothing to see," the guard said. "They're all dead."

"All dead?" Christal repeated. It was more of an exclamation than a question: "All dead!"

Even though Christal had been expecting the worst, and, so she thought, had prepared herself for the moment, his words smashed against her consciousness with sledge-hammer force. She felt the color drain from her face and though momentarily staggered by their jolting suddenness and his matter-of-fact tone, she struggled to regain her composure.

Viola, emitting an audible gasp, clung tightly to the baby with one arm while instinctively reaching out to grasp both mothers' hands. Rosemary felt her knees start to give way but managed to remain upright by leaning against a tree.

"Oh Lord—no! Please no!" Christal cried. Maybe she had misunderstood. "They're dead?" she asked incredulously. "They're all dead?"

The guard corrected himself. "One of 'em's still alive," he said. "But she's in pretty bad shape."

"One is still alive? Which one?" she asked and without stopping to take a breath, "You said 'she'—it's a girl? Which girl?"

Joe was stunned by the guard's seeming indifference, but then he quickly realized that the man was probably unaware that these two women were the mothers of the slain children.

"Ma'am," the guard said, "I'm really sorry but you can't go over there," as the two women tried again to breach the barricade. "Are you a relative or something?" he added.

"I'm their mother," Christal screamed in his face. "That man is my husband!" She pointed angrily at Rosemary. "That's her son down there! Now, please get out of our way!"

The guard continued to stand his ground. "I really am sorry, ma'am, but my orders are to let no one go down this road," and adding, "But I can tell you this—the little girl—she's not there. They took her to the hospital just a little while ago."

Christal pulled back as the guard said, "That's where you need to be."

Rosemary, now that reality had set in, clutched the guard's sleeve. "Please—it's my son—my only child," she pleaded. "Can't you let us through?"

But it was no use. The guard stood firm. Rosemary hesitated for just a moment. She released her hold on the guard's arm before turning to Christal.

"You go ahead, Christal. You need to be at the hospital. I'll wait here so I can see Michael, and then I'll get someone to take me to the church." In a firm, resolute voice she added, "Don't worry. I'm going to be alright."

Christal looked again into Rosemary's eyes and this time she saw a glimmer of hope instead of despair. She now turned her attention inward and to her own circumstances. She would have to deal with her own grief. It was impossible to comprehend that her family had been destroyed, one of them badly injured but alive and probably crying for her mother. Her husband and two other daughters were now beyond her help.

"C'mon, Sis," Joe, said. "You have to get to the hospital."

"Guard and the children will be taken care of." Placing a soft kiss on Rosemary's cheek, Christal turned to face Joe.

"Let's go," she said as calmly as if she were giving instructions to a taxi cab driver.

They raced toward Westwood, through and around the relatively light highway traffic, tires screeching with every bend of the road until finally reaching the clapboard building that served as the entire area's hospital.

Reno Revelry

Larry Shea stirred when the wake-up call came. Rolling over while still half asleep he slapped Lucille on her rear end. If she had heard the phone ring, she was ignoring it but either way, she wasn't going to be hard to wake up. Neither Larry nor Lucille had slept very well, both of them being deeply disturbed by the horrific story Jack had told them the night before. Now they were finding it difficult to function normally or carry on as though nothing out of the ordinary had happened. This was especially true of Lucille.

When they walked out into the hallway, Larry noticed the *Do Not Disturb* sign hanging from the doorknob of Jack and Bernadine's room. He sighed with relief. At that point, Jack Santo was the last guy in the world he wanted to talk to.

Larry had called the front desk to have their car brought around and it was waiting for them as they walked out of the hotel. He checked his watch and was pleased to see that they would have enough time for a quick breakfast and still get to the golf course in time to see the first players tee off.

While Larry and Lucille were making their way to the Washoe County Golf Course, Jack had given up on the idea of getting any kind of restful sleep. In addition to his being haunted by the images of yesterday's events, he found himself nursing a vicious hangover. After lighting up his last cigarette, he crumpled up the empty package, picked up the phone and dialed room service.

"You look like hell," Bernadine remarked, having awakened at the sound of Jack's voice. She was puzzled as to why Jack seemed to be so out of sorts. She lit a cigarette and with her head cupped in the palm of her hand, her elbow resting on the bed, she gazed at Jack through a combination of clouds of smoke and bleary eyes.

"Aw, come on, it's not that bad," she said. "You just had a little too much to drink," obviously thinking that the cause of his distress was his failure to perform.

"But I have to tell you, lover boy, that's not the same Jack I used to know."

Jack looked at her as if she were speaking a foreign language. "What the hell are you talking about, woman?"

"Don't worry about it, Jack. We'll make up for it tonight," Bernadine said as she rolled wearily out of the bed and half stumbled, half walked into the bathroom.

During the fifteen or twenty minutes she was in there, room service showed up with a pot of coffee, cigarettes and booze. The young bellhop was startled when, Bernadine, unaware that he was there, stepped out of the bathroom, freshly showered, hair combed, makeup in place and completely naked. She might easily have been mistaken for one of Harrah's showgirls. The bellhop gaped in astonishment as Bernadine, on seeing him, ducked back into the bathroom and slammed the door while an amused Jack, with a grin and a chuckle, paid the fifteen-dollar tab with a twenty-dollar bill.

"I'm sorry, sir," the bellhop said. "I don't have change for that."

"Nah," Jack said, waving him off. "You keep the change."

It was worth it, he thought, just to see the expression on the bellhop's face. Not only was the kid getting the biggest tip of his young life, but as a bonus, he had been given a cheap peek at Bernadine in the raw.

The red-faced bellhop rolled his cart back out into the hall and as he shut the door behind him, Jack called out to Bernadine, "Okay you can come out now, he's gone."

"Geez, Jack. You didn't tell me I'd be putting on a show," Bernadine said as she started to dress.

Jack grinned as he twisted the cap off the new bottle and after pouring the steaming coffee into both mugs until they were three quarters full, he topped them off with a quarter cup of whiskey.

"Here," he said, handing her one of the mugs. "This'll put hair on your chest."

Bernadine accepted the coffee and planted a playful kiss on Jack's cheek.

"Yesterday you said something about a shopping spree." She sipped her coffee. "Was that just a lot of bar talk or did you really mean it?"

"Yeah, we got a few hours to kill," Jack said, returning Bernadine's kiss.

This and another strong drink got Jack right back into a party mood. "Gotta go out to the golf course and meet Larry and Lucille, later," he said, "but I'm sure we can squeeze in some shopping if you feel up to it."

"Hell yes, I feel up to it. Let's see if we can relieve you of some of that cash," she said, and then added, "But first, how about my fifteen bucks?"

"God moves in a mysterious way, his wonders to perform;
He plants his footsteps in the sea, and rides upon the storm."

SEVEN

Pain

I n Westwood, the quiet morning ambiance was shattered by the shrill wail of Jeff Cooley's siren as his CHP cruiser raced through the town's narrow streets, arousing the curiosity of pedestrians, startling other drivers and putting the hospital ER staff on red alert. A few inquisitive onlookers watched as Cooley swung into the parking lot and skidded to a stop a few feet outside the Emergency Room door. Before he could switch off his siren, Mrs. Greenman, holding the half-conscious Sondra Gay tightly in her arms, bounded from the car, rushed past an intern holding the door open and carefully placed the semi-conscious toddler on a waiting gurney. Within seconds, Dr. Greenman, pulled in and parked in a space marked *Ambulance Only*. Grabbing his bag, he sprinted through the ER's doors and after first carefully washing up and being handed a clean lab coat by the duty nurse, he arrived at Sondra Gay's gurney before the staff had a chance to move her onto a bed.

After conducting his cursory examination, Dr. Greenman concluded that Sondra Gay's injuries, though serious, were not life threatening. He also noted that she was alert, wide-awake and fully aware of her surroundings and that she had sustained no brain damage or other permanent injury. She would survive and other than the actual perpetrator, would become the only living witness to the hellish events of the past twenty-four hours.

The doctor completed his report before turning to a concerned Officer Cooley.

"Well, Jeff," he said, "thanks to your quick action, this little girl is going to make it."

126

It was only a short time later when Christal arrived at the hospital with brother-in-law Joe at her side, whereupon a minor disturbance ensued when she tried to push her way past the nurse at the ER admitting desk.

"I'm her mother," Christal shouted to the harried nurse. "Please, let me go to her."

"She hasn't been completely cleaned up yet, Mrs. Young." The nurse tried in vain to prevent Christal from entering the room. "Please, won't you give us just a few minutes?"

When Christal saw the white-coated Dr. Greenman, and after he had given her Sondra's optimistic prognosis which allowed her to breathe a little easier, she continued to push her way past the nurse until finally, she was able to enter the Emergency Room.

Christal would later describe the experience of seeing her badly injured daughter for the first time:

"All I could see was a small body whose face was completely covered in blood. Two wide open eyes but absolutely no sign of a facial feature—no mouth, no nose—just two eyes blinking through a mask of blood."

The harsh reality of knowing that her husband Guard and daughters Jean and Judy were gone and the fact that her only surviving daughter had been beaten to within an inch of her life brought home the awareness of how suddenly and cruelly her world had changed, literally, overnight. It was a realization so overpowering that despite her determination to keep her emotional responses in check, Christal collapsed in a dead faint.

Upon receiving permission from hospital authorities, Christal would move into Sondra Gay's room taking the bed next to that of her rapidly healing daughter and from where she'd be able to hold her in her arms if or when she should require comforting. The staff had graciously even granted her permission to set up a crib for Wayne Robert.

Since no one at this early date had any idea of who could have committed this terrible crime or even why, authorities were concerned for the little girl's safety. There was a real possibility that the perpetrators, once they learned that Sondra Gay was still alive would probably be able to pick them out of a police photo lineup and so might decide to return to finish the job.

Neither the townships of Chester nor Westwood had the manpower nor the resources sufficient to provide for twenty-four hour security which, most agreed, was probably needed. Helping to watch over her, friends and family members would remain a constant presence during her recovery period. Concerns for Sondra's safety were real and would continue to mount.

Christal would soon solve the security issue by prevailing on a close friend in a small north coast town far removed from Chester who offered to provide a safe temporary home for the convalescing tot for as long as Christal deemed necessary. It was a home that Sondra Gay would soon come to call her "secret hiding place." In the meantime, Christal would continue to pray that those awful events of October tenth would gradually fade from her daughter's memory, but in truth, they never did.

The Investigation Begins

"The CII (Bureau of Criminal Identification and Investigation) is sending a criminologist up from Sacramento this morning," Sheriff Schooler told the gathering circle of local law enforcement personnel at the crime scene. "I don't want anyone touching anything until he gets here."

Sheriff Melvin Schooler was not your stereotypical small-town country bumpkin sheriff. A veteran police officer who had once attended the FBI Academy in Quantico, Virginia, he enjoyed a well-deserved reputation throughout the county as an intelligent, tough and thoroughly capable professional.

Schooler immediately instructed his office staff to send out teletypes to all neighboring jurisdictions outlining the situation, the ongoing investigation and where things stood at this point. He instructed them to describe the circumstances under which the four victims' bodies had been found and to include the probably unnecessary admonition that they should be on the lookout for anyone whom they might suspect may have been involved. "And be sure to add that the suspects, whoever they are, are probably armed and should be considered dangerous."

"Fan out around the area," Schooler directed the half dozen deputies and highway patrolmen who had shown up to offer assistance, "and see if you can find anything that might help us figure out what in the hell happened here."

The crime hit the national news wires soon following the discovery of the bodies, horrifying an entire nation. In the state capital of Sacramento, the state's Bureau of Criminal Identification and Investigation responded in force. The following morning, local investigators had been joined by three special state investigators including criminologist Everett Chamberlin.

In one of their reports they noted that *the victims' car, a light green 1950 Chrysler Windsor four door sedan bearing California license plates 2B9 949 had been found abandoned about a half mile from State Route 36. The bodies of the four murder victims together with lone survivor, 3 ½ year-old Sondra Gay Young, had been placed in the trunk of the car. Guard Young's hands had once been tied behind his back with sash cord or clothesline rope. But it was now found around his right wrist having the appearance that it had been cut. It measured 33½ inches in length. His face was covered with a blindfold fashioned from a piece of unbleached muslin which looked like it had once been used as an ironing board cover.*

After the bodies had been removed, the special investigators and the criminologists began their meticulous work of gathering evidence and dusting for latent fingerprints, even while realizing that before the area had been closed off, the crime scene had been crawling with curious onlookers, police officers and reporters, raising fears that whatever evidence the perpetrators may have left had already been compromised. They were able to trace with some success the path of the victims' car as it had been driven into the area, but the tracks made by the suspect's car, which they assumed had also entered the area, had been obliterated by the heavy foot traffic as well as by other cars belonging to various officials and so were of little evidentiary value.

Two calculator tapes were found; one bearing the logo of Young's Supermarket and the other stamped *Bank of America*. Both tapes bore the figure $7128.69, which was the amount that the bank teller said she handed to Guard Young before he left the bank.

A comb found on the ground near the car was identified as being the property of Christal Young who would later tell officers that the comb was always kept in the car's glove compartment, confirming investigating officers' assumption that the assailants had probably rifled through the glove compartment in search of the money. A small scrap of facial tissue was also found near the comb and on which was noticed a tiny, dark brown stain. It was initially expected that the stain would prove to be blood but a later presumptive analysis came up negative.

In a small pile of rubbish just off the clearing, officers found two intact ironing board covers, both bearing the same reddish-brown stains that had been found on the facial tissue and as officers noted, it was of the same material that the robbers had used to fashion the blindfold found on Guard Young. They surmised that there must have been a third ironing board cover, the remnants of which had been taken away by the killers.

Investigators were puzzled by a short piece of blood stained rope; the same type that had been used to bind Guard Young's hands, found lying in the center of the road several feet behind the car. In their attempt to reconstruct the crime, they concluded that this piece of rope, when coupled with the loose piece found dangling from the victim's left wrist, indicated that, with his hands bound behind his back, Guard and the children had been placed in the trunk in such a way that the killers had been unable to completely close the lid. Their conclusions were substantiated by the lacerations on Guard's hands that appeared to have been caused by being slammed by the trunk lid in a failed attempt to close it. At some point, officers surmised, the bindings on Guard's hands had been cut and after his body had been tossed atop the children, his left arm was repositioned further into the trunk. Their efforts however, seemed to have gone for naught since the lid had still remained slightly ajar, just the way it was found

From there, it appeared that the car had been driven another several yards into a clump of manzanita brush where, with the help of Mr. and Mrs. Bridges, it had been discovered by CHP Officer Jeff Cooley.

Probably the most significant piece of evidence found at the scene was an eighteen and a half inch length of slightly bent, ¾ inch galvanized steel pipe. The pipe was fitted on one end with a black cast iron elbow stained with what appeared to be blood smears embedded with human hair while the other end was threaded. Officers logically surmised that they had found the murder weapon.

Criminologists were quick to note that the pipe had been cut with a home-garage type roller cutter and had not been reamed and de-burred—a clear indication that it was not the work of a professional plumber. They also found traces of gypsum embedded in its threads, presumably from being forced through a sheet of drywall, as well as residues of Permatex No. 3 thread compound. Major disappointment came when criminologists were unable to lift at least one readable print from what they now presumed to be the murder weapon, due to the smudged and smeared condition of the stains.

The pipe had been found with one end stuck into a small pile of bark and leaf mold about eight hundred feet from the car and near the spot where the loose piece of rope had been found. Both items, investigators conjectured, had been thrown from the killer's car.

As the big Chrysler was being towed through town on its way to the garage for further processing, townsfolk looked on with mixed emotions. Some were just morbidly curious but others, as they stood on the sidewalks along the curb lined streets watching the car as it passed, were shaken by the realization that they were looking at the car in which the savagely beaten bodies of Guard Young and three young children had just been found, and some were finding it difficult to hold back tears.

Once it had reached the garage, investigators began the painstaking work of examining both inside and out, every inch of the murder car. They found that the steering wheel and gear shift knob, the window crank handles, as well as some of the articles that lay on the car's floor after falling from the glove compartment, were all smeared with what appeared to be blood, meaning that almost assuredly they had been handled by the killer or killers. They would be taken to the state crime lab for a more detailed forensic examination. The victims' clothing, now in the possession of the mortician at the Chapel of the Pines Mortuary would be turned over to investigators later in the afternoon.

The Mothers Mourn

It wouldn't have surprised most people who knew Christal that by nature, she would have assumed the role of a comforter even while having to deal with her own grief. Most mothers in Christal's circumstances and facing such unimaginable heartbreak, would themselves have been the ones needing comforting. The expected response from most any other mother experiencing the bitter anguish of the loss of a husband and two of her children, despite the contradictory sense of gratitude because one daughter had been spared, would be one of anger—maybe even rage—accompanied by a visceral desire to exact some kind of retribution. But Christal was not "any other" mother.

A devout Mormon, Christal would choose to deal with her loss in a much less reflexive manner. Although her loved ones had been taken from her on this Earth, her Mormon teaching assured her that through faith, her family will be *sealed together* for eternity, never again to be parted—even by death. Among the surviving members of Christal's family, there existed not the slightest doubt that one day they would all be re-united.

Christal was one of those rare individuals who actually lived her faith. In times like this, after having been struck by such overwhelming tragedy, just as she was four years earlier with the death of Gardner Lee, her first born son, she would weather the storm by appealing to that unswerving faith. The strength of Christal's character was best exemplified by her spontaneous reaction at the very moment she had first laid eyes on Sondra Gay's badly beaten body. While she looked down at her half-conscious daughter, the tiny body covered in blood and still suffering from the vicious beating, Christal, speaking of the person or persons who had committed this awful act:

"I could almost hate him," she said. She could not bring herself to actually hate anyone—even if that hate was only *almost*—including, even, the soul-less individual who had done this terrible thing to her family. It was indeed, a true example of the Christian edict that commands believers to *love your enemy and bless them that curse you.*

With that powerful faith and genuine compassion for others, Christal was able to share in Rosemary's bitter grief over her loss of Michael.

As the terrible news reached members of both extended families, relatives of the Young family began to converge on the Susanville home of Joe and Viola Hardy. Many would travel from points as far away as Utah to attend the funerals, bringing words of solace and to commiserate with each other over the family's loss.

Viola operated a day nursery in her home and even though it was a very large home, the Hardy's ability to accommodate the entire family was being stretched to the limit. Will and Ida Lister, Christal's mother and father, along with brothers Errol, De Rell and LuDean came. Sisters Opal, Gloria, Yvonne and Geraldine came with their husbands as well as Arnell, another sister, who, with her husband, drove up from Walnut Creek, three hundred miles to the south.

Aunts Stella and Catherine came as did other members of Guard's side of the family.

Geraldine would later tell of the challenge that Viola faced in trying to provide sleeping accommodations for such a large group.

"There were so many of us that we mostly had to sleep on the floor—side to side in spoon fashion," she recalled. "You slept like spoons—if one moved or turned over, then all of us had to move or turn over."

Christal expressed a desire to see for the last time, her beloved husband and her two slain children. Family members, fearful of the emotional trauma such a visit might provoke, advised her against going, suggesting that instead, she stay with Sondra Gay.

But Christal was determined to make that last farewell visit. She turned to her sister Geraldine. "It'll be okay," she said. "I know Sondra Gay is in good hands and besides, I'll only be leaving her for a short while." Pausing momentarily, she asked, "Would you and Ralph drive me to the mortuary?"

"Of course," Geraldine reluctantly replied.

Christal sobbed softly to herself during the half hour drive to Westwood's Chapel of the Pines Mortuary where Guard and the children lay in preparation for the impending funeral services. She still tried—though without much success—to keep her grief and her inner turmoil to herself.

On their arrival at the mortuary, the Walters learned that since they were not considered by the staff to be "immediate family members," they were prevented from entering. They could only watch Christal as she strode resolutely through the front door, disappearing inside the building where she would remain for the next twenty minutes.

Neither Geraldine nor her husband Ralph could have predicted Christal's reaction on seeing the battered bodies in their present state but knowing of her uncompromising faith, they were confident that she would find some kind of a silver lining in the midst of all the horror.

When she stepped out into the sunlight, as Geraldine would later describe, there was no evidence of the pain they were sure she must have experienced nor was there the slightest sign of sorrow on her face—not a single tear; not a hint of sadness. When she emerged, she was actually glowing—literally. Christal described the experience of being with her husband and children for the final time as one of extreme "serenity." Looking at the mutilated bodies of her most precious loved ones, she said she could sense the unmistakable presence of their departed spirits. In fact, she said, they actually "spoke" to her. Though she wasn't ready to reveal the substance of the conversation or any of its personal details, she said they talked as they had always talked.

It was her faith, she said, that gave her the strength to endure the heart-wrenching emotional pain, enabling her to describe the experience as a "sweet peace."

Big Spender

The bright neon arch stretches across downtown Virginia Street proclaiming: *Reno - The Biggest Little City in the World.* With its casinos, bars and hundreds of restaurants open for business twenty-four hours a day, seven days a week, Reno is, quite literally, a town that never sleeps.

Boisterous revelers with cocktails in hand stagger from bar to bar, casino to casino and back to the bars again. The *Battle Born* state of Nevada is a party animal's round-the-clock playground when compared to its next-door neighbor, California, where by law, bars close by 2:00 a.m. and most restaurants close their kitchens as early as 10:00 p.m.

When dawn comes, the party atmosphere and the glittery neon lighted streets are overtaken by the sounds of the trash collector and the hustle and bustle of delivery trucks of every description. All-night parties, desperation driven gamblers and left over barflies are beginning to straggle back to their rooms to nurse their wounds, count their losses, catch up their love-making and hopefully, get a few hours of sleep.

So when Jack and Bernadine stepped out onto the sidewalk on that bright, sunny Saturday morning, the downtown streets were not crawling with traffic and the sidewalks weren't jammed with people. Except for a few late running delivery trucks and an occasional diehard tourist still looking for a winning blackjack table, there were few signs of commerce with only a small number of retailers opening their doors for business; one of those being Florsheim Shoes. In her entire life, Bernadine had never owned a pair of Florsheims. Any shoe that carried a $19.95 price tag was way out of her league. Her shoes had always come from Karl's or Gallenkamp's and never once had she ever owned a pair of shoes costing more than $7.95.

When Jack noticed her gazing longingly through the store's display window at a pair of blue high-heeled pumps, he suggested, "If you like those, why don't we start here?"

"Don't be silly, Jack," she protested coyly, "they're way too expensive."

"Let me worry about that," he said as he pulled her through the front door.

Thirty minutes later they walked out of the store and Jack, now seventy dollars lighter was sporting a new pair of cordovan wing-tips and carrying a box of leather Hanover slippers for himself. Bernadine was wearing a broad smile and a brand new sexy pair of blue pumps.

Their next stop was Parker's Department Store where Jack treated himself to some new pants and a color-coordinated jacket, a couple of white dress shirts, a cowboy shirt and a deluxe pair of Tony Lama ostrich skin cowboy boots. Then it was on to a women's store specializing in western wear so Bernadine could pick up a pair of Jodhpur riding boots. While there, she also added a cowboy shirt and a belt with an over-sized silver plated buckle.

After a quick lunch, which for Jack, consisted of three martinis with extra olives and for Bernadine, a fruit-laced cocktail embellished with a tiny paper parasol alongside a Crab Louie salad, they hailed a cab to take them to the golf course. Their intention was to meet up with Larry and Lucille, but unfortunately, after having watched most of the day's play, the Sheas had returned to the hotel only to be informed by the parking attendant that "Mr. Santo and his wife" had left for the golf course. So after frustratingly having to double back, they were finally able to all come together.

"Looks like you guys got yourselves some new duds," Larry remarked, checking out Jack's new jacket, pants and shoes. Despite Lucille's dark mood, Bernadine's flashy new blue pumps did not go unnoticed.

"Wow!" she said, becoming animated if even for just a moment. "What a great pair of shoes! Where did you get them?" When Bernadine told her, not a little proudly, Lucille's eyes popped and she joked, "Florsheims? Well, ex-cu-u-se me!"

Larry, hoping to capitalize on what seemed to be Lucille's newfound exuberance suggested, "How about we go to Harold's Club? I could use a drink."

"You're talking my language, Larry," Jack said. "Harold's it is. Did you know they've got a great gun collection there?"

"Yeah, so I hear," Larry said, exhibiting little interest in being reminded of his current gun troubles.

At Harold's Club they quickly found their way to the famous Silver Dollar Bar saloon, one of Reno's favorite watering holes for tourists. With its curved and exquisitely polished bar in which more than two thousand silver dollars were embedded in its surface and a back-lighted translucent orange arm rail, the resulting effect was both unique and strikingly dramatic.

When the Silver Dollar Bar first opened in 1941, patrons had been treated to the stunning visual of a back-bar surrounded by huge, wall-size western landscapes show-casing a cascading waterfall and pool—except this waterfall and pool were not actually composed of water but rather, pure eighty-six proof Kentucky bourbon whiskey.

The Silver Dollar Bar was arguably the most unique drinking establishment in the entire state of Nevada.

Before leaving Harold's casino, on an impulse, Jack stopped at a dice table and in less than half an hour, despite his mind being fogged by the enormous amounts of alcohol he'd consumed over the past several hours, he managed to rack up a little over two hundred and fifty dollars in winnings.

At the Two Sixteen Club they enjoyed another expensive meal after which, as with every other tab this foursome had run up over the past two days, Jack paid.

On leaving the Two Sixteen and with Larry and Lucille several steps behind, Jack and Bernadine strolled arm in arm along busy North Virginia Street and as they approached the corner with its profusion of newspaper racks, Bernadine was the first to remark on the Reno Gazette's bold headlines; in fact, she was stopped in her tracks causing Jack to nearly lose his balance: *Extra!*, the headlines screamed; *California Family Massacre!*

"Wait a second, Jack. Let's see what that's all about," Bernadine urged.

As she scanned the story beneath the headline, Larry and Lucille, after catching up, walked past without making a comment. Jack on the other hand appeared annoyed that she would call attention to the headline. His entire demeanor seemed to change.

"C'mon," he said. "We're going to go home now. The party's over."

Larry, looking at Lucille, shrugged. "Okay, Jack. Let's go get the car and get the hell out of here."

Rolling out of Reno on I-80 with Larry driving, a bleary-eyed Jack Santo was slouched in the front passenger seat while the two women occupied the back. Jack had been drinking almost non-stop since even before leaving Chester two days earlier and now the liquor had started to exact its toll. He lapsed into what could only be described as a semi-coma. It was the moment for which Bernadine had been waiting.

"Lucille," she pressed. "If you don't mind my asking, what in the hell is wrong with you?"

"What are you talking about?" Lucille answered warily, obviously somewhat taken aback. "There's nothing wrong with me."

"We're not stupid, Lucille," Bernadine said, trying with some difficulty to be heard over Jack's loud snoring. "You were not having a good time. We could plainly see that. You hardly had anything to drink and didn't even touch your food. You just haven't been yourself. At first I thought you and Larry were having a fight, but then I realized that wasn't the case. It was like you just couldn't wait to get away from me and Jack."

Lucille looked at Larry for help but Larry kept his eyes riveted on the road so she turned back to Bernadine.

"Didn't Jack say anything to you at all?" Lucille asked.

"Say anything about what?" Bernadine wanted to know. "What the hell are you talking about?"

And then she realized. "Those newspaper headlines. There was something about those headlines, wasn't there, Lucille? Those headlines spooked all three of you. What's going on, Lucille?"

"Look, Bernie," Larry finally spoke up, "you're going to find out soon enough only it's going to have to be Jack who tells you."

Bernadine decided to give up but only for now and with Jack passed out and the two women drifting in and out of various states of wakefulness, the ride back to Chester was completed in near total silence.

Dead End Leads

That evening following a working dinner, police officers, investigators and others who were to play a part in the investigation gathered at the sheriff's sub-station in Chester where they compared notes, formed a strategy and compiled a list of possible suspects and witnesses.

One deputy recounted the two automobiles that had been seen in the area during the late morning hours of Friday: a black Buick, 1950 or '51 model bearing Arkansas license plates and apparently headed into Westwood; the other, an old brown sedan, spotted as it rolled down Route 36 toward Chester.

During the meeting, Sheriff Schooler took a call from Stanislaus County Sheriff Cecil Kilroy.

"Oh, hello, Cecil," Schooler said. "Listen, we're kind of locked up in a meeting right now. If you read that teletype, then you know we've got a few problems to deal with."

"That's what I called you about, Mel," Kilroy said. "I got your teletype this morning and it made me think of a piece of information you might find useful."

"About the murders?"

"Yeah, maybe so."

"Go ahead, Cecil. I'm listening," Schooler said.

"Well, this past summer," Kilroy began, "there was a couple guys who were doin' time in the Stanislaus county jail. A trustee overheard one of 'em—the guy from Chester—talking about how he had broke into Young's Supermarket one night but couldn't find no money, so he just left."

"Well that's pretty interesting all right, Cecil," Schooler said, "but what's it got to do with the murders?"

"Well, listen to this, Mel," Kilroy said, his voice rising. "The guy who was from Chester—well, he told the other guy that Young was in the habit of transporting big money from the bank in Westwood to his store in Chester—every other Friday, he said."

"That's pretty good. Is there more?" Schooler asked.

"He said the next day he went into the store to buy some groceries and he heard Young talking to people about someone burglarizing the store, but he was having a hard time trying to figure out why someone would bust in and not take anything."

Schooler waited for the punch line.

"But here's the thing, Sheriff. When that guy from Chester heard that story about Young carrying all that money, he says that one of these days he's going to go up there and take him."

"Now we're talking. Sheriff. You got the names of those two guys?"

"No, Mel. We don't have any names yet, but I can go back to that trustee and see if he can remember."

Schooler couldn't hide his disappointment. "You do that, Sheriff. When you find out that Chester guy's name, you got my number."

"Right, Sheriff," Kilroy said. "'Course I can't vouch for the guy's veracity. He drinks a bit."

"Great," Schooler said, knitting his brow. "Just let me know what you find out." He hung up the receiver making a mental note to check out Sheriff Kilroy's tip. Still shaking his head, he returned to the meeting.

Another message had come in while Sheriff Schooler was on the phone with Kilroy advising him that lone survivor Sondra Gay's condition was rapidly improving; information that would definitely go under the heading of welcome news indeed. The sheriff began to add things up in his mind and there was one thing of which he could be sure: this month of October was about to become his busiest month since taking office almost two years ago.

Saying Goodbye

On Monday, October 13, the streets of Chester were eerily vacant while store windows along the four-block business district displayed signs reading *Closed for Funeral.*

The thirteen miles stretching between Chester and Westwood is the same portion of Highway 36 on which four of their own, just three days ago, had met such a grisly fate. Normally lightly traveled, it was now jam-packed with what seemed to be hundreds of cars, many of them enroute to Westwood's little Church of Our Lady of the Snows where they would attend Father Hugh McTague's recitation of a Catholic Mass of the Angels funeral service for four-year-old Michael Saile. It would be the first opportunity for local townspeople, still not recovered from the shock, to pay their last respects to the four slain victims and for Rosemary Saile to say her final goodbyes to her son, Michael.

A relatively new arrival to the area, Rosemary was without the close family support structure that was there to comfort Christal over the loss of her loved ones so of course she was more than grateful when her sister, Margaret Crowley and lifelong friend Rita Brady traveled from Chicago to be with her.

"I guess he had to go," she sobbed, resting her head on Margaret's shoulder.

"But why, when he is still such a youngster?"

Yet, for the most part, Rosemary wore her grief in silence, weeping softly as she clutched her prayer book and rosary beads. She gazed wistfully at Michael's tiny white coffin as it stood within an arm's length, fronting the altar and surrounded by banks of flowers and funeral wreaths. One wreath, prominently displayed at Michael's feet, bore the inscription, *To Our Little Playmate.* It had been sent by Christal on behalf of the Young children.

When the ceremony ended, crowds of mourners solemnly gathered at the entrance of the little church to watch pallbearers carry

Michael's flower-covered coffin down the front steps and place it in the waiting hearse. Christal, who was struggling with her own grief and would be attending her family's funeral services the next day, came to stand beside Rosemary. Even under these difficult circumstances, Christal offered a comforting shoulder to her grief-stricken friend. The bereaved mothers embraced warmly and Rosemary, who until that moment had managed to keep herself somewhat composed, broke down and resting her head on Christal's shoulder, wept bitterly.

On the following day, with the morning bathed in bright autumn sunshine, most of the same congregation which had attended Michael's funeral re-gathered, this time at Westwood's little white Church of Jesus Christ of Latter-day Saints, where they would mourn the passing of Judy, Jean and Guard Young.

Inside the somber and sparsely decorated chapel, standing between the first row of seats and the altar, Guard's silver casket rested on a black cloth draped bier which, in turn, was flanked by the two small white caskets of Jean and Judy.

Funeral arrangements had been supervised by Christal, even while maintaining a vigil at Sondra Gay's hospital bedside. She asked that, rather than spend money on flowers, she would prefer that people donate to a fund which she had set up earlier to purchase equipment for a town playground that was now under construction. Most townspeople honored that request.

Bishop Jack Seipert's eulogy offered a powerful message of comfort and reassurance and, looking directly at Christal as she sat with both eyes glued on the three neatly aligned caskets standing only inches away, he said:

"Brother Guard was known to all of us as a brother in the gospel of Jesus Christ. I'd like to testify today that Guard is now in his place in heaven as are Judy and Jean."

The stirring piano strains of Norwegian composer Christian Sinding's *Rustle of Spring*, one of Christal's favorites, played softly over the poignant words of solace as delivered by Bishop Nason Hurst:

"Christal, there is a reason for these deaths. You and only you will know and understand and only you will be able to find that reason."

William Lister, Christal's father, sitting on her right was visibly shaken. He squeezed Christal's hand and silently wept as he listened to retired bishop Glen Thurgood's eulogy:

141

"In the minds of many here there will be questions about those who commit these abominable acts. We don't want people of this community to feel a sense of revenge in their hearts, for God will see that justice is done."

Near the back of the tiny chapel, store manager Dottie Elliott sat with her husband Howard. The fiercely loyal Mrs. Elliott, who over the years had become a fixture at Young's Supermarket and had worked closely alongside the Youngs since the day the store opened, sobbed unashamedly as she stared at the tiny coffins. She recalled the unbridled joy that reigned within the Young household on those days when each of the girls—first Jean and a few months later, Judy—had been brought home from the adoption agency and how over the succeeding years, they would turn the store into a veritable playground.

She thought about how it had been only a few short weeks since little Michael and his mother Rosemary had arrived on the scene and how quickly they were able to find their way into the hearts of the townspeople, especially those of Dottie and Howard Elliot.

Many within this saddened congregation, even despite the bishop's words and perhaps for generations yet unborn, would be haunted by a single nagging question: Why was this allowed to happen? The Young family was one of the most devoutly religious and—in every sense of the word—the most truly Christian family that anyone in Chester had ever known. How and why, they asked, could the God that this family had loved and worshipped so unconditionally—the God of boundless love and mercy—how could such a God permit an atrocity like this to befall a family that was so totally devoted to His service?

But for Christal there was never the slightest doubt or question. She found solace in the knowledge that, as in everything that happens in one's life, God has a plan. She leaned on the words of eighteenth century hymnist, William Cowper:

God moves in a mysterious way, his wonders to perform; he plants his footsteps in the sea, and rides upon the storm.

In 1952 the township of Chester had no burial grounds of its own so the Young family was interred in the small cemetery in neighboring Westwood, where Guard's brother Vance conducted the ceremonies at each individual Young gravesite, and only yards away from where Michael Saile had been laid to rest.

Christal was well aware that investigators would be looking to Sondra Gay, even while she was in the recovery process, to help them as they searched for the perpetrators of this crime.

Only Sondra Gay had been able to get a look at the monster that had attacked them. Only Sondra Gay remained alive to describe how he had raised the weapon above his head, ignoring their pleas for mercy and with chilling efficiency, brought it crashing down on their tiny heads, blow after bone shattering blow.

If and when there was to be a full recovery, Sondra Gay would be the only living person able to tell the complete story and yet at such a tender age, after having barely survived her own personal trip through hell, investigators wondered if she would be able—or even willing—to remember.

By late Tuesday, as the investigation began to heat up, Sondra Gay had recovered to the extent that she was now able to help investigators by answering a list of carefully prepared questions put to her by her mother who, alongside Deputy Art Bates, sat at her bedside.

She remembered how her father's car had been stopped by two men driving a blue car. When Bates questioned her further, suggesting that it might actually have been a green car, she was emphatic. "It was blue," she said.

To be sure that Sondra Gay, at three and a half, knew the difference between green and blue, Bates showed her two toy cars, one blue, the other green. Sondra Gay was adamant. It was *blue* she said, holding up and waving the toy blue car and immediately convincing Bates that the assailants were, indeed, driving a blue car.

She described the men as one wearing a mask and the other holding a "shiny" gun with a black handle. She gave contradicting descriptions of their clothing, at one time saying they were wearing blue trousers, like jeans, and another time describing them as yellow, which Bates took to mean khaki. She said that the man wearing the mask was bald above the mask.

It was becoming apparent to investigators that lone survivor Sondra Gay would, in the end, be of only limited help in solving this crime. They were facing the grim reality that the solution was going to have to come from other sources and from other clues—of which there were precious few.

"A pile of insurmountable evidence."

EIGHT

Perpetrators

The background noises in a typical rural sheriff's office in 1952 would have been the loud ringing of telephones intermingled with the annoying and incessant pounding of two or three typewriters, and certainly no office would have been considered state-of-the-art without the clatter of at least one teletype machine.

And so it was in the town of Redding at the Shasta County Sheriff's office when late that Saturday afternoon, Deputy Sheriff Darrell Wilson read the bulletin that had just come in over the teletype announcing that four bodies had been found just off a section of State Highway 36 between Chester and Westwood. All four had been apparently bludgeoned to death with a steel pipe and Plumas County Sheriff Mel Schooler was asking neighboring law enforcement personnel to be on the lookout for the perpetrators who he vaguely described as two white males, one tall, and possibly a white female, ages undetermined. "More details, as they become available will follow," said the communiqué.

Tearing the bulletin from its spool, Deputy Wilson shouted to his boss, Sheriff Charles Jones, "Hey, Charlie, take a look at this."

As Jones began to read, Wilson asked, "You thinking what I'm thinking?" He was referring to the three young hoodlums who, a couple of nights ago, had been arrested as suspects in a home break-in over in nearby Cottonwood, where, after viciously beating the occupants, the perpetrators had run off with a bagful of jewelry and an undetermined amount of money. Following a cursory investigation, the three young men had been released due to a lack of evidence.

Jones read the wire again, this time slowly. "This could be anybody," he said. "What are you saying? You think it's those three guys from the other night?"

"No, I'm just saying maybe we should notify Sheriff Schooler and let him be the one to decide," Wilson said.

"You do that, Darrell," the sheriff suggested, "And while you're at it, find out if he's got anything new on it. What we have so far is not an awful lot of information to go on." Almost as an afterthought, he added, "Find out if those three guys are still hanging around town."

Schooler took the call from Sheriff Jones' office in which he was informed that after receiving news of the Chester murders, the sheriff had placed the three young hoodlums in custody again.

"Sounds an awful lot like your Chester killings, Sheriff. Don't you think?" Deputy Wilson opined.

Schooler wasn't so sure. "I don't know, Darrell. They sound pretty young," he said. "We got witnesses who describe an older man." Then he added, "But I'd be crazy if I didn't at least talk to them."

The next day, Plumas County's District Attorney Bert Janes, Sheriff Mel Schooler and his deputy Roland Gillespie drove the hundred miles to Redding where they interviewed the three suspects. Ten minutes into the interrogation, it was clear that the young thugs had nothing whatsoever to do with the murders of Guard Young and the three children.

This would be only the first of a long series of blind alley leads that, in the weeks to come, would consume many valuable hours of the investigators' time.

In Quincy, an ex-convict named Guy Crocker had been seen flashing rolls of twenty-dollar bills, the same denomination as those that Guard Young had been carrying. He was a partially bald man and since Sondra Gay had described one of her assailants as being "baldheaded," Crocker was immediately placed on the list of possible suspects and taken into custody. A follow-up report stated that the man was exhibiting very odd behavior by "roaring" and shaking the bars of his cell in anger and refusing to tell authorities where he had obtained the money.

After spending a short time in his cell, Crocker changed his mind, claiming it was money he had saved. His story checked out and he was released.

Otto Black was another partially bald man who had recently been arrested in Placer County on an assault charge, the sheer brutality of which was strikingly similar to that of the Chester killings. He was handed over to Plumas authorities for questioning but was able to produce an airtight alibi for October tenth and so was quickly exonerated in the murders.

In the days following the Young murders, the Chester rumor mill had kicked into overdrive and even though manpower was exceedingly scarce, each rumor and each lead, no matter how far-fetched, was assiduously followed up.

Sheriff Schooler took heart when two women came forward to report that while driving on Route 36 near Malvitch Road around the time the murders were thought to have occurred, they had seen "two suspicious-looking men" driving a big black sedan bearing Arkansas plates.

At about the same time, Ralph Nelson, a Sacramento cab driver, reported being stopped near 7th and L Streets Saturday morning by two men in a dark sedan who asked for directions to "Frisco" and wanted to know how many towns they'd have to go through to get there. Nelson described the car as a "dark—maybe black"—Pontiac sedan. He said it was dusty and dirty with scratched door panels as though it had been driven around in heavy brush. He told Schooler that it bore out-of-state license plates—Arkansas, as best he could remember.

Schooler sent out another all-points-bulletin and that very evening as he was interviewing people who thought they "might have seen something," an excited Deputy Gillespie came rushing up to him as he sat at his desk.

"Sheriff, we got it—they're caught! He's on the phone now." Schooler picked up the phone to talk to Sheriff John I. Flaska of Albuquerque, New Mexico.

"Sheriff, we got the Arkansas Buick you boys are looking for. Picked it up on the highway not ten minutes ago, heading east. Three guys in it and they got at least two thousand dollars on them."

Schooler struggled to suppress his excitement. "That's great, Sheriff. What are their names and have they made a statement?"

"Well," Flaska said, "one of them is a guy named Ira Craig. And then there's Lawrence Gray and Charles Longing. Any of those names ring a bell?"

"No," Schooler said, "can't say that they do. Did they make any kind of a statement?"

"They're telling me they came from Las Vegas. They say they won the money at the dice tables."

"Do you believe them?"

"Don't know," Flaska said. "They're acting sort of suspicious, though. We'll be talking to them some more and, of course, I'll let you know how that goes. I just thought maybe you'd like to know your APB paid off. As soon as we find out more, I'll let you know."

"You do that, Sheriff. And thanks very much for your help."

It was the first promising lead but it was destined to be short-lived. A little after midnight, Schooler received another call from Sheriff Flaska.

"Bum lead," he said. "I'm sorry. These guys were sure enough spotted in Las Vegas at three o'clock Friday and they sure enough won a ton of money. It looks like they've been leveling with me." He said he'd given them back their two thousand dollars before sending them on their way.

Rosemary Sailes, Michael's mother, was questioned by the CII Bureau Chief to determine whether she might have known of anyone who drove a blue sedan. She said that on the Monday following the murders, she had observed a dark blue—what she thought to be a 1947 Ford or Chevrolet—stopped on Route 36 near the logging road where the murders had occurred. She added that she was too scared to obtain a better description of the car or its occupants. A short time later, Rosemary moved from her apartment over the Young's market and relocated five-hundred miles to the south in Sherman Oaks, California. In explaining to authorities why she made the move, she told them that even though her experiences while in Chester had been more than pleasant, the reminders of the horrible events of October tenth were so overwhelmingly painful, there was just no way she could continue living there.

The area's growing jumpiness was heightened when another local family was reported missing. Fearing a repetition of the Young murders, a posse of two hundred armed men took to the woods in search of three members of the Leonard Hawkins family, which in addition to Hawkins, included his brother-in-law and Hawkins' two year-old daughter. All had failed to return at the expected time after attending an out-of-town movie. They were reported missing by Mrs. Hawkins who had stayed home to entertain at a bridal shower.

Townsfolk breathed a little easier when the trio was found three hours later on Route 36 about twenty-three miles west of Chester. It seems that, instead of driving to Westwood to see the movie, they had gone in the opposite direction toward Redding and on the way back to Chester their car had broken down.

Chester's relatively undermanned law enforcement capabilities would be stretched to the limit as it struggled to deal with an event of such extraordinary magnitude. Not only were they expected to solve the crime in a timely manner, but at the same time, quiet the growing fears of an edgy citizenry.

One frequent report—worth noting in light of later developments— was that on the day in question, a woman named Mildred Smith had been seen on the highway near the logging road.

Mrs. Smith was a former clerk at Young's market and was reported to have been in a bitter ongoing disagreement with Guard Young over what she claimed were overcharges on her weekly grocery bills. Guard so resented the accusation that he eventually had her barred from trading at his store. The grudge had become so acerbic that Guard had mentioned to some of his friends that her disparaging remarks were upsetting him to the point that he had even considered selling out and leaving town.

When the name Louis Edmond Blair found its way to the top of the suspect list, from the anxious residents of Chester all the way to the state's investigation offices in Sacramento, a collective sigh of relief could be heard.

To anyone connected with the case in an investigative capacity, this looked like "the guy." Louis Blair was perfect. As the owner-manager of the town's movie theater, which happened to be located next door to Young's Supermarket, he was local. He had recently lost a court feud with Guard Young over property rights after which Young shut off Blair's water supply. As a result, he had been forced to install a well, an expensive undertaking under any circumstance. A

Chester woman had come forward to report that she had overheard Blair threaten to "kill the sonofabitch."

Sondra Gay had told investigators that the people who killed her father, sisters and friend Michael, and who "spanked" her, were driving a "blue" car. Her account was corroborated by Carl Roberts, a state forester based in Chester, telling authorities that he too had seen a blue sedan in the vicinity of the murder scene on Friday at around 5:00 p.m.

The clincher—as far as most investigators, the press, and much of the public were concerned—came when it was learned that Louis Blair drove a blue Chevrolet sedan.

Within days of the mass murders, Blair was placed under arrest in Reno where he had gone on holiday, and as Schooler, District Attorney Janes and the rest of the investigative team were preparing to announce to the world that the case had been solved—all that was missing now was a confession—thirty-seven-year-old Louis Blair would have other ideas.

Authorities also learned that he enjoyed dressing up in women's clothes after which he would haunt the seedy streets and bars of San Francisco's notorious "homo-haven" Castro district.

When a neighbor reported seeing Blair wearing lipstick and a woman's wig a few days earlier, Blair freely admitted that he was a cross-dresser. "Every once in a while tension builds up in me and I have to go down to the Bay Area and put on women's clothes," he told Sheriff Schooler.

Despite Janes' insistence to reporters that the state had amassed a pile of "insurmountable" evidence, including fingerprints, Blair proclaimed to anyone who would listen that his arrest was attributed to his cross-dressing proclivities or what some members of the press were describing as a "sexual aberration." There was nothing, he maintained, that could be called—by any stretch of the imagination— "insurmountable" evidence, as the district attorney had suggested.

His cross-dressing, he said, had absolutely nothing to do with anything and it certainly had not kept him from acting as the "Saturday afternoon baby-sitter" for the three hundred children who attended his theater and were placed under his care every Saturday.

"Why, I used to take that little Michael Saile boy up to my projection room so he could run the projector," Blair said. "He was a very bright boy. I would love to have a boy of my own like him."

About Sondra Gay, Blair was equally adamant. "And little Sondra. I knew her, too. A couple of days before this happened, I was digging a trench in back of the theater to lay some water pipe and some kids were watching and got too close. One of them was Sondra Gay. I remember telling her, 'You had better watch out or you'll get your toes cut off.'" He added, "If they would show me to her, I'm sure she would clear me."

Blair had difficulty explaining away his involvement in an incident that took place in the San Francisco suburb of Larkspur, a bedroom community at the northern entrance to the Golden Gate Bridge. Larkspur police records showed that in April, Blair had been arrested on charges of "loitering on the school grounds in women's clothes." Newspaper photographs pictured him in a woman's dark skirt, a blouse, women's shoes, no stockings and without the wig.

His wife, Vearl found herself struggling to fend off published reports that Blair had once tried to choke her on the darkened stage of his Chester movie theater. Denying those reports over and over again, she said, "Never did he ever threaten me or strike me."

Since pieces of what had appeared to be sash cord were left at the murder scene by the killers, she was asked to explain the presence of a length of sash cord found by investigators in the Blair home. Her terse explanation: "It was for a clothesline."

Investigators were further encouraged when a photograph of Blair was shown to Sondra Gay who recognized Blair as the "showman" and at first said that he was not one of the men, but when part of his face was covered to simulate a mask, she changed her mind and indicated that, yes; he was one of the men.

Christal described Blair as a "good, hard-working man, always friendly and nice to the children. I always especially liked his wife. Among the many cards of sympathy I received, one was from her which I appreciated to no end."

The district attorney's "pile of insurmountable evidence" had eroded into little more than a speed bump. The fingerprints, as it turned out, belonged to a person other than Louis Blair; two lie detector tests administered by the Washoe County Sheriff's Office in

Reno had produced "inconclusive results," failing to implicate Blair as the killer. In the absence of a formal criminal complaint, a writ of habeas corpus was filed making him free to go.

So, on October 18, all charges against Louis Blair were dismissed and he was released after having been held for nearly a week in the Washoe County Jail.

A battery of reporters and photographers had gathered at the courthouse to record his announcement:

"I do not blame the police for investigating me as they have a tough job ahead of them. I just wish it could have been handled in a different way."

When a reporter asked him to explain the transvestite accusations that had been leveled at him, he shot back, "Nothing to explain, I've already admitted that I do that sometimes."

He also told them that he would like to return to Chester and reopen his theater "if the good people of Chester will accept me." Later that week he issued a press statement pledging one hundred dollars to the growing reward fund that had been offered "for the capture of the true killers."

Following Blair's release in Reno, D.A. Janes made a statement to the press indicating he had other suspects who were still under suspicion.

"We don't feel we are at a dead end by any means," he said. "All other phases of the investigation came to a stop while Blair was our leading suspect, but we have other good leads," he assured the gathering.

But the truth was they had few promising leads, "good" or otherwise. They had been so sure that with Louis Blair in custody, the case had been solved and they had their killer. Almost all of their emphasis had been centered on Blair at the expense of all else.

Janes caught up with Schooler as both were leaving the courthouse. Now that their prime suspect had been eliminated, he wanted to get a quick status report from one of the lead investigators.

"Anything new, Sheriff?" he asked, after first assuring himself they were not within earshot of lingering and always inquisitive reporters.

"We got an anonymous call from some guy who claimed he saw someone painting a car just a day or so after the murders," Schooler said. "He said when he heard that the killer was driving a blue sedan and then he saw this guy painting a blue car—changing it to grey—he thought that was kind of suspicious. He didn't want to leave his name but he was sure willing to give me the other guy's name."

"What was this guy's name?" Janes asked.

"Larry Shea."

"So now what?"

"I'll have Mr. Shea come in tomorrow and we'll see if we can get it straightened out," Schooler said.

"You know this guy?"

"Yeah. So do you. We've been sitting on some pending charges against him over a bunch of stolen guns, among other things. He's kind of sleazy even though he tries to convince everyone he's Mr. Clean."

On October 19, Larry Shea was interviewed by Sheriff Schooler where it was quickly determined that Shea's 1951 Oldsmobile sedan still had its original paint job, which was grey. However, had Schooler dug a little deeper, he might have discovered that the car itself, which Shea readily claimed to be his, had been reported as stolen and the license plates had been issued to one Donald D. Read, a resident of Nevada City, California. They actually belonged on a 1935 Hudson touring sedan.

And so it went. Names from far and wide; witnesses, suspects—some were promising; a few were legitimate—but most were neither. It would have taken volumes to enumerate and describe the many false leads checked out over the length of the investigation. Hundreds of people were questioned and many were actually arrested on suspicion, only to be released in a day or two. But they all had to be thoroughly checked out and that meant untold hours of frustrating and at times, unproductive grunt work.

Sheriff Schooler subpoenaed the telephone records for the city of Chester and Westwood. On the off-chance that the killer had used the phone to communicate with a possible confederate outside the immediate local area, he wanted to look at the long distance logs of all calls made from either Chester or Westwood for October tenth and the week following the Young killings. If there had been any long distance calls made, there would be a record. This decision would finally put him on the right track toward solving these murders.

On October 29, Schooler got his information and it was an eye-opener. The records clerk at the phone company informed him that during that particular week, there had been one long distance call on October 10 at precisely 4:34 p.m. Within hours of the murders, a call had been placed from Chester to a number in the Marysville exchange. They checked a little further. "Who made the call?" Schooler asked the puzzled clerk. "Never mind the number—just give me the name."

"Looks like the call was made from the residence of a man by the name of Lawrence Shea. And it was a person to person call to a Bernadine Pearney at the Beale Air Force Base."

Schooler thanked the clerk and returned to his office. This is really weird, he mused. Shea's name keeps popping up. Now he's making long distance calls on the same day four people are murdered.

The name Bernadine Pearney was familiar too. The Sheriff recalled a phone call he had received early on in the investigation. It had come from Nevada County Sheriff Dewey Johnson in which he told Schooler about a conversation he had with one of his deputies. The deputy's wife worked as a waitress in a bar in Grass Valley where she had overheard a woman who apparently had enjoyed a few too many cocktails. She was shooting her mouth off about a lavish weekend spree in Reno during which she had been wined, dined and showered with gifts by her high-roller boyfriend. It happened to be on the same weekend as the murders.

Schooler had made a note of this information, even though he remembered thinking at the time that, like all the other leads he had chased down, it probably wouldn't amount to much.

It was time, he thought to himself, for another session with Mr. Shea and if it could be arranged, a contact with the woman who had been overheard in that Grass Valley bar—a woman whose name just happened to be Bernadine Pearney.

Larry Shea came into Sheriff Schooler's office with Lucille the next day. They were joined by State Agent Kenneth Horton, who was immediately struck by how obviously nervous the Sheas were.

"Is this about the car?" Larry Shea asked. "I thought we had that all cleared up."

Schooler told them to relax. "The car thing is pretty much settled." Shea breathed a quiet sigh of relief. "I want to know why you made a long distance telephone call to a Miss Bernadine Pearney," the sheriff asked.

Shea was obviously taken aback by Schooler's unexpected question because until now, he was pretty sure that Jack Santo's name had been kept out of the investigation. But once he answered Schooler's question that would no longer be the case.

"Oh," Shea began. "That was the day we had house guests. They come down to stay with us for a few days and do some hunting. It must have been one of them made that call. It wasn't me."

"What's the name of the person who made that call?" Schooler asked, and

it was at this point that the investigation received its biggest boost to date. "Jack Santo," Shea replied after a short hesitation.

With an occasional reminder from Lucille, Larry began to spin his version of events leading up to Friday, October tenth.

He stated that he had known Jack Santo since about 1945, having met him near Chester on a goose hunting trip.

"He was building some houses—I think it was near Auburn—and nails and plywood were kind of hard to get. There was a war on, y'know. So since I was a contractor, I could always get my hands on that kind of stuff so I sold him some stuff and we became pretty good friends."

"Tell us about that Friday, Larry," Agent Horton asked.

"Well, like I said, they come down here to do some hunting. . ."

Horton interrupted. "Who came down here? Who was he with?"

"His girlfriend, Harriet Henson."

Schooler and Horton exchanged glances as Shea continued. "The two of them come down that Wednesday towing an empty horse trailer. He had a couple of horses boarded out to a rancher near here goes by the name of Hank the Wrangler so he just dropped the trailer off there."

"What about Friday?" Horton persisted.

"Well," Shea continued, "We went deer hunting on Thursday—that would have been the ninth."

"Friday!" Horton demanded, growing more irritated by the minute. "What happened on Friday?"

"Well," Shea answered, "since we got skunked Thursday we all went out again Friday morning and stayed until about one o'clock.

154

Then we went home, had something to eat and then Lucille had to go downtown to pick up a few things for Reno and Harriet went with her and that's when Jack must have made the phone call. After that, me and Lucille left for Reno to attend a golf tournament."

"Do you know what was said in that phone conversation with Bernadine?"

"No. I left the room." Shea responded.

"Was Santo with you on the trip to Reno?"

"No. It was just me and Lucille." Shea paused for a moment. "When the girls got home from town sometime around four, Jack and Harriet left to go back to Auburn. When we got to Reno I took Lucille to Harold's Club to see their gun collection and then we had dinner and watched the floor show at the Bank Club. Then we checked into the South Virginia Hotel—room twenty-two I think—and the next morning we ran into Jack and Bernadine at the golf tournament."

He claimed that he didn't see Jack after that and on Sunday morning when they left Reno to come home, he left a note on Jack's door. In fact, he said, he has not seen Jack Santo since.

Neither Schooler nor Horton was convinced. The Sheriff was reasonably certain that this would not be the end of it. He intended to dig a little deeper starting with a call to Jack Goss, Washoe County Deputy Sheriff in Reno. He asked the sheriff to have a check run on the information just given him by Larry Shea.

Two weeks would pass before anyone acted on the tip about Jack Santo and his phone call to Bernadine.

On November 17, Jack Santo was paid a visit at his home near Auburn by Agent Horton and Investigator Bill Scott who was working out of the Placer County Sheriff's office. Santo's version of the events of that fateful weekend began to differ markedly—almost from the outset—from that of Larry Shea's.

"We'd like to know a little bit about your weekend hunting trip in Chester around the tenth of last month, Mr. Santo," Agent Horton queried. "We understand you and your lady friend were house guests of Larry Shea. Is that right?"

"Yeah, that's right. What's this all about?"

"On Friday, October tenth at precisely 4:34 p.m. you placed a long distance telephone call from the home of Larry Shea to a woman by the name of Bernadine Pearney. Is that correct?"

"Yeah, I guess so. What about it?"

"We're investigating the four murders and robbery of Guard Young on the tenth of last month. Can you tell us how you spent that day, what you did, where you went, who you saw?" Horton asked. "On what day did you arrive in Chester?"

Jack told them that he arrived in Chester on Wednesday evening, October eighth with his girlfriend, Harriet Henson and they stayed at the home of Larry Shea. He stated that on Friday, October tenth, he, Larry, Lucille and Harriet went hunting where they ran into a man they called "the Chinaman" who runs a small Asian grocery store in Chester. He said that the man had killed a forked-horn deer that morning.

They returned to Chester and in the afternoon they went hunting again in the Last Chance area and remained there until late afternoon.

Jack stated that he had decided to accompany Larry to Reno but since Harriet had to return to work in Auburn, rather than spend the weekend alone, he decided to call Bernadine Pearney, suggesting she meet him at the bus depot in Reno.

He said that Harriet had returned to Auburn by hitching a ride from someone she'd met at the Bear Club in Chester.

They drove to Reno in Shea's car, and after meeting Bernadine at the bus depot, he said, they checked into the South Virginia Hotel. He couldn't remember the room number but he recalled that it was directly across the hall from Larry and Lucille's room. He said they returned to Chester Saturday night.

Schooler told Jack about Bernadine being drunk at the bar in Grass Valley where she was overheard bragging about that weekend in Reno, saying the guy she was with was spending a lot of money.

"Well I like to show a girl a good time," Jack said, "but Bernadine was stretching the truth there. You don't have to spend a lot of money on a girl like Bernadine, if you know what I mean."

Schooler thought that at least for now, Santo's explanation sounded somewhat plausible, and they chose not to contact Bernadine at this time.

More importantly, after hearing Santo's story, it was time to haul Shea back in an attempt to reconcile the two distinctly disparate versions. The next day on Tuesday, November 18, Larry Shea returned to the hot seat.

Questioned again by Sheriff Schooler and Special Agent Horton, who had now been joined by his CII partner, agent Ray McCarthy, Shea admitted that he had lied during their last interview when he said that Jack had not accompanied the Sheas to Reno.

"Yeah," Shea said. "I'm sorry about that. Jack always has something going on with all his women and I was kind of worried about blowing his cover. Hell, you never know what some of these nutty broads will do. One of 'em got so mad one time, she took a shot at him." *(That, of course, was a lie)*

"The time for bullshit is over, Larry," Schooler said. "We're not asking you these questions just to hear our brains rattle. Have you forgotten about those gun charges? If you want to be indicted on stolen gun charges—maybe even armed robbery charges—then just keep on lying to us. I can make it happen that quick," he said, snapping his fingers.

Shea now sat at rigid attention and he began to tell the investigators how Jack had arrived in Chester on October eighth with Harriet Henson. He said that they went deer hunting on the ninth where they ran into George Locatell, offering him a cup of their whiskey-laced tea. At this point he veered again from the truth by saying that after returning to Chester, they resumed hunting, this time in the Last Chance area, coinciding with the account given by Jack. *(Another lie)*

"Tell us about Friday, Larry," Horton said. "And this time, no bullshit."

"Okay," Shea began. "Friday morning, Jack was still sleeping so I went into Westwood. I had to make a bank deposit. I got there a little early so I had to wait around a while for the bank to open. I made my deposit and then I went back to Chester." *(A third lie)*

"Was Jack there when you returned?" Horton asked.

"Yeah, he was eating breakfast. We had a couple drinks and then about one o'clock I went to the post office. That's where I ran into Sheriff Gillespie. You could check with him."

"I spent a little time at the post office and went home around two. After that me and Jack sat around and drank for the rest of the afternoon." *(Lie number four)*

"Did anyone see you and Jack at the house that afternoon?" Schooler asked.

"Yeah. Some guy who lived in Susanville but worked at Collins came by to see about renting one of my houses in Chester. I took him over to the house I had in mind but it was too small for his family so he left."

"Did you get his name?" Horton wanted to know.

"No. I wish I had. I didn't think it'd be necessary."

"Anyone else?"

"Three guys in a black sedan came by to rent a house but I didn't like their looks so I didn't rent it to them."

"Get their names?" Schooler asked with growing exasperation.

"No."

He related that he had gotten pretty drunk and had taken a nap but that, sometime later that afternoon, Jack and Harriet had gotten into some kind of spat and he sent her home to Auburn. *(Lies number seven, eight and nine)*

"How'd she get to Auburn?" Horton demanded, to which Shea replied that he had no idea. *(Lie number ten)*

"Jack called Bernadine Pearney, and told her to meet him in Reno at the bus station. We drove to Reno in my car, picked up Bernadine at the bus station and checked into the South Virginia Hotel."

"How long were you in Reno?" Schooler asked, eying Shea with unconcealed contempt.

"We got back to Chester the next night—Saturday."

Agent Horton lit a cigarette, took a deep puff and exhaled the smoke. He looked at Shea thoughtfully and decided this might be the appropriate time to bring up the other legal mess in which Larry Shea had found himself.

"Larry, maybe we ought to take a good look at where you stand in this quadruple homicide investigation." Horton's fixed gaze was making Shea visibly uncomfortable. As he started to squirm, Agent Horton laid it out.

"When you came in for an interview last month, you laid out such a load of crap that we had to regard you as someone who needed watching. The only thing we could think after that was, uh-oh, this guy's got something to hide."

Larry attempted to cover his mortification with a sheepish grin. He had thought after that interview, he had put one over on these guys. After all, just like Jack said, they were nothing but a couple of hick cops he could bamboozle with a half way decent story. Horton bore down.

"You are now looking more like a suspect in those murders, Larry. We've given you every opportunity to come clean but you just keep on lying to us. You may want to clam up now and ask for a lawyer and by law, we'd be obliged to cut off any more questioning until you get one." Larry seemed to brighten at Horton's suggestion of a lawyer, but his expectation for a quick end to this ordeal was short-lived.

"But before you do, Larry," Horton continued, "there's something you ought to know. We have a witness who has named you as the guy who's been attempting to sell him some rifles and shotguns at ridiculously low prices. Not only that, this witness says he's got proof those guns came from the Bremer Hardware job in Yuba City."

Horton took another drag on his cigarette and blew out the smoke as he stared at Larry Shea, who was now swallowing hard and feeling the sweat break out across his forehead.

"The stolen gun beef is not the half of it Larry," Schooler chimed in. "Yuba City is in Sutter County and Sheriff Earl Blackburn over there tells me that he has every reason to believe that you pulled that Bremer job. He says he can prove it, Larry, and he has a warrant for your arrest that he's asked me to serve. The charges are armed robbery, breaking and entering, and kidnapping, which, I'm sure you know, is a federal offense."

"Kidnapping?" Shea asked incredulously. He wiped the sweat from his brow with a quick swipe of one hand.

"That's what he tells me, Larry." Shea squirmed in his chair.

"It also just so happens, Larry," Schooler said, "that Earl is a close personal friend of mine. We kind of work together whenever we can, so I gave him the details on the Guard Young murders and I told him that you might be a valuable witness. I asked him if maybe we couldn't hold off on the Bremer charges—maybe quash 'em altogether—depending on what kind of info you give us."

Horton rejoined the conversation. "So if you want to shut down this interrogation, and call for a lawyer. . ." his voice trailed off and his tone had suddenly taken on an edge. "And that's what it is, Larry. It's not an interview anymore. It's an interrogation and you're a suspect."

"Yeah, yeah." Larry nodded. "I got it. Nah, I don't need no lawyer. I'll need some time to figure all this stuff out." His head was swimming. "I think I need a drink."

Larry would be willing to give up Jack and Perk—especially Perk—if he could avoid dirtying himself and Lucille in the bargain. Investigators would later learn from talking to both Larry and Lucille that throughout their relationship with Jack Santo, while there had been a genuine friendship between Larry and Jack, behind it, there had lurked an uneasy feeling of mistrust, even fear.

Lucille recalled one day when they were going to be away but knew Jack was coming to town, they put double locks on all their doors before leaving. When they returned a few days later, they found the locks broken and Jack inside the house. After the incident, he would joke with them about trying to lock him out and how they should have known better than to try that with someone like Jack Santo.

Lucille would frankly admit that she didn't much like Jack, but for Larry's sake, tried her best to maintain a cordial relationship with him.

During these series of interviews with Lucille Shea conducted by Agent Horton, it was learned that Lucille had been born in Iowa in 1909. After graduating in 1927 from high school, she enrolled in a business training school where she completed a course in bookkeeping. In 1928 she married a man named Clarence Lester, but he was a drunk so she left him in 1930. In 1935 she married Kenneth Dunkin. He turned out to be another loser; an alcoholic with a vile temper whom she finally dumped in 1952. Shortly thereafter Lucille met Larry Shea, who at the time, happened to be visiting in his home state of Iowa. In July, she left Iowa and returned to Chester with Shea and had been living with him ever since. One fact getting the attention of the investigators was that barely a month after the Young murders, as the investigation had begun to zero in on them, Larry and Lucille had gone off and gotten themselves married in Lovelock, Nevada. The date was November 17, 1952, the very day before this interview.

It was enough to make Schooler and Horton even more suspicious. Was this a deliberate attempt to avoid having to testify against each other by invoking the Marital Privilege Law if and when the killer or killers were caught and brought to trial? The Marital Privilege Law is a California law which, in most criminal cases, allows a wife or husband to refuse—without penalty—to testify against his or her spouse.

Lucille Shea would prove to be a fountain of information, although, like that of her husband, was replete with distortions, half-truths and outright lies, the bulk of which would have to be discounted.

As the days turned into weeks and the weeks became months, despite a growing list of witnesses but a narrowing suspect list, it was becoming obvious to Sheriff Schooler that the key to solving this crime would in all likelihood, depend on how much Larry Shea knew and to a lesser degree, his wife Lucille.

But even more importantly, how much of what either of them knew would they be willing to share with authorities? That was not to say that Larry—and again to a lesser degree, Lucille—were not themselves suspects but they were moving down the list as other names ascended. Names like Jack Santo and Emmett Perkins.

Christal Moves On

In Chester, the sensational nature of the four murders continued to attract the very worst of the tabloid press. Christal found herself being hounded day and night by aggressive reporter types until finally, after having had as much as she could be expected to take and with the events and images of October 10, 1952 still indelibly etched in her mind, Christal realized that as long as she chose to remain in Chester she would continue to be confronted with cruel reminders at every turn.

The idyllic lives they were enjoying before their paradise had been shattered forever; her hopes and dreams of any semblance of a future for her and the children were being overwhelmed by the stark reality of having to move forward in the face of constant harassment by a voracious press.

After first trying to erect a virtual protective wall around herself and the remnants of her shattered family and hoping—in vain as it would turn out—to keep the media wolves at bay, Christal turned the store's operation over to Guard's bother Vance. She then picked up her now fully recovered daughter, Sondra Gay from her "secret hiding place" on the coast and along with her not quite one-year old son, Wayne Robert, bid a reluctant farewell to the township of Chester.

It would be in Provo, Utah, while enjoying the more salubrious surroundings of the traditional Mormon community where Christal would be able to remove herself from center stage in Chester and be in a place where she could grieve, away from the ever-present glare of the media—and somehow get on with her life.

She would pen a poignant letter addressed to the entire town of Chester and printed in the town newspaper. It was yet another illustration of the inner beauty of this extraordinary woman—the heartfelt concern she constantly felt for others while still having to bear the weight of her own cruel circumstances.

Dear Friends of Chester,

For the past two months I have hoped to write to each of you personally to express my appreciation to you. One by one the days have slipped by, Christmas has come and gone and now the new year is upon us. Somehow, I just couldn't go away without telling you the feelings within my heart. This letter is written in the hopes it will reach into your home to each one of you. A writer once said:

"There is a destiny that makes us brothers
None goes his way alone
That which we give into the lives of others
Comes back into our own.

The past months have helped me to know and realize the great amount of love and goodness that can come out of a community. There are many things for which I am deeply grateful. Just to mention a few: First of all, the long dark night in which you men left your homes after a hard day's work to search the woods for our missing loved ones. Next, the warm sustaining arms and prayers that were reached out to us when the search was ended. The delicious food which you brought into our home, the beautiful floral offerings, the many expressions of encouragement and hope. Then your magnificent response to the Children's Playground Fund. (May great joy and satisfaction be yours next summer as you see this project completed.) In the days that followed I felt your warmth, your cheery smiles and your willingness to help. These are the things that have lifted me up and given me strength.

We have appreciated our business relationship with you and your patience in the adjustments we have had to make.

Conditions made it necessary for me to go away with Sondra and my baby son Wayne for a while. Vance, Guard's brother, will continue on in the store. He has the same feeling for all of you as I have, and it is his desire to continue on, with your help, to make the store a better and more pleasant place to shop.

Somehow I feel sure that Guard, Jean and Judy are fully aware of all that has been done in our behalf—and they join us in saying "Thank You". May the blessings of Our Heavenly Father be with you in abundance throughout the coming year.

Sincerely
Christal, Sondra Gay and Wayne Robert Young

Christal and her now abbreviated family were warmly welcomed into their new surroundings—Provo, Utah—the very core of Latter-day Saints' culture.

As they began to rebuild their lives that had been so devastated by the horrific events in Chester, one of Christal's first steps in this process was to become a student at Provo's Brigham Young University, enrolling in classes preparatory for a new career as a school teacher. It was a role for which she, in the opinion of most of the people who knew her, was perfectly suited and eminently well qualified.

Christal's departure from Chester, understandable though it was, did not diminish in the least her keen interest in the progress that was being made by investigators, nor did her determination flag in the dogged search for those responsible for the murders of her family members. A letter written to District Attorney Bert Janes indicates her active involvement as well as her frustration over the lack of information she'd been receiving from the authorities in Chester. The letter was dated January 26, 1953.

Dear Mr. Janes,
We are all settled here in Provo, and for myself, up to my neck in school. Sondra Gay is well and very happy here.

I have watched the papers and listened to the radio in hopes there may be some report as to the progress of the case. But as yet, I have heard not a word and no news has come from Chester. Have there been any new developments yet? Are the two state investigators from Sacramento still working in Quincy? Although away from there, I am still desperately involved in the case.

I had felt that Sondra had given all that she was able to give before we left. She really tried to cooperate with all she could remember and I decided that I would not mention it to her at all here. However, one day in her play she picked up the little blue car Mr. Bates had brought to her to play the game of 'blue and green cars' and came to me saying, "this is the blue car like the bad men drove." Immediately we talked about it in hopes something new would come out of it. "Did Daddy know the bad men?" "Yes, Mr. Blair." In questioning her further, she repeated the same. Then I got the papers out with his pictures, she recognized them as Mr. Blair, the showman, but she said the man in the pictures was not one of the bad men. She is still as clear as ever as to the details of what happened, but as to identity she is lost. The name Blair may have come to her as a carryover from hearing his name discussed, but she came forth with it without questioning. Is he still being watched?

Has Mr. Everett Thompson been questioned? He was the plumber in Chester at the time, and he had a definite grudge against Guard. He left town shortly after this happened. I mentioned this name to Mr. Gillespie but he brushed it off as unimportant. He was the one man I felt might could [sic] have been implicated like Mr. Blair.

I still have the gun that was brought to me but I do not know to whom it belongs. I brought it with me while traveling with Sondra, but I do not feel there is a need for it here. Should I send it to you?

I surely hope that before too long something will break. I do appreciate all the efforts that are being put forth. If there is anything that we can do at all let us know.

Yours truly
Christal Young

Christal would not have to wait much longer to get her wish. Although it would not be the way Christal or anyone else would have wanted or expected the case to break, sinister events were taking place some five hundred miles to the south and the state of California was about to be rocked with news of yet another horrendous murder. The circumstances and the *dramatis personae* surrounding that crime would lead unerringly back to Northern California's Sierra foothills and to the solving of the four Chester murders.

Bodies found stuffed in trunk of car. UPI Photo

Jean, Judy, Sondra Gay, Michael, Guard. UPI Photos

Guard with daughters Judy, Sondra Gay, Jean. UPI Photo

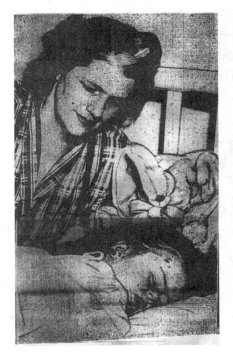

Christal prays beside injured daughter's bedside. UPI Photo

Michael's mother Rosemary follows his tiny casket from the church after funeral services. UPI Photo

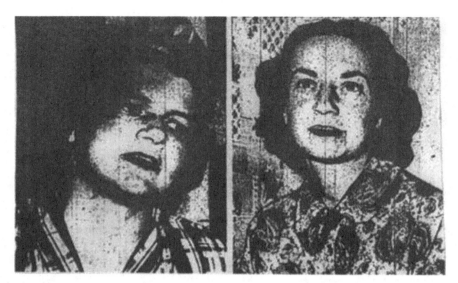

Bereaved mothers; Christal (L) Rosemary. (R) UPI Photos

Jerry Bridges: discoverer of murder car. UPI Photo

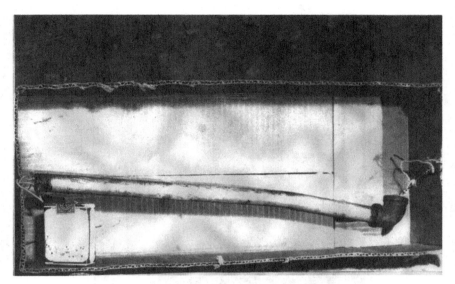

The Murder Weapon UPI Photo

Sheriff Mel Schooler Photo courtesy of Plumas Co. Sheriff's Dept.

District Attorney Bert Janes and Sheriff Mel Schooler examine the tire tracks left at the scene. UPI Photo

Jack Santo (L) Emmett Perkins UPI Photo

Jack Santo (L) Emmett Perkins UPI Photo

Harriet Henson being escorted to court UPI Photo

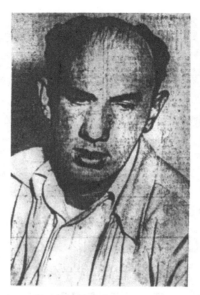

Suspect Louis Blair UPI Photo

George Boles (R) signs confession under the watchful eye of Nevada County Sheriff Wayne Brown. UPI Photo

Harriet Henson consults with her lawyer UPI Photo

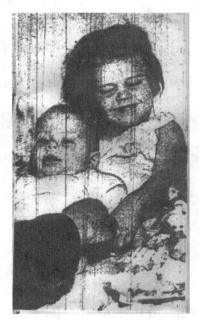

Sondra Gay cuddles with little brother Robert. UPI Photo

The Sheas: Lucille and Larry UPI Photo

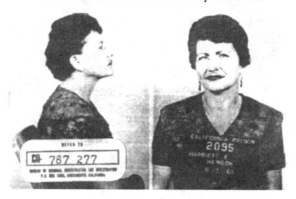

Harriet Henson's Mug Shot. UPI Photo

Jack Santo (L) Emmett Perkins (Ctr) Barbara Graham (R) At defendants' table during the Monohan murder trial. UPI Photo

NINE

Predators

In 1953, the Southern California megalopolis known as Greater L.A. included more than five thousand square miles and was populated by nearly 10,000,000 people. It was also an area that teemed with privately operated gambling parlors, only some of which were legally licensed. Any visiting tourist seeking to satisfy his primal urge to lay down a bet or two needed only a fat billfold and a reasonably well-connected cab driver. Within thirty minutes he could find himself sitting in front a stack of poker chips at a green felt-covered table with a drink in one hand and five cards in the other.

In an abandoned warehouse turned grungy rooming house tucked away in the L.A. suburb of El Monte, Emmett Perkins had set up his unlicensed "home game."

With no advertising other than word-of-mouth, the "right people" somehow had become aware of its existence, the "wrong" ones had not and the smart ones wouldn't go anywhere near it.

For Emmett Perkins, the clientele, which included an almost endless supply of tourists looking for action or cash-fat businessmen or salesmen with generous expense accounts, provided more than just a diversion; they accounted for a major portion of his livelihood.

But of late, the fishing hadn't been as good as it once was. The fish had been hard to find, even when he used hookers for bait. The suckers were becoming a scarce commodity.

The money from the Chester job was all but gone and Perkins knew that Jack wasn't exactly rolling in dough either. If Jack didn't come up with some kind of a score pretty soon, Perkins was afraid he wouldn't even be able to front his poker game.

Both he and Jack had been keeping a low profile since doing that nasty little job in Chester and although he still had some concerns because they had carelessly left a couple of loose ends dangling in the form of Larry and Lucille Shea, maybe it was time to come out of hiding. It had been almost six months and there had been almost no word as to how the investigation up there was going.

Their only connection to the Chester murders, insofar as he could tell, were the Sheas and since Jack had already gone to great pains to ensure that Larry understood—in no uncertain terms—what would happen to people who can't keep their mouths shut, so far, those threats appeared to be having their desired effect. He still wondered though, should things start to get hot up there, just how much of that heat would it take to get Larry Shea to roll over just to save his own sorry ass?

For the past couple of months, Jack had been lamenting the lack of what he called, "good situations" around the Southern California area—meaning by that, opportunities that would allow them to replenish their bankrolls. They'd both been keeping their eyes and ears open for that one big score that would put them back on Easy Street but because of their being holed up and out of action, any job that would provide them with some desperately needed cash was going to be very difficult, if not impossible to find. Perkins wondered just where and when that next big hit would happen.

"Things aren't looking so good down here Perk," Jack said. "Maybe I'll head back up north. At least up there I can run a few gold scams. Maybe I'll get back in touch with John True; maybe we can cook something up."

"John True!" Perkins exclaimed. It had been over a year since, during one of his poker games, John True had spun that fantastic tale about an old lady and a shoebox full of money. Ever since first hearing it, the name "John True" had remained etched in Perkins' brain, as did True's crazy story of *Luther the Tutor,* and his rich old mother-in-law who lived by herself in a big house in Burbank. There had been talk about a safe and a shoebox supposedly stuffed with a hundred grand in cash—money that Luther the Tutor had skimmed while working as a pit boss in Vegas.

"I don't know how well you can trust this guy, Jack," Perkins drawled, sounding more than a little dubious, "but he swears the story is true and if it is, it sounds like it would be easy pickings for us."

Jack came out of his funk. "I'll call John in the morning. I'll find out if he was just throwing a lot of bullshit around or if there's any truth to it. He'll level with me—he always does."

By mid-morning of the next day they had their confirmation. According to John True, every word of his story was the God's honest truth, and not only that, there was every reason to believe that the one-hundred grand stash had even grown over the past several months. Jack's phone call to True had produced a small but totally unexpected complication. If Jack was making plans to go after that 100 G's, John True wanted to be let in on the action After all he reasoned, he was the guy who had first brought it to Perk's attention and if it hadn't been for him, they wouldn't even be talking about it now. And God knows, he could sure use the dough.

It meant another mouth to feed, so to speak, but since only True knew the location of the house where all this money was supposed to be stashed, he was reluctantly accepted into the gang.

Things Keep Getting Uglier

In the early evening of March 9, 1953, the four conspirators, plus another, met for dinner at the nearby Smokehouse restaurant in Burbank. In addition to Jack and Perkins, there was Baxter Shorter, the safe-buster who had agreed to join the group in exchange for a full share, John True and Barbara Graham, the fifth member who had not attended their earlier meeting, but who both Jack and Perk now considered to be an essential part of his plan.

Jack had decided that in order for them to gain entrance to the house without attracting the undue attention of the otherwise quiet neighborhood, it would be helpful to bring along a female whose soft, little girl's voice might better persuade the old lady to open the door.

Perkins agreed and suggested Barbara, one of the girls he employed to steer suckers to his poker game and with whom he'd been shacking up for the past couple of months.

"Maybe with her cut of the 100 G's she'll be able to buy her own dope and I won't have to keep springing for it," Perkins said.

In typical Jack Santo fashion—exercising as much precision and preparation as one would devote to planning an afternoon shopping excursion—Jack laid out his "plan," the predictably clumsy execution of which would jump-start a chain of events that would end, inevitably, in total disaster.

With Jack and Perkins in one car and with Shorter, Graham and True leading the way in another, they drove the short distance from the restaurant to the well-kept, suburban ranch-style house at the corner of Parkside and Orchard Avenues. Jack pulled up directly in front of the house and as the men watched, Barbara got out and proceeded up the walkway to the front door. She rang the doorbell and seconds later the porch light came on, the door partially opened and while an anxious Santo gang looked on, Barbara and the woman now standing inside the doorway engaged in conversation. Within minutes, the door swung fully open and Barbara disappeared inside.

Jack jumped from the car, walked up the concrete path and after quietly signaling to the others to join him, together, they entered the house through the now unlocked door, closing and locking it behind them.

Another Murder

Two days after Jack Santo and his gang had visited the Monohan residence, Mitch Truesdale, Mrs. Monohan's twice a month gardener, rolled into the Monohan driveway in his red pickup.

After entering through the slightly ajar front door, almost immediately Truesdale was confronted by what he would later describe as a "ghastly sight." At the base of the blood-spattered hallway wall, Mrs. Monohan lay sprawled face down on the floor. Her hands had been bound behind her head. She was motionless and to Truesdale, very obviously dead.

"Jesus!" he gasped, spinning around and scanning the room as he looked frantically for a phone. Seeing none, he raced to the house next door and pounded on the neighbor's door.

"They've killed Mrs. Monohan!" he screamed. "Call the police!"

Within minutes, officers from the Burbank Police Department were on the scene. They found Mrs. Monohan's fully clothed but severely battered body lying on the floor amidst blood spattered walls, shards of broken glass, scattered papers and other indications that the house had been ransacked, although not as thoroughly as had first appeared. The motive for the murder was almost certainly robbery but when detectives took a closer look, they noticed several anomalies.

In the bedroom closet where Mrs. Monohan kept many of her personal belongings, they found a small pile of luggage, several pairs of shoes and a number of purses. All had been strewn about the over-sized closet with the purses lying open. Hanging from a separate hook, apparently overlooked by the robbers, they found one handbag containing several pieces of jewelry. To the detective's trained eye, the jewelry was genuine and worth in excess of at least ten thousand dollars.

"Do you really think they could have been that inept?" one of the investigators asked.

"Well, it happens sometimes," the detective said. "These people usually aren't brain surgeons."

An autopsy would later disclose that Mrs. Monohan had suffered severe head trauma with asphyxiation as the cause of her demise.

An investigative team under the leadership of the Los Angeles Police Department was hastily assembled and it wasn't long before they received a welcome assist from—of all places—far away New York City.

Iris Sowder was Mabel Monohan's daughter from her marriage to Luther *The Tutor* Scherer, and from her Manhattan home, Mrs. Sowder posted a five thousand dollar reward for any information that would lead to the arrest and eventual conviction of the killer or killers of her beloved mother.

This would prove to be the turning point, not only in the solving of the Mabel Monohan murder, but would, through an unlikely series of events, lead investigators to the killers of Guard Young and the three children murdered in Chester the previous year.

When newspapers reported that a five-thousand dollar reward was being offered, calls began to inundate the LAPD's switchboards. One tip in particular caught the investigators' attention.

A gaunt, rough-looking L.A. street crawler who said his name was George Allen but answered to his street moniker *Indian,* came to police headquarters with a scrambled tale about a poker game during which an elderly rich widow living alone somewhere in the Burbank area had been discussed. When pressed for details Allen was forced to admit that when all that talk was crossing the table, he had been a little buzzed and could recall only a few details. But there was one thing he did remember. There had been a lot of money involved— something like $100,000—but the dough was in a safe and that would require someone who knew how to bust it open.

The Indian remembered another guy at the game by the name of Willie Upshaw. It was Willie who had recommended Baxter Shorter as the best guy for the job—the best in the business, he had claimed— the guy who could crack open that safe.

It wasn't a lot, the detectives agreed, but since the investigation was less than a week old, it did represent progress.

"How about that five grand reward?" Allen asked with just a hint of sarcasm. "Do I get it or is it going to go to one of your relatives instead?"

"We'll see where this leads, George," Burbank Detective Robert Covney advised the visibly disappointed Indian, "but in the end, it's going to be the D.A.'s call."

No sooner had George Allen walked out the door—grumbling something under his breath about "crooked L.A. cops"—lead investigator Dick Ruble suggested the obvious:

"Let's get this guy Baxter Shorter in here and have a talk with him. Hopefully his memory will be a little sharper than the Indian's."

Baxter Shorter wasn't hard to find and the entire team of investigators waited anxiously for his arrival at the office of L.A. District Attorney Ed Milton.

Milton decided to tell Shorter that George Allen had given up his name as a possible person of interest in the robbery and murder of Mabel Monohan.

"What the hell? Why would he do that?" the incredulous Shorter asked.

"You know what murder I'm talking about, right?" Milton said.

"Yeah, I may have heard something about it," Shorter answered warily.

"I guess you haven't heard about that five-thousand-dollar reward that was posted by the old lady's daughter. Am I right, Baxter?"

"Five grand?" Shorter, indeed, had not heard about any such reward.

"Right," Chief Andrews said. "And if by throwing your name into the hat, it should lead to our solving this murder, guess who gets the five grand reward?"

He pondered the dilemma in which he now found himself. He could blow this case wide open for these guys and hopefully collect the five thousand dollar reward or he could clam up, keep his name completely out of it and thereby stay out of jail.

While that was very tempting, he also realized that if he wasn't extremely careful, he could very easily bury himself by saying the wrong thing.

"Okay," he blurted. "Maybe I can give you guys something. But I want you to understand, I'm not admitting to anything."

As the detectives reached for their notebooks, Shorter began spitting out names, places, times and other details faster than they could write them down.

"This guy Perkins called me a few days ago—says he heard I was a good pete man. It kind of threw me a little . . . I mean, coming out of the blue like that.

"Yeah," I told him," and not missing an opportunity to do a little self- promoting, Shorter added, "I told him I was the best around. I told him that because I am."

"What else did Mr. Perkins have to say?" the D.A. asked.

"He told me he might have some work for me if I was interested." Beads of nervous sweat began to form above Shorter's upper lip. "He told me he got my name from Willie Upshaw, one of the guys at his poker game. He said he was putting together a few people to do this thing."

"What thing?" Milton asked. "And who were these people? Why did they need a pete man?"

Shorter thought for a moment. "Let's see, he mentioned couple of guys I didn't know—someone named Jack—I didn't catch the last name and there was a guy named John. I think he said his name was 'True—John True." Shorter paused. "Oh, and he mentioned a broad, a hooker named Barbara. He said she was a real looker." And then he smiled. "A looker hooker, I guess you could say."

When it came to street smarts, Baxter Shorter was no fuzzy-faced rookie. He fully realized that by copping to his involvement in the Monohan murder, he could be digging himself a very deep hole—reward or no reward. He decided he'd better end this interview right now and even though he would have little more to say to the detectives at this time, maybe, he reasoned, he'd be able to cut some kind of a deal with them at a later date.

"Look guys," Shorter said, rising and taking a step toward the door. "I think I've said enough for now."

The D.A calculated that at this point there was just not enough evidence to charge him with anything.

"Baxter," D.A. Milton said as Shorter reached for the door knob, "you've been hanging out with some pretty heavy-duty characters." His voice suddenly sounded more menacing. "I'm not saying that you know who did the Monohan murder but if you do—and if they should find out that you're talking to us, your life could be in danger." He placed his hand on the door, preventing Shorter from opening it. "Maybe you ought to think about staying with us for a while, just until we can get some of this stuff straightened out. You'll be a lot safer if you're in our protective custody." He waited for a response.

"Nah," a grinning Baxter said. "I'll be OK. I'll probably be a lot safer at home than I would be with you guys."

When Baxter Shorter walked out into the street closing the door behind him, D.A. Milton and Chiefs Andrews and Brown exchanged knowing looks, anticipating the wealth of information Shorter could be expected to share with them the next time he sat in that interviewee's chair. That would be when, they were quite sure, this case would break wide open.

But that day would never come. The last time they—or anyone else—would see Baxter Shorter, was the day he walked out of the D.A's office.

Baxter Shorter would vanish from the face of the earth when, according to his wife, he was kidnapped by two men and a woman who came to their house, forced him at gunpoint into a waiting car and aside from his abductors, would never be seen by anybody ever again.

Having been hit with the unwelcome news of Baxter Shorter's abduction, the investigators had no way of knowing that at least three of the four names Baxter Shorter had dropped so incidentally: "Jack," whose surname would turn out to be "Santo," his partners in crime, Emmett Perkins and John True—would not only pry open the Monohan investigation, but would provide a big assist in helping investigators unravel the as yet unsolved quadruple murders that had recently occurred hundreds of miles north of the seedy suburbs of Los Angeles.

The Chester Connection

In early April of 1953, the investigation into the Guard Young killings had begun to bear fruit. In Chester, the mere mention of the name "Jack," coupled with the news about the Monohan case coming out of the southern part of the state was enough to bring the entire team of investigators to a state of red alert. In the flurry of statewide police bulletins and reports and requests for information between the various law enforcement agencies, it would not be long before Emmett Perkins' name would begin to appear in the same text alongside that of Jack Santo's, the juxtaposition of which was becoming much too obvious for investigators to ignore.

CII Agent Kenneth Horton suggested that there may have been some kind of connection between these two guys and Guard Young that needed to be looked into.

"Sheriff, did you know Guard Young?" Horton asked.

"We were acquainted," Schooler answered. "I didn't know him personally, but after the murders I talked to some of his family members, as well as several friends and business associates, and they had quite a bit to say."

"Like what?"

"The guy was a saint, Ken. Great father, good husband, didn't smoke, didn't drink. When I asked them if he even cussed, well, nobody was willing to go that far but they told me he was a big time churchgoer and had even attained some kind of official status within the Mormon Church. He had been talking seriously about becoming a missionary. All in all, he was a pretty straight guy," Schooler said.

Agent Horton could only nod in agreement. "Yeah, it sure doesn't sound like he would have had anything to do with the likes of Jack Santo and Emmett Perkins, does it?"

Schooler was quick to concur. "It sure doesn't, Ken."

Detective Ray McCarthy, one of the investigators the state had assigned to the case, chimed in. "Was he a veteran? Did he serve in the Army or Navy during the war?"

"No, I asked about that," Schooler said. "He was 4F—they turned him down because he had asthma—but I understand it wasn't a dodge. He really did try to join up. He was living with his mom in San Francisco before going to Reno to volunteer as a pilot trainer because he already knew how to fly."

"Sounds like a hell of a guy," McCarthy said.

"Yeah," Sheriff Schooler said. "I'm sure we can dispense with any notion that Guard Young knew those two scumbags."

Schooler thumbed through the growing file as the three detectives continued to brainstorm, looking for any small clue that may have been missed. A single entry listing a phone call he had received early in the investigation caught his eye.

"This call came in from Dewey Johnson," Schooler remarked. "He's the sheriff over in Sierra County. I didn't give it a lot of thought at the time because we had been focusing most of our attention on the Louis Blair interrogation."

"You think maybe this call might have some significance?" Agent Horton asked.

"Now that I look back on it," Schooler said, "that's exactly what I'm thinking."

Schooler now had the full attention of the two state agents.

"Dewey said he had some information that might help us break open the Chester robbery/murder case," Schooler began. "He told me that the wife of one of his deputies who's a bartender at this bar in Grass Valley—*The Golden Gate*, I think he said—was telling him about this floozy who had been mouthing off at the bar about a big-spending weekend trip in Reno that she had taken with an old boyfriend."

Although the phone call had come many months ago and was only one of many that he had received during that hectic period, the conversation, for whatever reason, stuck in the Sheriff's mind.

"Now remember, at the time this call came in, we had been concentrating on Blair and while I thought Dewey's call might have had some minor relevance, I sure didn't put it at the top of the list. I remember asking him what that had to do with the four Chester murders."

Agent Horton, who was present when Schooler had taken the call, attempted to recap the conversation for Detective McCarthy. "Yeah," he said. "Sheriff Johnson asks Mel if those murders happened on October tenth and Mel says 'yes that's right' and then Johnson says, 'If I'm not mistaken, the money that was taken was all in twenty dollar bills—right?' and Mel says 'yeah, that's right.'"

McCarthy, sensing that he was about to hear of a new angle that might help get this investigation off dead-center, had come out of his slouch and was now sitting fully upright as he listened to Sheriff Schooler and Agent Horton lay it out.

"Get this, Ray, he says that this big spending weekend in Reno took place on the night of October tenth—the same night of the murders."

"Holy jumping Jesus!" McCarthy bellowed. "This could be just what we're looking for! How could we have overlooked something like this?" It was a question to which Schooler took immediate exception.

"It wasn't overlooked, Ray," Agent Horton was quick to point out. "I went up to Auburn with another detective to interview Jack Santo about his trip to Chester, his phone call to Bernadine Pearney and his big weekend in Reno. He told us there was nothing to it—nothing at all like that broad had implied. He said he spent a few bucks, money that he had made on some kind of a gold deal, but that was it. He said she was just blowing a lot of smoke."

"And you bought it?" McCarthy asked incredulously.

"What he said seemed to make sense compared to the third hand story about some boozed up barfly, and besides we were chasing down other leads at the same time we were zeroing in on Louis Blair," Schooler reminded them. "We wasted so much time on him because the D.A. was so absolutely certain that Blair was the right guy."

McCarthy backed off. "Okay, so what do we do now?"

"We have the name and address of that loudmouth barfly," Horton said. "She lives in Grass Valley. And wait until you hear this, Ray: Her name is Pearney—Bernadine Pearney!"

"Bernadine Pearney?" McCarthy recalled seeing that name on a report having to do with the questioning of Larry and Lucille Shea back in November and recognized it immediately. It had appeared in connection with the long distance phone call that came from the Shea home placed by Jack Santo. A person to person call to a Bernadine Pearney.

"I think it's about time we have a sit-down with Miss Bernadine Pearney," Agent McCarthy suggested. A few days later, Agent McCarthy along with fellow CII Agent Henry Cooper did exactly that.

McCarthy had noted in his reports that if Pearney was at all surprised or shocked that two investigators would be paying her a visit to inquire about her relationship with Jack Santo, she didn't show it. "She was cool and calm but evasive," McCarthy would later report. "She admitted to having had a relationship with Santo but she vehemently denied knowing anything about the Young murders."

When asked about her Reno weekend with Jack Santo, she told them, in very guarded terms, that after he had phoned her on the Friday afternoon of October 10, she agreed to meet him at the Reno Greyhound bus depot. At around ten p.m., Jack, accompanied by Larry and Lucille Shea, pulled up in front of the bus depot. According to Bernadine, they had partied that night, got a little drunk and then the next day, after a couple hours of shopping—"so she could pick up something decent to wear"—they went to a golf tournament to meet up with the Sheas.

"And after that?" Cooper probed. "Where did you go? What did you do?"

"From there, we just drove back to Chester."

When the agents brought up the subject of the Golden Gate Saloon and the story about her loud boasting of the Santo spending spree in Reno as had been told by barmaid Fern Waters, Bernadine played it down as nothing more than meaningless braggadocio by a girl who had had way too much to drink and who was trying to impress the other patrons.

"Didn't you tell everybody that Jack Santo was blowing money like there was no tomorrow, buying you dinners, drinks, shows, even took you downtown and bought you a bunch of new clothes? Wasn't that you saying all that stuff?" Cooper had asked.

"It really wasn't like that at all," she said. "Yes, he bought me a couple of things, but I paid for most of what I got."

When asked about the denomination of the bills with which Jack had paid the tabs, she claimed she either "couldn't remember" or "didn't notice."

They asked her if she was aware of Jack's relationship with Harriet Henson. She told them that although she knew about it, she wasn't pleased with it but she assured the agents that she was really Jack's favorite.

The next day, when summarizing their interview with Bernadine Pearney, agents McCarthy and Cooper reported that she was either unable or unwilling to place Jack at the scene of the murders or to offer any additional information that could be used in the investigation.

At this stage of the Chester investigation, it was not apparent to any of the investigating police officers that this interview would not be the last time that the paths of Ray McCarthy and Bernadine Pearney would cross. It would take a call to McCarthy from the Burbank police department, now involved in the investigation into the March ninth murder of Mabel Monohan, to keep this strange connection intact.

On April 3, 1953, Sheriff Schooler paid an official visit to the Auburn home of Harriet Henson where Jack Santo was living at the time. He was keenly disappointed when he learned his trip had been for naught. Jack wasn't there.

On the following day, officers from the Los Angeles and Burbank police departments arrived in Auburn to take Jack Santo into custody for the Baxter Shorter abduction, as well as for his involvement in the Mabel Monohan murder and again, Jack was nowhere to be found. They did however, speak with Harriet Henson who told them that the last time she had spoken with Jack was "weeks ago" when he had called from Medford, Oregon, but claimed to know nothing more than that.

Her visitors had no sooner left her front door than Harriet put in a call to Jack who, rather than being in Oregon, was actually somewhere in Los Angeles.

"They're looking for you, Jack. I told them I thought you were in Oregon."

"Good," Jack said. "If anybody else wants to know where I am, tell them the same thing."

A visit to the Chester sheriff's office by Dick Ruble, now lead investigator in the Monohan murder case, was the beginning of a growing professional rapport between Ruble and State Agent Ray McCarthy. It was an association that would later prove to be invaluable in helping Ruble build the case against Jack Santo and his killer confederate, Emmett Perkins.

The Chase Is On

Digging through their records, Ruble and MCarthy found that in 1949, Emmett Perkins and one of his buddies had been arrested near the L.A. airport shortly after assaulting and robbing a tourist couple from Iowa. The charges were dropped however, when the couple declined to return to California to testify. Investigators smiled knowingly when they learned that Mr. Perkins' buddy was a guy named Jack Santo.

They had four of the names in question—Willie Upshaw, John True, Jack Santo and Emmett Perkins and a quick look at Perkins' bio sheet gave up the fifth.

A cursory investigation into the Barbara connection had revealed that she was a junkie hooker, street name: *Bonnie;* real name, Barbara Graham. She had been shacking up with Emmett Perkins for the past few months while working as a hook for his illegal card room enterprise.

Bingo! The cast was now complete—at least for the moment.

Their first move after learning the identities of the five people Baxter Shorter had named would be to bring them all in for questioning. Unfortunately, that would prove to be easier said than done.

Although they knew where they could lay their hands on Upshaw, True and Graham, it seemed that Santo and Perkins had both disappeared into the underground.

Jack Santo's rap sheet disclosed that a greater part of his time was spent in the northern part of the state but since he was presently being considered as a possible participant in a $300,000 San Francisco jewelry heist, he hadn't been seen by any of his known acquaintances for months. To the best of their knowledge, he was still somewhere in L.A.

Los Angeles' Chief of Detectives, Thad Brown was quick to surmise that if police were able to find Perkins, Santo wouldn't be far away. And finding Perkins might be made possible by tracking Barbara Graham.

Barbara had continued to maintain the El Monte residence she occupied with Perkins, which made it a simple task for Chief Brown to assign detectives to conduct a twenty-four hour stakeout and tail, confident that she would lead them to Jack Santo and Emmett Perkins, which is exactly what happened.

No sooner had Barbara stepped foot out of her apartment door than female L.A. undercover officer Kay Sheldon was—as Chief Brown would later characterize it to the press—on her like "stink on a skunk."

The officer was close behind as Barbara boarded a street car that took them downtown to the Greyhound bus depot. She made a prearranged dope deal and after a quick trip to the restroom to shoot up, and with the detective closely on her tail, she boarded a crosstown bus that took them to Lynwood, a gritty, blue collar Los Angeles suburb some twenty miles to the south.

After getting off the bus, Barbara led the detective straight to a rundown apartment building which appeared to be some kind of a converted warehouse.

The officer was uncertain as to whether or not this was to be their final destination and as she watched Barbara enter the building, her eyes searched the area for a place that would allow her to wait without attracting attention—for how long, she had no idea.

Her dilemma was solved when in a matter of minutes, a man she easily identified as Jack Santo emerged from the building, walked to the corner liquor store to make a purchase and then returned to the apartments. She had been told early on in preparation for this assignment, "Where you find one you will find the other," and she quickly realized she had just hit the jackpot.

In response to her call-in, within minutes, police had the apartment building virtually surrounded and once they were able to determine which apartment would be their target and with Chief of Detectives Thad Brown leading the charge, a squad of uniformed officers forced their way into the fugitives' lair and took all three into custody.

On May 4, 1953, Barbara Graham, Jack Santo and Emmett Perkins were booked into L.A. County jail on charges of first degree murder.

Pondering the seriousness of the predicament in which he now found himself, a furious and unrepentant Jack Santo was just thankful that they had one fewer big-mouth to worry about since Baxter Shorter had "mysteriously" turned up missing. Both Santo and Perkins were convinced that Shorter would have turned stoolie in a New York minute had he been offered any kind of a deal that would have kept him out of jail.

But now Shorter's wife was still out there lurking around and she could identify them as Baxter's abductors, and that, of course, could prove to be an enormous problem. The lesson they should have taken from the botched Hansen job back in 1951, Jack mused, was as prudent as it was simple: Witnesses talk. By leaving Hansen's wife alive, she was in a position to finger them as her husband's killers. Now Baxter Shorter's wife posed the same kind of threat. Big mistake, Jack told himself.

"I came like water, and like the wind I go."

TEN

Pas de Trois

J ack Santo and Emmett Perkins were taken downtown and booked
into the Los Angeles County Jail. Barbara Graham was delivered
to the Century Regional Women's Detention Facility in Lynwood.

In large metropolitan jurisdictions such as Los Angeles, it was
common practice for district attorneys to plant informants in the
same cells with otherwise tight-lipped cellmates, hoping they'll
let something slip that prosecutors could use against them during
their trials. In the case of Barbara Graham, despite her well-touted
street smarts, this was the ploy used by the Los Angeles D.A. and it
turned out to be eminently successful. As a consequence, Barbara's
indiscretions would prove to be her eventual undoing.

Hardboiled ex-con Emmett Perkins, and to a lesser degree, Jack
Santo, over their previous periods of incarcerations, had learned to
survive in hostile prison environments. Because they now had each
other to lean on for "moral support" they were able to keep mostly
to themselves. Authorities were quick to realize that no "jailhouse
snitch" tactic was likely to loosen the tongues of these two prison-
hardened criminals. The District Attorney's office had long since given
up on the idea of being able to squeeze anything useful out of either
one—at least anything that would remotely resemble actual evidence
that could be used against them—much less a confession. Instead,
insofar as the trio of Graham, Santo and Perkins was concerned,
they decided to focus their efforts on *flipping* an accomplice with an
offer of leniency in exchange for damaging trial testimony against the
accused. This decision would turn out to be more successful than they
ever could have imagined.

It wasn't long after the trio had been booked and charged with first degree murder than the situation turned even darker for Emmett Perkins. On the following morning, Olivia Shorter, after viewing a police photo lineup where she was unable to name Santo as one of the men who had abducted her husband, nevertheless identified Perkins—"positively"—as the man who, at the point of a gun, had forced Baxter into a waiting car from whence he would never be seen again.

It took only minutes before the first degree murder charge which he already faced was amended to include "kidnapping," another death penalty offense.

Enter Bernadine

At about the same time that the three fugitives were being booked downtown, Los Angeles police were responding to a citizen's complaint concerning a blue 1950 Oldsmobile sedan—apparently abandoned and parked just about a block and a half from the seedy apartment building which had been serving as the trio's hideout. The car, the complainant had reported, bore expired out-of-state license plates and had not been moved for at least the past two weeks. A cursory check revealed it was registered to a Miss Bernadine Pearney whose address of record was in Grass Valley, California.

Initial efforts to contact Pearney were unsuccessful. Absent any kind of interview, her links to the Jack Santo/Emmett Perkins gang or to the Mabel Monohan and Guard Young murders were not immediately obvious. Detective Dick Ruble's curiosity was nevertheless aroused the minute he noticed Bernadine's name on the abandoned vehicle report.

"I recognize that name, Chief," he said. "She's somehow mixed up with Jack Santo up there in Chester."

"How would you know that?" Chief Brown asked.

"Last month when we went up north to get Jack Santo, I was talking with one of the state's investigators who told me that Santo is a suspect in the Chester murders and he said he'd be surprised if this Emmett Perkins character wasn't in it with him," Ruble explained. "While we were driving around, he filled me in on how the case was going and that's when the name Bernadine Pearney came up. She's one of Santo's honeys, a real dish I understand."

"Nice work, Dick," Chief Brown nodded. "Maybe you could give this guy a call, find out what's with this Pearney gal and see if you can find out what they have on Santo and Perkins and any of the rest of our suspects. I got a feeling this guy might be able to save us an awful lot of legwork. What did you say his name was?"

"Agent Ray McCarthy. He works for the CII." He's been ass-deep in the Chester case so, other than the sheriff, if anyone knows about these people, it has to be him."

Ruble was sensing a positive swing in his own case. He put in a call to the Plumas County Sheriff's office where he knew McCarthy had established his temporary base of operations. The detectives exchanged warm greetings before Ruble came to the point:

"Ray, it's about that Bernadine Pearney gal. We'd like to get some info on her. Her unregistered car with Washington plates was found—apparently abandoned—on an L.A. street and we think it might have something to do with the Mabel Monohan murder. It was parked a couple of blocks from where we nailed Santo and Perkins and some woman named Barbara Graham."

McCarthy pondered. "The Mabel Monohan murder? I'm not sure I'll be able to help you, Dick. I'm pretty much occupied with our case up here. I know absolutely nothing about the Mabel Monohan case."

"Yeah Ray, I realize it may be a little out of your area of interest but would it be possible for you to talk to her again on our behalf?" Ruble asked. "I'll brief you on the stuff we want to know. Since she already knows you, she'll probably feel more comfortable if you're the one asking the questions. Plus, it would save us the time and expense of having to make the trip up there."

Because his initial contact with Bernadine Pearney had proved to be less than productive, McCarthy had intended to have another talk with her anyway. He readily agreed to Ruble's request and so, accompanied by Agent Henry Cooper, McCarthy returned to Grass Valley to pay Bernadine Pearney a second visit.

Visibly ill at ease, the uncharacteristically demure Bernadine fidgeted nervously as McCarthy began to dig deeper into her relationship with Jack Santo and her involvement in his criminal activities. She admitted that she and Jack had once been lovers and as such, he had used her to pass a few forged checks. "But that was all in the past," she hastened to add.

McCarthy's primary area of interest focused on their weekend Reno trip and his no-nonsense, aggressive style convinced Bernadine that lest she becomes tangled up in two murder investigations by feeding him evasive answers as she did the first time she was questioned, her best bet would be to just come clean and let the chips fall where they may.

"Yeah, he did spend a lot of money that weekend," she told them. "I'd never seen him with so much money."

"Did he tell you where the money had come from?" McCarthy asked.

"Well," she recalled, "when I asked him about it, he said it was from a store robbery he had done in Redding."

She confirmed that he had paid for everything with mostly twenty-dollar bills, and she even described his odd reaction when she called his attention to the Saturday evening newspaper headlines.

McCarthy then brought up the subject of the car. "Tell us how your car happened to be parked outside Jack's apartment in L.A. for the past two weeks. How did it get there?"

She explained that on Jack's instructions, Harriet Henson had called her a few weeks ago to tell her that Jack needed to borrow her car for a while and that she—Bernadine—should drive it to Southern California and bring it to him. "So that's what I did." She told him that after she delivered the car, she flew back to Sacramento where Harriet met her at the airport.

After receiving McCarthy's report on the Pearney interview, Detective Ruble focused on its central observation which was: no matter how much she tried to play the innocent, she is deeply involved with these people.

He relayed this information to his Chief of Detectives, Thad Brown.

"So Bernadine Pearney is mixed up with this bunch?" Chief Brown's suggestion was more of a statement than a question.

"Up to her pretty blond ass," Ruble replied. "As it turns out, she was Santo's main squeeze and another *mule* in his stable of flunkies.

He and Perkins would use these people to pass stolen or forged checks or help out in other scams like insurance frauds or gold high-grading."

"How do you plan to use this stuff?" Chief Brown asked.

Ruble smiled. "She'll make a dandy prosecution witness when we get to trial. Olivia Shorter should be able to identify Pearney's dark blue Olds as the car that drove off with her husband and now we can put Santo in possession of that car."

"And Pearney's got an interesting story on this John True fellow," Ruble continued.

"Listen to this, Chief—we found out that just before Baxter Shorter was snatched, Pearney had loaned John True twenty bucks to purchase a silencer for Santo. When True learned that Pearney would be driving to L.A., he gave her a message to relay to Santo. The message was: He "wasn't able to get it."

"Okay," Brown agreed. "That's pretty good stuff if we ever get to a Baxter Shorter kidnapping-murder trial. But what did she have to say about our case?"

"Nothing, Chief," Detective Ruble was forced to admit. "She said she had nothing to do with the Monohan job and McCarthy believes her."

Chief Brown was clearly disappointed that the Pearney interview had produced so little information that could be used in charging Santo and Perkins with the Monohan murder. "Is that it then?" he asked, his frustration apparent.

Ruble nodded, and then said, "But she was able to come up with a little more on Baxter Shorter. McCarthy says she told him that Santo had called a guy named George Boles, one of their boys up north, and asked him to help them 'knock off' Shorter. She said Boles turned 'em down and later when she asked Santo what happened to Shorter, he told her that Shorter 'had been well taken care of' and 'they will never find him.'"

With his star witness in the Monohan investigation having mysteriously vanished, Chief Brown had now been presented with another possible—even probable—murder to investigate. Three of the suspects in both crimes, Santo, Perkins and Graham, had been arrested and only the fourth, John True, remained at large.

Within days after the arrest of the three fugitives, Bob Covney, Burbank Chief of Detectives, in the company of two of Burbank's finest, along with a Los Angeles police officer drove five hundred miles north to the Sierra foothill town of Grass Valley. There, without fuss or fanfare they arrested a totally shocked John True, charging him with the first-degree murder of Mabel Monohan.

By May 9, two months to the day after Mabel Monohan had been savagely beaten and strangled to death in her own home, all four suspects in the brutal slaying were now in custody.

The Monohan Trial Looms

While investigators were gathering evidence that would point to Barbara Graham's involvement in the Monohan murder, officially, Barbara was being held on a previous check forging charge. It would not be long before that charge would be amended to include a charge of first degree murder when, as her court-appointed attorney, Jim Hardy, relayed to her the stunning news that Jack Santo's friend and accomplice John True was planning to turn state's evidence. He would testify that it was she—Barbara—who had actually committed the brutal murder.

Shocked to her bones when told of True's intended self-serving treachery, Barbara realized that there was now good cause to worry about her defense strategy. She began to think that the only thing that might save her from the gas chamber would be a credible alibi proving she was somewhere else that night and couldn't possibly have had anything to do with Mrs. Monohan's murder.

The trial date had been set for August 14, 1953, so it was obvious to Barbara that time was of the essence. Enter fellow prisoner, Donna Prow.

It hadn't taken long for Miss Prow to befriend Barbara who, in her now depressed state over the dire turn of events in her own case, had become desperate as she looked for a friend in whom she could confide. In Donna Prow, she seemed to have found such a friend—so much so, that they quickly became lovers.

With the connivance and assistance of a friendly guard, they would hold their clandestine trysts in one of the jailhouse's vacant cells, and it was during one of those occasions that Donna Prow had come up with a defense strategy for Barbara:

She had a friend, Donna said, who could solve Barbara's entire problem. His name was Sammy and she was sure that if she asked him—and maybe greased his palm with a little hard cash—Sammy would testify that Barbara couldn't possibly have done this crime because she was miles away with him at the time.

Miss Prow assured Barbara that Sammy was an expert liar and his testimony would be so convincing that she'd be acquitted and she'd walk out of that courtroom a free woman. And Barbara went for it.

When Sam Sirianni walked into the visitors' area he immediately drew admiring glances from guards, inmates and visitors alike. One writer who later chronicled the event in a local newspaper described him as a "dead ringer for John Derek, except he had a better build." It was a reference to the handsome Hollywood heartthrob who in 1953 had co-starred with Humphrey Bogart in the classic thriller *Knock on Any Door.*

But Barbara's interest was not so much in how the man looked, but rather what he had to offer that would get her out from under the rock where she now found herself. But first she had to make sure he was the guy that Donna had sent and not some imposter trying to run a scam on her.

She introduced herself. "I'm Barbara," she said, to which Sirianni replied, "Hi, Barbara. I'm Sammy."

After they had both taken their seats, she peered at him through the metal screen divider, looking directly into his eyes *"I came like water . . ."* she said to which he replied:

". . . and like the wind I go."

It was a passage from Omar Khayyam's *Rubiyat,* one of Barbara's favorite poems; a somewhat melodramatic prearranged signal that she and Donna had cooked up. With the formalities out of the way, they got down to business.

"Donna tells me you're in a little bit of a jam," Sirianni began.

"Yeah, I guess so," Barbara answered, her eyes darting furtively around the room to be sure no one was eavesdropping. "She tells me you can swear that I was someplace else when that old lady was killed."

"Yeah, I might be able to do that," he said, his jet black eyes burning holes in hers. For the ensuing fifty minutes, Barbara and Sirianni concocted a scenario that would place her with Sirianni at the Encino

Ritz Motor Hotel on Ventura Boulevard on the Monday evening of March ninth, far from the Mabel Monohan residence in Burbank.

Like two storytellers crafting the plot of a best-selling mystery novel, no detail—no bit of minutiae—was left unattended.

But at the trial, and to her utter shock and dismay, *Sammy* Sirianni turned out to be an undercover Los Angeles police officer and Donna Prow was a jailhouse snitch looking for a deal in her own case.

When, from the witness stand in a hushed courtroom, Sam Sirianni played back the recorded conversations that had taken place between him and Barbara in which they had set up her fake alibi, her doom was sealed.

And so it went. The trial played out in anti-climactic fashion and in the end, the three defendants were found guilty of the murder of Mabel Monohan and the kidnapping of Baxter Shorter.

The Sentencing

On September 19, 1953, Jack Santo, Emmett Perkins and Barbara Graham were sentenced to die in the gas chamber at San Quentin. As payment for his testimony, John True was released from custody and allowed to walk from the courtroom, all charges against him having been dismissed.

Up until now, the L.A. media had been relatively sanguine with respect to the actual trial proceedings, but when Barbara Graham was sentenced to death, even the city's most cynically hardened trial-watchers were aghast.

Newspapers jumped on this sensational turn of events by running special headline editions, all about *Bloody Babs* and her newly imposed death sentence.

Still, Santo and Perkins refused to behave like two men who had just been sentenced to receive the "ultimate punishment." They smirked at spectators and wisecracked to members of the press as they were led from the courtroom. It would later be learned that they had firmly believed that Barbara would be their salvation. Their rationale was well founded because tradition was on their side. In the state's entire history of putting people to death, only one woman had ever been executed. Up until that time, of the more than six hundred court-ordered executions that had taken place in California, every one, save that of Ethel Leta Juanita Spinelli in 1941, had been a male.

"They'll never send Barbara to the gas chamber," Jack Santo had boasted. "And if she gets a commutation, then they'll have to give us one too." Barbara hoped he was right but Perkins muttered, "I'd rather be executed than have to spend the rest of my life in prison."

Another Robbery—Another Murder

As the Los Angeles trial of Santo, Perkins and Graham was coming to a head, in Nevada County's gold country, four hundred miles to the north, police were being stymied over yet another murder that had occurred in their neck of the woods. But thanks to the efforts of authorities in L.A. and information received from Bernadine Pearney, another name had surfaced that would eventually prove to be the key in helping detectives solve the Nevada County murder whose investigation had been stuck in neutral for over two years. That name was George Wilson Boles.

On the evening of December 29, 1951, in the northern California town of Nevada City, Edmund Hansen and his wife Mary had been enjoying a quiet Saturday evening at home watching the popular hit show *Your Show of Shows* on their recently purchased Philco television console. Hansen, owner-operator of *The Last Chance* gold mine, had started to doze off when Mary, who had just stepped into the kitchen for a quick glass of water, thought she heard noises coming from the other side of the front door.

"Someone's trying to get in," she had shouted at her half-awake husband. "Wake up, Ed. Someone's trying to open the front door."

Before he could respond, two strange-looking men crashed through the door and into the foyer. One was wearing a Halloween type mask; both were wielding guns.

"This is a robbery," the mask wearer said. "Just do as you're told and nobody will get hurt."

Mary took one look at the man who was pointing the gun at Ed's face and before the man had a chance to notice her presence, she had already taken three steps toward the kitchen's back door. On seeing her, the intruder spun while simultaneously firing off two shots. Both shots missed and Mary was able to slip through the door. She ran screaming to the neighbor's house next door, "Call the police! We're being robbed! Call the police!"

Thinking he could take advantage of the ensuing pandemonium, Hansen had bolted in the direction of the kitchen, hoping he might be able to flee out the same door through which his wife had just escaped, but he was neither as quick as Mary nor as fortunate.

Enraged over Mrs. Hansen's successful run to freedom, one of the gunmen emptied his six-shot .32 caliber revolver into Hansen's midsection.

As the critically wounded Hansen staggered toward the kitchen door, both intruders, empty-handed and without a dollar to show for their efforts, fled in panic through the front door.

Rushed to a local hospital, Hansen clung stubbornly to life for another two weeks before finally succumbing to his wounds.

The anticipated $20,000 score that had precipitated this ill-fated home invasion had now become nothing more than the stuff of which dreams are made; another bungled effort that would continue to hallmark this murderous cabal's dubious *modus operandi*.

A Confession

In September of 1953—almost two years after the Hansen murder and about the same time the Monohan murder trial was being wrapped up—Nevada County Sheriff Wayne Brown talked on the phone to Edward Bonner, his counterpart in Placer County.

"Ed, there's a guy down there we'd like you to talk to. He works as a nurse in the sanitarium at Weimar."

"Sure, Wayne," Bonner said. "What's the deal?"

"His name's George Wilson Boles. We got some information that he might be involved in that Ed Hansen killing a couple years back."

"Yeah, I remember that one," Bonner said. "You think he's your guy?"

"Well, strange as it may seem, his name popped up when one of the suspects in the Mabel Monohan case. . ."

Sheriff Brown stopped him. "The what case?"

"The Mabel Monohan case," Brown explained, "Down in L.A. It seems that he's mixed up with the people who were on trial for that job. He's part of that same bunch of guys that did the Monohan job, and we know damn well those are the same guys who did the Hansen killing. We just can't come up with the evidence."

"Well, hell yeah, Wayne," Bonner said. "What do you want me to do?"

"Can you pick him up and hold him? I'll send a couple of deputies to bring him up here so we can talk to him. I have a feeling he's going to get us off dead center."

"George Wilson Boles at the Weimar Sanitarium," Sheriff Bonner repeated. "You got it, Wayne."

Nineteen months after the still unsolved slaying of Edmund Hansen, George Boles found himself uneasily seated across the desk from Nevada County Sheriff Wayne Brown asking about his activities on December 29, 1951.

"I don't know what the hell you're talking about, Sheriff." It was not a surprise to Brown that Boles would open with this timeworn defense. "How do you expect me to remember something that happened so long ago?"

Boles' attitude and his body language, to Brown, was a clear indication that before this man was going to cough up any information of value, he was going to have to be ground down. One interview was certainly not going to do it. This particular interview lasted two hours, and aside from confirming that, yes, Boles was acquainted with Jack Santo; and yes, he knew Emmett Perkins and okay, they had been involved in a few bad check capers over the past few years, but Edmund Hansen? Nope. Never heard of him.

But before allowing Boles to climb out of the frying pan, Brown was careful to embed in his brain the one central theme of this interview.

"Here's something you need to know, George," Brown said ominously. "You're a prime suspect in the Edmund Hansen murder. I'm going to talk to Santo and Perkins and anyone else whose name comes to my attention. We're talking death penalty here, George. Maybe they'll clam up and maybe they won't. Maybe they'll figure they'll get a deal if they roll over on you. Maybe you'll be the guy who ends up holding the bag." Brown pushed his chair back and stood up.

"Think about it, George. There's only going to be one deal. Do they get it . . . or do you?"

For the following month, Boles did a lot of thinking. He thought about how stupid he was to ever let himself become involved with the likes of Jack Santo and Emmett Perkins and just when it was looking like he had run out of aces, his phone rang. It was his old friend Bernice Freeman. Back in the days before he had started on this spiral of petty crime—long before meeting Jack Santo—Boles had been a cub reporter for the San Rafael Independent Journal where he had worked under the watchful aegis of Bernice Freeman. For whatever reason, this matronly mother of four daughters, one of them older than the 28-year-old Boles, had taken a liking to the brash young man and, like a mother hen, took him under her wing. Bernice was now working as a reporter at the San Francisco Chronicle and when she spotted the news clips coming over the wires with stories about her friend's Nevada County arrest, in addition to feeling concerned for his welfare, she smelled a story.

"What's going on, honey?" Bernice asked, her voice wavering slightly. "This Hansen thing has me plenty worried. What's the real story?"

"It's not looking good, Bernie," he said. "I just got myself caught up in a crazy web of circumstances." Boles maintained his innocence and Bernice was ready to believe him.

"George, if you tell me positively that you had nothing to do with this murder, I'll do everything I can to see that you get a good criminal lawyer to help you out of this jam."

Boles was clearly affected by Bernice's willingness to go to bat for him, and after a moment's thought he said softly, "I can't do that to you, Bernie," his voice dropping to an almost inaudible whisper. "I did it."

For the next hour, Bernice, though utterly shocked by Boles' candid admission, listened intently as he spilled out the whole gruesome story—Santo, Perkins, Henson—everything. The police had it right. When he related Sheriff Brown's parting words to him and his offer of a "deal," Bernice jumped on it.

"You have to tell them, honey," she said. "You have to take the deal. If you don't and they put it all together, you could be looking at the gas chamber."

George reluctantly agreed. "Looks like you've got your page one exclusive," he said glumly. He hung up the phone and immediately began searching for the card that Sheriff Brown had given him. Finding it and after staring at it for a few seconds, he took a deep breath and dialed the number.

For George it was coming down to the realization of a life gone horribly wrong; a life of ups and downs and stumbles and bad decisions. Becoming involved with people like Jack Santo and Emmett Perkins—the excitement and easy money of it all notwithstanding—was probably the biggest mistake he ever could have made. About the only thing for which he could be thankful, he reminded himself, was that time back in '52 when he was arrested on bad check charges and so, fortunately, was in jail during the time the Guard Young job went down. At least, he thought, he wouldn't be facing four more murder charges.

Two days later on September 13, Bernice Freeman's front page story broke in the Chronicle: "Nevada City Murder Confession; Implicates three others."

The baffling twists and turns of a statewide five-year string of murders and mayhem—a bewildering maze in a hall of mirrors— its bloody trail of human carnage confounding investigators from Northern California's wildernesses to the palm trees and crowded freeways of the Los Angeles suburbs had now entered its own death throes.

When the story of the Edmund Hansen murder would finally be written, just as in the Monohan murder and the slayings of Guard Young and three small children, the guilty party in every instance would turn out to be Jon *Jack* Albert Santo leading his pathetically inept gang that couldn't shoot straight.

ELEVEN

Probe

T he arrest and confession of George Boles in the Hansen murder was to have major implications in solving the 1952 quadruple murders in Chester. Boles' confession, in which he named Jack Santo, Emmett Perkins and Harriet Henson as co-conspirators in the killing of gold mine operator Edmund Hansen, turned out to be an event that would prove to be critical not only in solving the Hansen killing, but would breathe new life into the Chester multiple murder investigation which had become stuck in neutral for the past several weeks. The information provided by Boles would be the final lock-down piece of evidence that the State would need to secure convictions for the cold-blooded murders of Guard Young, his daughters Judy and Jean and their four year-old playmate, Michael Saile.

Harriet Henson had been arrested in Grass Valley and brought to Nevada City to be indicted as an accessory in the Hansen murder and was now being held in the Nevada County Jail.

However, at the request of County Prosecutor Vernon Stoll, the charges against Harriet Henson had been almost immediately dismissed, citing as his reason, "the furtherance of justice."

Expecting a quick release from custody as a result of the dismissal, Harriet was stunned to learn that at the very moment she was being cleared in the Hansen murder, she was about to be charged in Plumas County with four counts of first degree murder in the Chester slayings and would not be getting out of jail any time soon.

After agreeing to cooperate with investigators in the Chester killings as well as expressing a willingness to testify as a witness for the prosecution in the trial against Santo, Perkins and Boles for the murder of Edmund Hansen, Harriet would remain in custody for the duration of the Nevada City trial.

Defendants Jack Santo and Emmett Perkins were driven in separate cars from their death row cells in San Quentin to the county jail in Nevada City to face trial for the 1951 murder of Edmund Hansen. Because of Jack's well-known penchant for engineering jail house escape attempts, they were accompanied by two heavily armed guards.

Through one hundred and fifty miles of verdant valley farmland and over rugged snow-dusted Sierra Nevada mountain passes, the trip would require more than five tension-filled hours to complete.

Once having arrived and true to his reputation, Santo wasted little time in plotting an escape. After befriending a fellow inmate who was due for release in a matter of days and hoping to skirt the jail's less than vigilant small-town security system, Jack had arranged for his new friend to smuggle a packet of hacksaw blades into his jail cell. After being quickly discovered by Sheriff Brown's deputies, the plan was foiled and Jack stayed put. For his trouble, the "friend" found himself doing an additional two years.

In Nevada City, the Hansen murder trial was now set to begin on December 18, 1953, while in Chester at about that same time, the investigation into the quadruple Young slayings was drawing to an end.

On the Monday following the Christmas weekend, Sheriff Melvin Schooler sat down in his Quincy office with State Agent Ray McCarthy and District Attorney Jack Keane to discuss the filing of formal charges in the Young multiple murder case.

While sipping at a cup of hot coffee, Schooler flipped through his voluminous stack of notes. "Let's take a look at what we've got so far," he said.

"I think we're putting a pretty good case together, Mel," McCarthy said. "We can put Santo and Perkins at the scene. Larry Shea, too. In fact, if you ask me, I think we might have enough right now to indict the whole bunch." He looked at Keane and waited for a reaction.

"Really?" Keane answered. "Okay, lay it out for me."

Schooler consulted his notes. "We have Harriet Henson's tapped jailhouse conversations with Santo. We've got her admitting she got a cut of the stolen money."

McCarthy joined in. "Right, Jack. Our agent Harry Cooper is an expert with these bugging gizmos. He sweet-talked her into wearing a wire and she let him go in there and set Santo up for us. She was very cooperative. She did everything we asked her to do but he had to promise we'd cut her a break if and when we file charges. Harry thinks she'd be amenable to turning state's evidence."

Keane frowned and shook his head. He had no intention of using Harriet as a witness for the state. "If she's a defendant in this case, there isn't going to be any deal," he said.

McCarthy was taken aback by the D.A.'s sudden recalcitrance. He shot a quick glance at Schooler, whose expression of hope was turning into one of disappointment. He was concerned about any promises his CII colleague, Agent Cooper, might have made in exchange for Harriet's cooperation. How would Cooper react when he learned that the D.A. was not going to cover him?

McCarthy turned to Keane. "When Harry finds out that you're not going to back him up, he's not going to be too happy."

It was an oblique but unmistakable reference to an unwritten code among all law officers. No agent wants to be the cop who would betray an informant's trust.

Keane, unmoved, continued. "If she was in on it, she's going to stand trial Ray, just like the other two." He paused before changing the subject. "Let's see what else we have."

Schooler returned to his notes. "We've got a Chester rancher who will testify he saw Perkins standing out there on Route 36 beside Young's car with Henson in the back seat around the time the murders went down."

"Are you saying that not only does he put Perkins at the scene, he can identify Henson as being there as well?"

"Absolutely!" Schooler responded.

"Not bad," Keane said. "Let's go back to Henson. What if she doesn't take the stand? If her lawyer doesn't let her testify, I'm wondering if that wire will be enough to stand on its own."

"Oh, it's enough all right," McCarthy said. "What Santo says on that wire is damn near an actual confession."

It was obvious to Keane that the two investigators were still concerned about a deal for Harriet Henson. Maybe, he pondered, weakening just a bit—maybe he was being too tough on her. Maybe she deserved a break. So many of these dumb broads let themselves get caught up in their lover's criminal activities, and even though they might have nothing to do with their actual crimes, they find themselves in hot water.

"Tell me, Mel," Keane said to Schooler, "what's the deal down there in Nevada City with Henson? Why are they charging her?"

McCarthy glanced apprehensively at Sheriff Schooler. "It's that Ed Hansen thing. She's admitted to driving the getaway car."

"She drove the getaway car?" Keane exclaimed in near disbelief. The room went eerily quiet as, weighing for the first time the full extent of Harriet's involvement in the Hansen murder, Keane suddenly shifted into his no-holds-barred prosecutor's mode. The fact that she had been an active participant in the commission of a cold-blooded murder was news he hadn't heard before.

"You're telling me that she aided and abetted in the attempted robbery and murder of that gold miner?"

In his job as a county prosecutor in the D.A.'s office, Jack Keane had established and nurtured a well-deserved reputation within the legal community as a no-nonsense, by-the-book pursuer of justice. He had become known for his uncompromising, almost ruthless prosecutorial approach who always pressed for the harshest punishment that the law would allow. After having been recently promoted to the top job of District Attorney, he had given little reason for anyone to think he might have softened.

"There's not going to be any deal in the Chester case," Keane said, making it clear that, following a formal indictment, Harriet Henson would be charged as an accomplice in the multiple murders of the Young family and the Saile boy. He hastened to add, almost as an afterthought, "And in all three of the indictments, we'll be asking for the death penalty."

"Will you be handling the prosecution, Jack?" Schooler asked. The sheriff was not at all convinced that Harriet Henson had been an actual participant in the murders, and that because of her cooperation with authorities, he was hoping that she would not be charged. Obviously, District Attorney Keane had other ideas and Schooler's concern now was that if it was going to be Jack Keane—with his go-for-the-groin prosecutorial style arguing the state's case—not only would Harriet Henson have to stand trial for a murder she probably didn't commit, she may well have to face the gas chamber if convicted. Schooler also knew that in exchange for Henson's cooperation, she had all but been guaranteed that she would not be indicted and that Harry Cooper, the CII agent who had originally worked out the deal, would be predictably livid when he learned of the D.A.'s unyielding stance.

Schooler pressed on. "OK, there's that Reno shopping spree on the very weekend of the murders and the fact that Santo picked up all the tabs and paid for everything with twenty dollar bills. And we got a recorded conversation between Shea and that Pearney woman."

Keane interrupted. "Who?"

"Bernadine Pearney. She's the hot tamale who accompanied Santo on his spending spree in Reno. She's his former girlfriend and we have a bugged conversation between her and Larry Shea. She got Shea drunk and he said a lot of stuff that's pretty damning for Santo and Perkins. It's all on that wire recording."

"Will she testify for the prosecution?" Keane asked.

Schooler nodded. "I think she will. She's scared shitless and I think she'll do whatever we ask her to do just so she doesn't have to go down with the rest of them."

"Don't forget that truck salesman from Modesto," McCarthy added. "His name's Jack Furneaux. The L.A. cops sent him undercover and he turned out to be a valuable witness in the Monohan trial. He was able to testify about several conversations he had with Harriet about providing phony alibis for Santo."

"Yeah, that was good stuff," Schooler said. "Furneaux is a pretty straight shooter. He volunteered to do the same thing for me with Shea's meeting with Pearney. I would have used him too, but in the end it just wouldn't have worked out."

Keane nodded. "Anything else?"

"That's about it, Jack," Schooler said. "Isn't that enough?"

"It's enough for Santo, but what about Perkins? Henson? Shea?"

McCarthy chimed in. "We can show Perkins lied about being in Chester on October tenth. We've got both Sheas testifying he was there with Santo. He's hanging out at the bank—stalking that Locatell guy and when that fails, Guard Young."

Keane liked the way this was adding up. The cops had done a good job in gathering evidence and it was starting to sound like it might be enough to go to trial. But still, he seemed troubled.

"Let's go back to the Harriet Henson thing," he said. "Tell me exactly what it was this woman said on that wire that was so incriminating."

McCarthy consulted his own notes. "Harriet and Santo—along with Perkins and a guy named George Boles—are on trial in Nevada City for the Hansen murder. They're being held in separate cells up there of course, but Sheriff Brown let Agent Cooper and me put a wire on Henson and then we let the two of them get together for a little while. I wanted to see if either one of them would say something we could use in the Guard Young case."

"And you got something?" Keane prodded.

"Yeah, I'll say," McCarthy exclaimed. "They talked about the Young job. Santo chewed her out for blowing Perkins' cover when she told us she left Chester with Perkins on the day of the murders. See, she was supposed to say she got a ride back to Auburn with friends or something. That would have kept Perkins out of Chester."

"Anything else on Perkins?"

"We've got Henson's statement that Perkins split up the loot with her when they got to her house in Auburn," Schooler said.

Keane looked from Schooler to McCarthy. "That's pretty good Ray, because it actually brings her in. Anything else?"

"We've got Larry Shea," McCarthy said, "and Mr. Shea is a very interesting case. We have caught this guy so many times lying his ass off on just about everything. He lied about what time Jack and Harriet left the house, saying first he was asleep when they left and didn't know what time it was, but when he finds out they're using him for an alibi, he says four-thirty. He says Perkins was in Chester on the tenth and then he says he never saw Perkins. He lied when he said he and his wife drove to Reno alone and Santo and his girl joined them later, but after we pressed him, he finally admitted that Santo went with him. Then, of course, we have Harriet's testimony that he was in on the job and got ten percent as his share."

Not to be outdone, Sheriff Schooler spoke up. "We have a guy named . . ." he looked at his notes, "Bacalla—Calvin Bacalla—he'll testify that he was driving on Route 36 and saw two men standing beside the green car, one of whom was Guard Young, around the exact time of the murders."

Keane asked. "Did he see anyone else?"

"He said he saw a man sitting behind the wheel of the blue car and a woman in the back seat," Schooler said. "We showed him photos of Henson and he thinks she was the woman. We wheeled him down to Nevada City so he could get an in person look at her."

"And what happened?" Keane asked.

"He made her. He says she's the woman who was sitting in the back seat when he drove by. He's absolutely certain of it."

"Okay." Keane said. He was finding it difficult to conceal his excitement. "I have to admit, I've tried cases with a lot less than that," he said before adding, "'course not always resulting in a conviction." He smiled. "Is there anything else? What about Shea? What have we got on him?"

"Well, Shea might be a problem," McCarthy said with concern. "If we're going to put the other three at the scene, we're going to need his corroborating testimony."

"What's the problem?" Keane asked.

"The problem comes if you indict him," Schooler said. "I'm sure there's enough to charge him, but if we make a defendant out of him, and he testifies against the other three, you're going to need someone to corroborate his testimony."

He tried to explain: "As a witness, Shea's testimony could be huge. I mean, he knows that Santo was at his house and left that morning before the murders happened, and all the other stuff, too. He can testify about how they chased that other grocer and then when they screwed that up, all of them went back to the bank to wait for Young."

"That would make a pretty strong case," Keane agreed.

McCarthy looked at Schooler, then at Keane. "Here's the thing about Shea, Jack. Even though we all know he was probably involved, he's going to deny it to the bitter end. We're going to end up having to prove it." He paused. "That will be very hard to do."

"So what are you getting at Ray?" Keane asked, skepticism creeping into his voice. "Are you talking about another deal?"

McCarthy had an answer. "Remember what happened in that Monohan case earlier this year?"

He continued: "the prosecution had to get one of the defendants to flip and testify against the others in order to obtain convictions. They got three death sentences out of the deal even though, in the end, the guy walked."

He went on to recount in detail how the prosecutors had persuaded defendant John True to testify for the state in order to gain a conviction against Santo, Perkins and Barbara Graham.

"In that case, they turned one of the perps—a guy who admitted to being right there when that old lady was killed—and they gave him a deal anyway. They ended up convicting the whole bunch."

"Yeah, I remember," Keane responded. "I also remember that they didn't actually convict the whole bunch. The rat who got the deal got a pass."

"Maybe so, Jack, but he's the only reason Santo and Perkins and that Graham broad are on death row right now," McCarthy countered.

"What makes you so sure Shea will go for a deal?" the district attorney asked. "Unless he's convinced we've got him cold, he might want to take his chances with a jury."

"I haven't told you everything, Jack. There's some other stuff in this guy's file that I'm sure will be enough to persuade him to cooperate," McCarthy said.

"What do you think we can get?" Keane asked. "Second degree? Manslaughter maybe?"

Schooler had a ready answer. "We don't charge him at all if he puts Santo and Perkins anywhere near the scene of the Young murders on Friday afternoon between three and four o'clock. If he does that, we got 'em. If not, you're going to have a very hard time convincing a jury."

"How about a reduced charge?" Keane mused. "Maybe we don't file murder one. Maybe murder two. Or maybe even involuntary manslaughter. What about that? Would that be enough to get him to cooperate?"

"I don't think so Jack," Schooler said. "He won't go for it. He knows he's got us by the balls and if we don't agree to let him walk, he'll clam up so tight you wouldn't be able to drive a needle up his ass with a sledgehammer."

Again, the room fell uncomfortably quiet while the D.A., in his own mind, wrestled with his better judgment over how—despite being convinced that Larry Shea had played a part in the commission of this crime—how could he possibly allow this man to come out of it completely unscathed?

"Okay, fellas." Keane finally said. "I guess it won't do any harm if we had another talk with Mr. Shea." Schooler exhaled and looked at a likewise relieved Agent McCarthy as Keane continued.

"But we have to make sure his information is credible. The defense lawyers will probably try to throw cold water all over his testimony by pointing out that he lies all the time and he's lying about this too. If the jury believes the lawyers, any testimony Shea provides won't be worth a warm bucket of shit."

He let that sink in before pointing out, "He's going to have to come up with some pretty convincing stuff." And adding as a caveat, "We better get him here and talk to him before we decide what to do."

Schooler agreed.

"OK, guys," Keane finally said. "I think you're right. I think we have enough. Let's go ahead and charge the bastards."

Squirming Off the Hook

On New Year's Eve of 1953, while Harriet Henson was being brought from her jail cell in Nevada City to Quincy for arraignment in the Chester murders of Guard Young and the three children, Lucille and Larry Shea sat uncomfortably opposite Sheriff Melvin Schooler in his office to discuss the advisability of their cooperating with authorities in the investigation of those murders. Also present were D. A. Jack Keane, and CII Special Agent Ray McCarthy. Much to the relief of the investigators, as had been their practice on all the previous occasions when being interviewed, the Sheas showed up without an attorney.

Sheriff Schooler was aware that Lucille Shea was not going to be an easy nut to crack. Sporting a pair of round horn-rimmed glasses with lenses much too large for her petite face, Lucille struck Schooler as a reasonably intelligent and attractive but somewhat docile housewife who would probably say whatever her husband told her to say. McCarthy and Keane, perhaps using the same reasoning, were of the immediate impression that Mrs. Shea would not be doing much of the talking today.

Since neither of the Sheas had previously met Keane or McCarthy, Sheriff Schooler completed the introductions before sliding a thick manila folder that had been resting on the side of his desk to front and center. With a slightly exaggerated flourish, Schooler proceeded to flip it open and then stared at the Sheas.

"I asked you to come in today because we'd like to go over the events of that day back in 1952 when all those folks were killed."

"Yeah," Shea said. "I figured you'd be calling again, even though I've already told you everything I know about that day."

In contrast to Larry's contrived bravado, Lucille fidgeted nervously. "How many times do we have to keep going over this, Sheriff?" she asked.

"Well, Lucille," the Sheriff replied, "We've got a couple of other items on the agenda today."

While Keane's attention remained firmly fixed on Larry, Schooler was shuffling through the folder and after finding what he was looking for, removed a single sheet. "Do you remember this past September there was a warrant issued for your arrest on that stolen car?"

Shea was quick to counter as he felt Keane's steely eyes boring holes into his defensive wall. "Sure, I remember," he said while trying to avoid eye contact. "And I came in the very next day. Do *you* remember? You interrogated me about Jack Santo. I even came clean on the Reno trip."

Keane interrupted. "But we have never executed that warrant, Larry," he said, "so I'm sure you understand; that's still an open proposition."

Shea looked stunned and Lucille continued to fidget. "Is that why you brought us in here?"

"Did you think that's all been forgotten?" Keane asked, making a subtle threat which he made no attempt to hide.

"We haven't made the arrest yet but that doesn't mean we're not going to." He paused to give Shea a chance to assess the precariousness of his situation. Larry started to sweat and Keane continued to pour it on.

"There's also that pesky Bremer Hardware matter over in Yuba City ..." Keane pretended to be reading from the sheet. "Let's see here . . . armed robbery. . . . stolen guns . . ." He looked up as he continued. "You remember that, don't you?"

Shea's agitation was beginning to show. "Oh yeah?" he retorted. "Is that what this is all about? Sure I remember it. I remember it's a bad beef, too. You got a couple of lying so-called witnesses, is what you got. I wasn't nowhere near that store when that robbery went down and I can prove it," he lied.

"Maybe so, Larry—maybe, like you say, it's all a big mistake—but it's still hanging around out there. It still needs to get cleared up."

Larry shot a look at Lucille as if he expected her to suddenly jump up and give this guy a good swat, but all she could do was return his questioning gaze with the same bewildered expression. Where, she wondered, was the D.A. going with this stuff?

Beads of sweat had formed across Shea's brow. Rather than wait for the next shoe to drop, he turned to Schooler.

"Okay, Sheriff, spit it out. What is it you want me to do?" He thought for a second before adding, "and when or if I do whatever the hell it is you want me to do, what's in it for me?"

"I'm not the one to talk to, Larry—you need to be talking to Jack, here," Schooler responded. "He's the one guy who might be able to get you off the hook."

"Let's go back to the Young murders, Larry," Keane began. "When you were interviewed by Sheriff Schooler and the others, you gave them a story that you didn't know Emmett Perkins—had never met him—so as far as you knew, he wasn't in town on October tenth." Larry continued to sweat while Lucille dabbed nervously at her nose with a Kleenex. "You remember that?" Keane asked.

Larry didn't answer. "Then, in another interview," Keane continued, "you said, well, maybe you really had met him once or twice, but you hadn't seen him recently. Remember that?"

"I gave you the full story. You know that," Larry said. "I lied at first because I was just trying to stay out of it. I thought that if you couldn't link me with Perkins . . ."

Schooler didn't let him finish, "You told us that you and Lucille drove up to Reno on the night of the tenth" He glanced at Lucille who had begun to dab a little more vigorously. "And it was only after you were cornered that you finally came clean, as you put it, and admitted that Santo went with you."

He slammed shut the folder and coldly stared into Shea's eyes who, while squeezing his wife's hand, could only wonder what was coming next.

"I'll be frank with you, Larry," Schooler warned. "I'm not the only one who thinks that both of you are involved in this crime. Maybe not as the actual perpetrators, but I think we can make a pretty good case," and casting an accusing glance at Lucille, "that both of you were accessories—probably before as well as after the fact," adding, "and that would make it—at the very least—conspiracy to commit murder."

Agent McCarthy, who had been quiet up to that point, feigned exasperation. "Hell, Jack. Let's just charge these two," he said, trying to sound as if his patience had run out. "We've got more than enough evidence."

Larry had reached the limit of his forbearance. He was in big trouble and he realized that playing the "know-nothing" game with these guys would almost surely turn into an exercise in futility. His mood was approaching despair. Breathing an audible sigh and bowing his head, he said in a near whisper, "Alright, we're listening."

"Maybe we can make a deal," Keane said and watched them both exhale. "We want Santo and Perkins. Henson too, if she was part of it. It's not you we're after."

One of Keane's chief concerns was that, even though he and Sheriff Schooler along with the entire team of CII investigators, were convinced that the Sheas—particularly Larry—had taken part in the Guard Young killings, they were just as convinced that the evidence they'd need to secure a conviction was sadly lacking. Keane rationalized that by using the Sheas' testimony to impeach Santo, Perkins and Henson, in all likelihood, he'd be able to cinch the case against all three. As things stood right now, Larry Shea's testimony was the *sine qua non* of their entire case.

Had the Sheas come to this interview in the company of a lawyer, Keane had little doubt that his doing so would have produced a vastly different outcome. Any lawyer worth his law degree would have seen from the get-go that the state lacked the necessary evidence against the Sheas to make any kind of a murder charge stand up. But if he could persuade them that the prosecution had enough to put them, if not in the gas chamber, certainly behind bars for a very long time, they would sing like the Mormon choir. He just had to make it sound sufficiently compelling.

Keane lit a cigarette and leaned back in his chair to give what he'd already said a chance to sink in. He took a long drag on his cigarette and exhaled before he spoke again. "Do you recall a meeting that took place between you and Bernadine Pearney some months back?" Keane asked. "I think it was at her husband's cabin up in the mountains somewhere around Truckee. Do you remember that?"

Shea corrected him. "It wasn't at her husband's cabin. It was at some two-bit motel just outside of town," he said. "Yeah, I kind of remember it. I was pretty squashed, so it's all a little blurry."

Lucille shot her husband a dagger-like glare. Apparently this was a piece of news that Larry had somehow neglected to share with her.

In point of fact, early on in the investigation, Schooler had arranged for Bernadine to call Larry and set up this meeting by telling him that she was calling at Santo's behest because he wanted Larry's help in concocting an alibi for the day of the Young murders. Schooler was confident that Shea was so far under Santo's thumb he would probably do or say just about anything Santo asked of him. Shea was unaware, of course, that the conversations would be bugged.

In the early 1950's, law enforcement investigators, always on the prowl for new investigative tools, had discovered and were now starting to make use of the revolutionary *Minifon* portable wire recorder. Made in Germany and using technology considered to be "state-of-the-art" at the time, this amazing device featured two crystal microphones concealed in a man's wristwatch from which a series of wires were routed through the wearer's sleeve down his arm to a spool attached to a recording unit. The entire package was about the size and weight of a paperback book. The Minifon could be worn underneath a man's jacket either in a harness arrangement or carried in an inside pocket. One may only assume that the twenty-first century term "wearing a wire" had its origins in investigators' 1940's deployment of wire recording devices such as the Minifon.

It had been no small trick getting Bernadine outfitted with the device, which, almost certainly would have been quite bulky and clumsy, especially in her attempts to conceal—or at least camouflage—an oversized man's wristwatch crammed with microphones (in those days, women simply didn't wear men's wrist watches) hiding the wires as they trailed up her arm and then having to struggle with some kind of a harness arrangement or pouch holding the recorder; all concealed underneath an outer garment.

When Schooler got his first look at the contraption after it had been assembled, it had appeared so improbable that he seriously considered scrapping the whole idea, but in the end, he could only hope that Shea would be so drunk he wouldn't notice.

"Why don't you tell me what you remember about that meeting?" Keane began to probe.

Hesitantly and while glancing nervously at Lucille, Shea began to recall his conversations with Bernadine Pearney during the drunken rendezvous and the events that had taken place over a year ago. "Well, as best as I can remember, about a half hour after I get there Bernadine shows up and she's got a couple bottles. She starts pouring the booze down me and I'm getting' pretty hammered and all she wants to talk about is the Guard Young thing. She tells me that Jack—she means Santo—if anybody asks me, she says he wants me to swear he wasn't in town that day."

"And was he?"

"Yeah," Shea said. "He was there and so was Harriet. Perkins came later."

"And you told her that you knew they did it, right?" It was Schooler who asked the question.

Shea's nod was barely perceptible. "I think I told her that. I probably did but it's kind of hard for me to remember everything. I remember I was scared. I figured that if he could do that to those little kids, no telling what he'd do to me if he found out I was talking too much. But like I said, I was pretty boozed-up and I guess I said a lot of things."

"Well, you don't have to worry about Santo and Perkins now, do you?" Schooler reminded him.

"No," Shea said. "They're in prison now. I'll be okay as long as you keep them there."

Schooler played his trump card. "Larry, this is going to come as a surprise, but we bugged that whole meeting. We've got you on a wire saying that Santo and Perkins, with Harriet's help, did it, and you said that you know they did it."

Shea appeared to be puzzled. "If you got that on a wire, what do you need from me?"

"The quality of the recording is not that great," Keane broke in. "We could cut a transcript and show it in court but there's a better way."

Shea held Lucille's hand tighter as Keane laid it out. "When we get this case into a courtroom, besides giving your other testimony about when they were at your house, when they left, how they waited outside the bank and how you fingered the victims, Santo's big spender trip to Reno—anything else you know—besides all that, you're going to get on the witness stand and narrate this recording as we play it back so that every word, every syllable you uttered on that wire, will be unmistakably clear to the jury, as well as to every single person in that courtroom."

Assimilating all this, Shea looked again at his wife and wondered if she was thinking the same thing he was thinking. Santo had told them the whole story. How much of what he had told them would he have to spill? How much did they already know?

Shea shook his head. "Jesus God," he cursed under his breath.

But it was Lucille who would break. It was just more than she could stand. It had been tearing at her soul since the day that Jack had told them the whole sickening story. It was a weight that was much too heavy for either of them to carry around any longer. Santo and Perkins were already on death row. There was nothing to be afraid of anymore.

"You have to tell them, honey," Lucille said softly. Keane looked at Schooler who looked at McCarthy.

"She's right, and you know it, Larry," Keane said. "If we find out you held out on us, there's no deal. We'll amend the complaint right now and you'll be charged right along with the rest of them. We want the full story—everything you know."

Shea heaved a sigh of resignation. With Lucille's hand tightly gripping his, he cleared his throat and began. In a matter-of-fact monotone and speaking barely above a whisper, he vomited up the whole sordid story as he had heard it from Jack Santo. He described the robbery, the ensuing fight between Santo and Young culminating in Guard's death. Reiterating Jack's vivid depiction of Emmett Perkins savagely beating and slaughtering the children, he even included in his narration—as Jack had done—Harriet's appalled reaction to Perkins' orgy of killing and her horrified response, even to remarking on the copious amounts of blood created by the carnage.

Without elaborating on or adding to Santo's narrative—with Lucille adding a point or two should her husband falter or stumble— the three officers listened in shocked awe as Larry retold Jack's remorseless description of how four innocent people had been slaughtered in cold blood. It was enough to make the three veteran lawmen recoil in utter revulsion.

The relief felt by both Larry and Lucille when Keane had finally dotted the last "i" and crossed the last "t" was palpable. It was done. They slumped back in their chairs and each lit a cigarette.

"What now?" Shea asked after a moment's silence. "You got everything we know. There is no more."

"I think we've got enough for now," Keane replied. "As it stands right now, you folks won't be charged in this. You need to bear in mind though, charges can always be amended—defendants can always be added—even after the trial. But as long as you're completely truthful with us, you won't have anything to worry about. But try to pull a fast one and you'll be right back on the hook."

After the Sheas had departed the office, a satisfied Agent McCarthy remarked, "Whew! Not a bad day's work, Jack. That should give us more than enough to convict those ghouls."

But D.A. Keane had his doubts. "It's pretty obvious that we've got our killers all right—" he said, "but I'm not so sure that a lot of what Shea has been telling us is going to be of much use."

"What?" Schooler asked incredulously. "It locks it up, doesn't it? I mean we got Santo admitting to the crime and pointing the finger at Perkins as the actual killer. What more do you need?"

"Mel, it's only inadmissible hearsay. If we try to bring in a Santo admission of guilt that happened to come out in a conversation between Santo and the Sheas, the judge is going to shoot us down faster than any of us can say "guilty!" Not only that, we've got one accomplice fingering the other without a single word of corroboration. There's not a judge alive who's going to let that kind of evidence come in."

Schooler looked at McCarthy. "What the hell was this all about if we can't use Shea's testimony?"

Keane continued, "But I'll argue that it's a whole different ballgame with the wire recording. I'm betting that the wire will be allowed in, and with Shea doing the voice-over, it'll be just as effective—maybe even more so."

The cast iron steam radiator tucked under the window kicked in and the loud hissing noise provided the dingy office's only sound as Keane studied the two officers' astonished reaction to his intended trial strategy.

"If Shea's direct testimony would be considered hearsay, how is it that the wire recording isn't hearsay, too?" McCarthy wanted to know.

"Because we'll have Shea—the guy who actually spoke the words the jury's hearing on the wire—doing the narration," Keane countered. "It'll make all the difference in the world."

McCarthy cocked his head. "I'm just a tad leery, Jack, but you're the expert. If you say it'll work, then I guess it'll work."

"Trust me," Keane smiled.

"So what do we do now?" Schooler asked as they all rose in unison and headed for the door.

"We go home and kiss our wives at the stroke of midnight. Happy New Year to you both," Keane said with a grin. "Now," he said matter-of-factly, "we go to trial."

Waiting for News

The press was having a field day reporting on the story of the Chester massacre, labeling the as yet publicly unidentified band of thugs and killers, *The Mountain Murder Mob*. The ongoing investigation into the murders of Guard Young and three small children was steadily moving ahead with developing events now pointing an accusing finger at Jack Santo, Emmett Perkins and Harriet Henson. The Year 1953 had ended and with it, the life-long criminal careers of two of the most vicious predators ever to roam the Golden State.

But those last three months in Chester, although it had been a full year later, had not been erased nor even blurred from Christal Young's consciousness. From her new home in Utah, she had been keeping herself abreast of the investigation's progress and despite the bitter recollections those terrible events evoked, among the heartaches she had been able to find memories—however few—which could still be cherished.

Prolific writer that she was, Christal felt compelled to pen this letter to the editor of the Sacramento Bee:

In the last few days when the case that has baffled the world has appeared to be in its final stages of being solved, the papers have been filled with the daily developments. The horror and cruelty of it has been predominant. And I have found myself reliving those terrible days immediately after last October 10th when my kingdom crumbled at my feet. Naturally I find myself again involved in the midst of it with questions constantly put before me: "Mrs. Young, what are your feelings toward the individuals who are responsible for this crime?" "Has the past year been hard for you?" "Do you have anything to say?"

There have been many, many things that I have wanted to say, to tell to all that may be interested; that out of the horror of all of this has come much sweetness, much beauty, much goodness, and knowledge that there can be victory and good come out of death. It is of this beauty that I want to tell, humbly realizing my inability to say in words the things that are in my heart.

I'm certain that last October 10th when several individuals for the sake of a little financial gain for personal satisfaction, stopped a green car filled with happy children and a wonderful father, took their money, and then for fear of recognition brutally took their lives, could not really know what they had done. How could they know how important and valuable each of their lives and personalities was? How could they know what price had already been paid just to have those lives?

To help you understand how beauty can come out of all of this, I must first let you glimpse the sanctuary of our home. Though it contained very little of grandeur or worldly wealth, there was so much love that at times it seemed almost to burst at the seams. In those few rooms which were temporarily built above the back supply room of our store was our "Castle in the Clouds" which housed our "Kingdom." Even the building of those rooms played an important part in cementing and welding our little family together.

It was in the afternoon of March 7, 1947, while making final arrangements to open our business in Chester, that a telephone call came informing us that a little baby girl was available to come into our home! Only those who have never been privileged to have children can possibly realize what it means, after eight years of childless marriage, to finally receive a baby by adoption.

But our immediate problem was that we had no home. Ideal living conditions are one of the specifications of the adoption agency. Hurriedly, Guard and I built a room for the baby in one of the corners of the attic over the store where we lived. It was a dream room though, off all by itself, papered in soft blue and white colors, fluffy white curtains, a crib and much love. Almost in a like manner our little "kingdom" grew. A few months after Jean arrived, Judy made her appearance, by adoption, and became another member of our family.

Each year for the next six years a new room was added here and there as needed. Next a kitchen, then a bathroom, and a bigger room in-between for "mom" and "dad". Just like topsy it grew! But out of all of this, since we were not carpenters, every inch of those walls represented our sweat, blood, laughter, tears and a very part of us.

Then suddenly magic began to work, as we realized we were going to have a baby of our own. No one can possibly know the joy of those months until that final day came and a son was born to us! This joy was short-lived, however. Our little son was not well. He remained with us only two days, and gently we were called to give him back to our Heavenly Father, who had loaned him to us for only a few brief moments. With it came also our first contact with the sweetness of death! But always there is good yet to come in life we learned as little Sondra came to us and then another son, Wayne.

Love abounded in our home, the pattern was set by the children's father who at the age of two had lost his own father, and knew the longing of wanting a dad. He tried to give his children all of the father's love that he had been denied. Some of our most precious moments were the ones in which our family gathered together once a week for our family "Home Evening". Each child took their turn performing with a little song, or dance, or played a piece on the piano. There always had to be a little play acted out (their favorite was the Nativity Scene) with all the costumes a necessary part. Their chief delight was when it came Daddy's turn to sing. Of course Daddy never dared to raise his voice in song outside his home, but he gave with his rich, deep, vibrant voice his favorite hymn:

Bless this house, Oh Lord we pray,
Keep it safe by night and day.
Bless the folk who dwell within,
Keep them pure and free from sin.
Bless us all that we may be
Fit Oh Lord to dwell with thee.

Refreshments were then served by the children and it was Daddy who led them off to bed and listened as their goodnight prayers were said. It was usually a half an hour longer before he could emerge again. He was pinned down with a little girl on each side with Sondra in his lap begging for their favorite stories, which came from their Bible picture book. As he told them the characters came to life and were real to them.

After being gone away from home for a day on his trips to Sacramento for groceries, the children would wait eagerly for his return. At the first sound of his motor as he maneuvered the truck into position – even if it were late into the night – three little pajama-clad tykes bounded out of bed and little feet fairly flew down the stairs. They usually met in the middle of the stairs and were all caught up in one embrace. Then he would look up at me and say, "This is worth going away – just for the welcome home."

Little Michael Saile also became almost like one of our family. He stayed with us while his mother worked. He was a lovable little fellow, all boy and deeply religious for his tender age as a result of his mother's teaching. We used to almost pretend he was ours—he was just the age our little son would have been had he lived.

Each child so vibrant, so alive, so loving life, each with their own personality. Jean with her heart-warming laughter, her dancing rhythmic feet, her love of people, always a wave of the hand and a cheery "Hello". Judy with her quiet sweet smile, with all the wonder, faith and glory of life in her eyes, whose faith was that "of a little child" who often said, "Tell me more about the gospel, mother", and whose one ambition in life was to learn to cook and sew so that when she grew up some man would fall in love with her and she could be married and have children.

All of this accounts for the reason the children were with Guard that day. Believe me, when I learned that this wonderful "kingdom" of ours had broken in half and crumbled at my feet, it took all the faith within my grasp to withstand the terrible shock. I had to dig deep into all my past understanding and faith to understand. Why? Why? Why? All my life I had been taught that God was real. Not a myth, not something intangible but a real, live Heavenly Father who loved his children here upon the earth, who heard and answered prayers and was mindful of our happiness. Couldn't He have heard their prayers and protected them? Then as I looked down on Sondra in the clean white hospital bed and knew that she would live, then I knew there WAS a God—that He heard and answered prayers.

But now what about the rest of my family? Guard, Jean, Judy, yes, and even Michael. They were here yesterday and gone today. Again I had to dig deep and from this reserve came the calm assurance that our lives are eternal. They have no beginning or end. They cannot be destroyed. They had lived previously with our Heavenly Father in a spirit world before they were born here upon this earth. Their life here was a necessary schooling which they had to pass through that they might prove themselves before Him. Then when they had completed this earth life, regardless of the manner in which their lives were taken, they only lay their bodies away for a little while. But their spirit, the real personalities of Guard, Jean, Judy and Michael are just as real and alive as ever. They have just slipped into another stage of their progression. They will continue to grow, learn and have work to do, preparing for that day of the resurrection when their bodies and their spirits will again be reunited. At this time all of the blessings and privileges that would have been the children's had they lived, will be granted unto them. Later I would again be given the privilege of holding my little girls in my arms and rearing them to maturity.

But what of the family unit which had brought us so much joy here upon the earth? Again I dug deep and found therein my most precious possession. This unit, which began years ago when Guard and I decided to become as one, this sacred ceremony was performed in our temple and sealed under a covenant which would last not for this life only when death might us part but for this time and all eternity!

Believe me, there have been many moments of longing and hurt that comes from contact with their personal belongings—clothing— which is a hurt as deep and real as if a knife were placed in your heart and slowly turned. But always following each hurt a sweet peace seemed to permeate as though to say, "Peace I give unto you, not as the world gives, give I unto you . . . let not your heart be troubled, neither let it be afraid."

Someone said once, "The deeper that sorrow carves into your being, the more joy you can contain." So you see, these are the reasons plus all the wonderful goodness of all the people, plus all the united prayers that have been offered in our behalf and were answered, plus filling each day to capacity so that sleep came immediately at night have I been able to go through these months with a song in my heart.

As to how I feel concerning those who are responsible for this experience—all they have taken from me—there is still something they cannot reach, that only I can destroy. It is out of my hands to pass judgment; that is up to the laws of the land which must preserve our freedom, and to God to whom we all must answer. Each of us is given our free agency to choose whatever path we wish to follow. But those who commit sin must pay the price. But to be bitter—how can I be bitter when so much has been given?

It can all be summed up in the words of Shakespeare who had a way with words, of saying things.

"And they, sweet love remembered, doth such wealth bring . . .

I would scorn to change my place with kings"

Christal's life, as well as those of Sondra Gay and Wayne Robert, in the impending year of 1954, were destined to take a definite and well deserved turn for the better.

"Call your first witness."

TWELVE

Preparations

N amed after the Illinois city of the same name, the quaint hamlet of Quincy is the seat of California's Plumas County. Quincy is a community steeped in gold rush lore, with origins dating back to the mid-nineteenth century. It's a township of fewer than two thousand souls, mostly white, decidedly Republican, bravely scraping out a living. Picturesquely situated on the gravelly banks of the Feather River, Quincy is well within shouting distance of scenic Lake Almanor, a natural wonderland and virtual year-round sportsman's playground where the Sierra Nevada Mountains meet the Cascades. During fishing and deer hunting seasons, nearby recreation venues can easily double the population of this not quite isolated mountain outpost.

Bitter cold mountain winters bring ten-foot snowdrifts alongside rustic country roads. Fog-breathing townspeople go about their daily errands while finding it necessary to wrap themselves in layers of warm clothing to ward off the icy winds. Due to the sometimes harsh weather conditions, there is a tight-lipped-ness about the place as its shivering citizenry eagerly looks ahead to the fulfillment of Mother Nature's annual spring promise of warmer days just around the corner.

Less than two years earlier, Plumas County had been the scene of one of the most horrific crimes ever committed in this area; certainly within anyone's living memory: the brutal murders of Chester grocer Guard Young, two of his daughters and their neighbor boy.

As the three suspected perpetrators of this barbaric crime were being prepared for trial, the eyes of an entire nation had become focused on this tiny dot on the California map. Oddly though, the community buzz that would normally accompany the build-up to such a momentous event had up until now, been nowhere in evidence, but as the start of the trial drew closer, that situation was about to change.

During the early stages of the investigation, District Attorney Bert Janes had personally assumed an active role in the questioning of suspects and the interviewing of witnesses and it was during this process that Janes had received his appointment to the Plumas County Superior Court bench, throwing the entire trial process off track. The Chester multiple murder case was now scheduled to be tried in State Superior Court in Quincy with newly appointed Judge Bertram Janes presiding. The uncertainty over this obvious conflict of interest was finally settled to everyone's satisfaction when Janes recused himself and neighboring Lassen County's Superior Court Judge Ben V. Curler was brought in to try the case. Bert Janes would now be relegated to the role of spectator in the biggest trial to hit Plumas County in all of its one hundred and fifty year history.

The Jury

As Judge Curler reviewed the case, he was immediately able to determine that in the matter of impaneling a jury, he could be faced with his first problem. In 1954, Plumas County was comprised of fewer than 14,000 residents and Curler realized that the probability of ending up with twelve impartial jurors culled from such a small population pool would be slim at best. After all, the "Chester Massacre" was not just local news—it had been making headlines in newspapers across the country for well over a year. Curler was keenly sensitive to the strong feelings and opinions generated amongst the local populace by the four murders, and with that in mind, he requested and was granted the importation of two hundred prospective jurors from his own Lassen County jurisdiction.

On the morning of March 25, 1954 in an adjacent courtroom, one hundred and eighty potential jurors gathered. Chain-smoking cigarettes and drinking county-provided coffee, they waited anxiously for their names to be drawn from a metal box that rested on the court clerk's table in the main courtroom.

As their names were called, the prospective jurors took their seats in the jury box where each would be subjected to the process known as *voir dire*—a Latin legal term meaning, *speak truth*—in which they're obliged to respond truthfully to questions posed by opposing lawyers engaged in a kind of strategic sparring match in an effort to gain even a minor tactical trial advantage. The questions could range from the innocuous to the uncomfortably probing. Some could be intensely personal but all are purposefully framed to elicit information that might reveal to the questioning attorneys how a particular juror would be likely to vote in deciding a defendant's guilt or innocence.

Other questioning might be more pointed. William Lally, Harriet Henson's attorney, sought to prevent parents of small children from being impaneled perhaps presaging his intended trial strategy by repeatedly posing to prospective jurors, "If it appears that my client aided in this horrendous crime, but only in a peripheral way, you would not take from that that she was a party to the actual murders, would you?"

It was a line of questioning that, on more than one occasion, prompted Judge Curler to interrupt by reminding the panel, "You should understand that Mrs. Henson is charged as a principal in this case."

Frequently, and adding to Judge Curler's frustration, prospective jurors would inform the Court that they had already made up their minds and would not be able to serve impartially.

After several days of intense questioning and legal wrangling, on April 1, both sides expressed satisfaction with the final complement of twelve jurors plus, on Judge Curler's recommendation, the swearing in of three—rather than the customary two—alternates.

The jury's final makeup would consist of seven men: a lumber company executive, a mill-worker, a garage owner, a garage manager, a school janitor, a building contractor, a retired mechanic and five women. Each of the women selected described her occupation as "housewife". The panel's average age was forty-five.

After completing the final seating of the jury, the judge called a recess until the following Monday morning at which time Assistant District Attorney Milton Schwartz would open the State's case.

The Defendants

Harriet Henson had been driven to Quincy from her cell in the Nevada County jail where, since the preceding January, she had been under indictment for her participation in the Hansen case and where, although charges were dismissed, she was still being held as a suspect in the Young murders.

Hypersensitive to rumors that Jack Santo might be engineering an escape plot similar to that of his recently foiled Nevada City attempt, and having been on edge for the several days leading up to the trial, Plumas authorities had taken every conceivable precaution with all three defendants.

Already under death sentences for their part in the murder of Mabel Monohan, Santo and Perkins were placed in shackles and leg-irons while being driven the two hundred miles from San Quentin's death row under the watchful eye of Sheriff Mel Schooler and two of his deputies. Schooler himself had been armed with a sub-machine gun while each deputy, in addition to his sidearm, carried a sawed-off shotgun.

Although ultimately, their transfer from San Quentin would be accomplished without incident, the mere threat of an attempted escape created a palpable tension throughout the courthouse that continued to linger in the air as heavily armed guards took up posts at all entrances and exits of the Quincy courthouse building. Even the judges' chambers and jury room were not exempt from the heightened security.

Extraordinary measures included the installation of new floodlighting at the rear of the jailhouse as well as the hiring of additional guards whose sole duty was to conduct periodic bed-checks.

Sheriff Schooler announced to the press that a meeting of state, county and local police officials had been convened in order to map out plans for the implementation of roadblocks on all city streets, roads and highways leading in and out of Quincy. On the off-chance that a prisoner would somehow be able to get out of his cell, Schooler was confident that his office was fully prepared to prevent any and all attempts to actually make good an escape. He deliberately let it be known that he has assembled a posse comprised of more than a hundred deputies from five counties, a contingent of

California Highway Patrol officers, as well as a dozen fire department personnel—all equipped with searchlights and bullhorns and posted at all the roads coming in or going out of town.

Other trial preparations were being made but not without difficulties. Larry Shea, a key prosecution witness, had claimed that he had been receiving telephoned death threats which prompted his request for a bodyguard for both himself and his wife. After a short discussion with the district attorney and other officials, Schooler denied Shea's request.

No Plumas County criminal proceeding in anyone's living memory had ever before been beset with so many pre-trial procedural snags, but despite the many difficulties and delays, Judge Curler was at last convinced they were now ready to proceed with the trial of Jack Santo, Emmett Perkins and Harriet Henson.

The Scene

Standing imposingly above Quincy's downtown business district, the Plumas County Courthouse rises from the center of an expansive lawn with six towering California sugar maples guarding the front entrance. The four story neo-classical stone structure features a stately array of blue-grey marble columns cut from nearby Tuolumne quarries and grandly positioned above the main entrance. A rich motif of variegated marble extends throughout the building's interior, adding to its over-all elegance.

On the third floor, the main courtroom is a graceful, hall-like—though somewhat space limited—area, well-appointed with rich dark oak wall paneling. A large ornate crystal chandelier hangs from a vaulted ceiling; an arched cathedral window accented by a dark marble sill is set beside evenly spaced old-world wall sconces on luxuriously adorned wainscoted panels of aged oak.

In the gallery behind the art-deco oak balustrade, several rows of theater style chairs are fastened to a parquet tiled floor, comfortably accommodating up to one hundred and twenty-eight spectators.

On this crisp April morning in 1954, with painfully vivid images of the four victims still etched on their collective psyche, droves of grim-faced citizens would soon be filing through the heavy oak doors and into the Plumas County courtroom.

Christal Young, after having traveled from her home in Utah, was determined to be present at the trial—for every minute of every day—and for however long it turned out to be. After placing her two children in the care of friends, she had flown back to California where she rented a hotel room in Quincy.

On the morning of the trial's first day, she made the short block-and-a-half walk from her hotel to the courthouse and on approaching the building's front entrance, she found herself smack-dab in the center of a milling crowd of restive citizens waiting for the courtroom doors to open, some having traveled from places as far away as Los Angeles and who were now hoping to secure one of the few unreserved spectators' seats pre-allotted to the general public.

Viewing the noisy queue as it streamed through the hallway and out onto the front lawn, Christal was dismayed but not surprised to see moving about in the crowd of plain everyday citizens, several of those same over-assertive media people whose aggressive behavior had driven her from her former home in Chester.

Their notepads at the ready, extra pencils protruding from the bands of their fedoras and accompanied by the ubiquitous popping of photographers' flashbulbs, they prowled amidst the crowd like hungry wolves.

Pushing her way through the surging mob and doing her best to keep her head down, Christal searched for some sort of a clear pathway into the courthouse, hoping desperately that she wouldn't be recognized. It was a hope that was quickly dashed when a loud voice in the crowd called out:

"Hey! Aren't you Christal Young?"

Almost instantly she was besieged by reporters thrusting microphones in her face and photographers snapping shutters from every angle.

"Mrs. Young," one reporter yelled, stepping in front of her and blocking her path. "Can we get a statement?"

It required every ounce of fortitude she could muster to resist the urge to rip the microphone from the reporter's hand and bang him over the head with it. She responded instead with a look of undisguised contempt as she continued to elbow her way through the crowd.

A photographer waved: "Mrs. Young, over here! Hey, Mrs.Young, over here!" Christal ignored him.

A security officer had been posted at the courtroom door in order to prevent the general public's admission until all court VIPs, credentialed press and immediate family members had been seated. In the meantime and in the officer's own judgment, people who did not fit into any of those categories waited in the hallway for the courtroom doors to swing open to the public.

After having pushed and struggled her way through the throngs of people crowding the hallway, Christal would still have to convince the officer at the courtroom door that she was indeed who she said she was.

To Christal's great and pleasant surprise—appearing seemingly out of nowhere—a uniformed security officer who had recognized her, quietly stepped up to offer her his arm. To Christal, taking that arm was like grabbing a life preserver in the middle of a stormy sea.

He ushered her past the line and after exchanging polite nods with the officer at the door, they entered the courtroom where, in sharp contrast to the raucous commotion in the hallway, she was struck by an aura of solemn, somber quietude—a most welcome relief from the cacophony taking place on the other side of the courtroom walls.

A grateful Christal smiled appreciatively at the burly officer, squeezing his hand before finally settling into her pre-assigned seat to await the start of what the press had now dubbed *The Mountain Massacre Trial*.

On that morning and to no one's surprise, when the courtroom doors finally swung open to the hordes of anxious would-be spectators who, several hours ago, had begun to gather in the hallways, a wave of humanity streamed in through the open doors and the jostling for seats began. With members of the print and broadcast media competing with the general public for seating space and in order to handle the overflow, additional chairs had been set up on the lawn but it was only a matter of seconds before every available seat—both in or out of the courtroom—was occupied and for the duration of the trial, seating of any type would remain at a premium.

Once the gallery had been filled with spectators, a sullen Jack Santo, dressed in prison-issued blues, was brought into the courtroom and seated at the defense table next to his attorney, Public Defender Morris Durrant. Although the shackles had been removed from his wrists, under the table, clearly visible to courtroom spectators as well as members of the jury, leg-irons and chains were still securely wrapped around his ankles. At the same table, also in prison blues and unshackled except for leg-irons, Emmett Perkins sat beside Public Defender-defense counsel Winslow Christian. Harriet Henson had taken her place at the far end of the table beside her court-appointed attorney, William Lally.

On the right, opposite the attorney's podium, District Attorney Jack Keane and Assistant D.A. Milton Schwartz occupied the prosecutor's table while at front center, directly facing the litigants' tables and placed unobtrusively next to the standing bailiff, the court reporter sat at his stenotype machine. Slightly fronting, but adjacent to the judge's bench, the jury box sat within whispering distance of the witness stand.

Seated in the gallery's first row, oblivious to the boorish glances of curious spectators, Christal Young, grim-faced and alone, had taken scant notice of the insensitive stares that were being directed her way and instead, would document her impressions of the proceedings in a small loose-leaf notepad which she held in her lap. It was something she would do regularly throughout the trial.

As the defendants took their respective places at the defense table, Christal made an effort to study their faces, looking into their eyes, searching for even the faintest glimmer of regret or remorse for what they had done. She saw none.

Christal was expected to be called as one of the state's first witnesses and under normal circumstances, those who were scheduled to testify, for obvious reasons, would be sequestered or otherwise barred from the courtroom until they had completed their time on the stand. But because of this trial's unique circumstances, Judge Curler had waived standard court protocol and allowed her to remain in the courtroom throughout the trial.

Rosemary Saile, mother of victim, Michael Saile, who had long since changed her residence by moving to Southern California and, having no desire to attend the trial where she'd be forced to relive those dark October days, chose instead to remain at her Sherman Oaks home, relying on newspaper accounts to keep her updated.

The Mountain Massacre Trial

"All rise," intoned the bailiff as the door to the judge's chamber burst open and with robe flowing, in typically grand fashion, Judge Ben V.Curler entered the room and seated himself at the bench. The court clerk, reading from court documents intoned:

"In the Superior Court of the State of California in and for the County of Plumas, the people of the State of California, Plaintiff, versus John A. Santo, Emmett R. Perkins and Harriet E. Henson, defendants. Charges: Murder, First Degree, Four Counts; Attempted Murder, One Count; Armed Robbery, One Count. Honorable Ben V. Curler, Judge Presiding."

Looking out over his rimless bifocals, Judge Curler surveyed the packed courtroom before nodding a greeting of good morning to opposing counsel. He directed his initial remarks toward the prosecutor's table:

"Is the State ready to proceed with opening statements?"

"Yes we are. Thank you, your honor," Assistant D.A. Milton Schwartz said as he rose to his feet and strode slowly toward the jury box.

After a dramatic thirty-second pause for maximum effect, he began:

"On the Friday afternoon of October tenth 1952," he said, locking eyes with first one juror and then the next, "supermarket owner Guard Young, drove from his store in Chester to the town of Westwood, twelve miles away, to do some banking. He decided to take with him his three young daughters and their friend and playmate Michael Saile so that when he finished his banking business, he could treat them all to popsicles." Schwartz went on to paint a verbal portrait of three winsome little girls and their irrepressible friend, Michael. After pausing so as to allow the verbal pictures to sink in, he continued to draw mental images of a loving father and four giddy, squealing, happy children.

"You will hear how, after leaving the bank, this young father with seven thousand dollars in cash in his hand and with these four deliriously joyful children clinging tightly to their popsicle treats, the completely innocent, totally vulnerable victims were viciously set upon by three sub-humans who would steal their money and, for no reason other than their fear of being identified, would take a lead pipe and brutally bludgeon them until three of them were dead, leaving only one to survive. A lead pipe!" He paused. "Think about that, ladies and gentlemen; a three pound lead pipe!"

It was obvious his words were having their desired effect. All twelve jurors, particularly the five women, listened in horror-stricken silence.

Schwartz continued. "You're going to hear testimony so graphic and so frightening," he said, "it'll make you question whether those responsible for this horrible crime are actual human beings. You will be shown photographs of the victims—the loving father and those sweet little girls and that little rascal Michael, and you'll see the condition in which they were left after these predators had finished their dirty work. It's a scene that I guarantee will stay with you long after this trial is over."

The prosecutor elaborated by describing the crime in vivid detail, choosing colorful words and phrases in order to impress on each juror the images that would remain fixed in their minds throughout the trial and into the deliberation process.

"We must never lose track of what happened on that day. We must never forget the five occupants of that car and how they were smashed over their heads with a three pound piece of pipe, swung with such force that their little skulls were crushed like melons," he said, as he stared into the eyes of each juror, his face contorted in a mask of anger, "and then stuffed in the trunk of the car and left to die."

Christal sat mesmerized, her eyes fixed firmly on the prosecutor as he proceeded to synopsize the state's case to the jury in the most dramatic terms imaginable. She listened as he painted a word picture of stark horror, describing in meticulous detail—right down to the children's clothing—and in his words, calling out the "sheer depravity" of the crimes for which these three defendants were now being tried.

Drawing curious but sympathetic glances from the jury, Christal could feel herself cringe as she absorbed Schwartz's vivid imagery. She stiffened with each jarring word as he described her loved ones lying battered and lifeless in the blood-drenched trunk of their car and a knot began to form in the pit of her stomach.

With head bowed, she closed her eyes. Her soft sobs could be heard over the almost palpable hush that had settled over the packed courtroom.

"And finally," Schwartz said, though he had no reason to believe that any of the defendants would testify, "you're going to meet the three individuals who committed this unspeakable crime."

Like an actor playing the lead in Macbeth, Schwartz suddenly swung his arm around, and while pointing a dramatic finger toward the defense table and in a voice loud enough to startle everyone in the room, he roared, "There! Sitting at that table! The state will show, beyond any doubt whatsoever, there sit the murderers of Judy Young, of Jean Young, of Michael Saile and of Guard Young."

Santo and Perkins returned Schwartz's accusatory gestures with menacing scowls while Harriet simply stared blankly at the floor.

Schwartz would continue his opening remarks by occasionally motioning in Perkins' direction to which Perkins' response suggested that these entire proceedings—insofar as they concerned him—were little more than an unpleasant inconvenience. From time to time he would look up from the newspaper he was pretending to read and, narrowing his beady eyes, would squint contemptuously at the jury. It was as though their decision—whatever it should turn out to be—mattered little if it mattered at all. Or he would sit, unmoved and unmoving—even grinning at some of the more graphic verbal imagery—with those grins, at times, turning unmistakably into smirks.

Upon concluding his opening soliloquy, Schwartz returned to his table while the courtroom buzzed with anticipation. How, the stunned spectators wondered, would the defense counter the prosecutor's opening statement? Jack Santo—defiant and unashamedly displaying contempt for the entire process—reacted to Schwartz's remarks by squirming uneasily in his chair.

Emmett Perkins exhibited almost no reaction; his gaunt, pasty face—save for an involuntary tic at the corner of his mouth—remained expressionless as he glared at the jury. Harriet's audible sobs broke the courtroom's stillness and she continued to stare at the floor.

From her front row vantage point, Christal had been given an unobstructed view of the defense table, making it possible to observe the three defendants as they reacted to the manner in which they were being depicted. Despite being sickened by the cold callousness displayed by both Santo and Perkins—but especially Perkins—Christal was determined to sit through these proceedings to the bitter end no matter how gut-wrenching or how repugnant they might become. This resolve however, would soon be tested beyond anything she could ever have imagined.

The Defense

William Lally, court-appointed attorney for Harriet Henson, in his opening statement laying out his client's defense, suggested to the jury that even if they should find Mrs. Henson guilty for having had knowledge of the four murders, the evidence would show that this knowledge came only after the fact and that she had not taken part in the actual commission of the crime. He further would argue that although she may have been remiss in failing to bring this information to the attention of the police, she was guilty only of having "loved too well but not too wisely."

In his opening statement, Winslow Christian, attorney for Emmett Perkins suggested, "Rather than being able to place Emmett Perkins in Chester on the day of the murders, the state will present not a single scintilla of evidence that would link my client, Emmett Perkins to these murders."

He reminded the jury that "no matter your personal feelings with respect to my client—if it happens that you disapprove of his lifestyle, his prior felony convictions or his alleged life of crime—despite all of that, if the evidence offered by the state is so weak, so un-compelling and so un-persuasive that it fails to convince you—beyond a reasonable doubt—of Mr. Perkins' guilt, then you are bound by the oath you took just a few days ago to return a verdict of not guilty on all counts."

But it was his next line of attack that brought the gallery to its feet, throwing Christal into a near state of shock and sending the media types scrambling for the nearest telephone.

After Christian had gone through the usual pro-forma defense arguments, calling the jury's attention to the state's "lack of evidence" before predictably segueing to what he called, the sheriff's "rush to judgment" by singling out his client, along with co-defendant Jack Santo as their *only* serious suspects, he dropped his bombshell.

"We're going to look into the activities of Mrs. Young just prior to October tenth 1952," he announced to a stunned jury. All eyes in the courtroom turned to an obviously perplexed Christal, who, still struggling with the prosecutor's opening remarks, frowned, thinking perhaps she had not heard the lawyer's words correctly.

At the prosecutor's table Milton Schwartz and Jack Keane exchanged puzzled glances. What the hell was this all about, Keane wondered. There had been no prior indication that the defense was working on a trial strategy that would include a personal assault on the wife and mother of the victims.

Christian continued. "We're going to examine the rumors that had been circulating around Chester at that time and we're going to ask questions about Mrs. Young's personal and possibly clandestine relationship with a mysterious 'Mr. X'. Is there any truth to those rumors? We're going to find out."

Immediately Schwartz was on his feet to object vehemently to Christian's sudden and totally unexpected attack on Christal Young. A lengthy and somewhat animated sidebar discussion was immediately followed by Judge Curler's warning to the defense that the statement would be allowed at this time but only on the condition that the defense produces credible evidence during the trial. On that basis, Schwartz's objection was overruled.

Christal was totally nonplussed. "Rumors?" What were these *rumors* he was talking about? Could it be Clair? Was he talking about Clair?

Shortly after re-locating her family to Utah, Christal had been surprised—and probably annoyed—to see the entire story of her tragedy, complete with graphically lurid photographs splashed across the front pages of the Deseret News, a Salt Lake City metropolitan newspaper which enjoyed broad circulation throughout the state. She had moved away from Chester in a vain effort to circumvent the often oppressive media scrutiny to which she had been so mercilessly subjected. In Utah however, she discovered that the newspaper coverage recounting the events of the previous October had begun to generate the same kind of public attention that had chased her out of Chester and she had begun to fear that this harassment by the media had followed her all the way to Provo.

Considering the paper's wide circulation, it wasn't long before her phone began to ring. There were calls from the morbidly curious, calls from opportunists hoping to somehow turn her misfortune into a quick buck for themselves, calls and letters from all manner of individuals with all manner of motives. But one in particular caught Christal's attention. It was a letter from a man named Clair Mathis, a widower with two young children. No one knows what magic might have been contained in that letter that would have made Clair Mathis stand apart from all the rest. Maybe it was Christal's sensing of the fact that because he, like her, was a single parent raising two children and making an effort to infuse them with the strong Mormon values that had played such a large role in his own life. Or maybe it was her sensitivity to what she felt was her now fatherless children's need for a male role model at this stage in their young lives. Maybe it was just her vulnerability of the moment. Whatever Christal's motivation, after much thought and prayer, she agreed to his suggestion that they meet. They did so and it would not be long before their shared interests in church and family gradually evolved into a deep mutual affection; so much so that a little over a year after their first meeting, Christal and Clair had become engaged to be married.

Christal stared quizzically at Winslow Christian as he addressed the jury and wondered if this is where he was going with this. Did he intend to use Clair as a pawn in trying to defend a guilty client who many observers believed—rightly or wrongly—was utterly indefensible, and who, even now, sat glaring at the jury, his pasty facial features twisted into a malevolent smirk? It was a suggestion so patently absurd, she reasoned, that no one on this planet could ever believe such a preposterous idea.

No one was prepared for what was to come next: "We're going to see if the rumors that Mrs. Young and this mysterious 'Mr. X' might have colluded in these murders. We're going to ask the question: are they only rumors?"

Christian asked the stunned jurors, "Would Mrs. Young have had anything to gain by eliminating an unwanted husband?" It was such a contemptible idea that if not for its total outrageousness, Christal thought, it would have been laughable. Was he actually suggesting that she had a hand in the murders of her own family?

Milton Schwartz, with D.A. Jack Keane at his side, was on his feet, waving his arms, furiously objecting to Christian's completely off-the-wall suggestion. Schwartz was almost speechless. "Your Honor, this is unconscionable! There has been absolutely no groundwork laid by counsel for such an outrageous and completely unfounded suggestion."

Judge Curler didn't hesitate. "Sustained," he said, banging his gavel and glaring at Christian. "Mr. Christian," he said, almost shouting, "that's enough! You know better than that." He instructed the jury to disregard Winslow Christian's remarks.

A mortified Christal watched in astounded disbelief as, grinning smugly, Christian walked back to the defense table, satisfaction written across his face.

"Call your first witness," Judge Curler said to the prosecutor.

During that first week, after having listened to witnesses describe—in vivid and excruciating detail—the grisly sight that confronted them at the murder scene; the shock of seeing four blood-drenched bodies, three of them children, lying in crumpled heaps like so much dirty laundry, Christal would retire each evening to the solitude of her hotel room where she would dwell on the events of the day.

When this nightmare is finally over, she mused, there would be some small comfort in the knowledge that at last justice will have been done and the guilty would finally receive the punishment due them. But she realized too, that their executions—if indeed that was to be the jury's decision—would very likely not bring her satisfaction but instead, a paradoxical sense of guilt in knowing that she had played a role in causing the deaths of other human beings, no matter how reprehensible their crimes might have been.

Lying in her bed while staring at the ceiling—trying to fight off the tears she knew were only a blink away—Christal would pray long into the night, pleading for the strength to endure just one more day in court until finally—overtaken by the sheer mental fatigue brought on by the crushing stress of the sights and sounds of the trial—mercifully, sleep would at last come. There would be time to cry later.

"She was all covered with blood, her clothes and all,
and I could barely make out her face."

THIRTEEN

Payback

The tabloid press was characterizing the Chester multiple murder trial as *The Mountain Massacre Trial* while other mainstream media outlets had dubbed it *The Trial of the Century*. Either way and typical of most cases that involve the death penalty, the trial itself got off to a somewhat mundane, most unsensational start.

"The state calls Joseph Watson," intoned Assistant D.A. Milton Schwartz, who would be handling most of the prosecution's questioning of witnesses. Schwartz's announcement caused puzzled onlookers to strain their necks, allowing their eyes to follow a balding, diminutive middle-aged man stride down the center aisle on his way to the witness box.

After being sworn in and after having established the fact that he lived in Quincy, Watson was asked by Schwartz about his occupation.

"I am the Plumas County Surveyor," he answered proudly.

He explained to the court that he had been commissioned by Sheriff Schooler's office to create a map of the murder scene and its surrounding areas; the same map which prosecutors would be entering into evidence as State's Exhibit Number 1 in the presentation of their case.

Next to testify was Mary Bell, the clerk who was behind the counter at Bennight's Variety Store on that fateful day. She told of selling popsicles to Guard Young and the children and how she had to admonish Mr. Young for seating one of the little girls on the lunch counter, reminding him of the state's stringent health regulations. Bell described how, after paying for their popsicles, she watched Guard and the children leave the store, get into their car and drive away.

Bank of America teller Carly Dunn took the stand to testify how Guard, with his daughter Sondra Gay, had entered the bank on October 10 at two-fifty p.m. Dunn said she helped Mr. Young transact his business before departing the bank at three p.m. She identified the calculator tape that had been found at the murder scene as the one that she had given to Mr. Young and confirmed the $7,128.69 figure as the cash amount he had received.

She described in detail how she handed Guard Young the cash. There were eight bundles of twenty dollar bills," she said, "six containing fifty twenties plus two others containing twenty-five, both wrapped with rubber bands." Additionally, there were four bundles of twenty-five "very dirty" one dollar bills, plus two tens, one five, three more singles and sixty-nine cents in change. She said that before leaving the window, Mr. Young had placed the money in a bag marked with the Bank of America logo.

Bank manager John Woods took the stand to establish the fact that Young and Sondra Gay had departed the bank shortly before the three p.m. closing time and almost immediately thereafter, he had locked the door.

Thus the *Mountain Massacre Trial* had begun with a procession of witnesses, some critical to the prosecution's case but more than a few, only marginally relevant.

Christal

One of the first witnesses to testify, Christal Young strode purposefully to the witness stand, her head still reeling from the defense attorney's scurrilous opening remarks but nonetheless determined to keep her tightly wound emotions in check. A respectful quiet descended over the gallery as Christal, with her typically classic grace, mounted the two steps and seated herself in the witness chair.

Schwartz, speaking in his most deferential manner, began by asking her to recount the activities of her family in and around the Young Supermarket on the early afternoon of October 10, 1952, particularly with respect to her husband and the four children as they prepared to embark on their bank errand to Westwood.

"Guard had come up to the apartment for lunch," she stated. "It was about that time when he told me he would be going to the bank. We had a new baby and Guard knew how much work that can be so he said he would take the girls with him so I could have a little rest."

Her voice was firm and clear and except for the wringing of a small, white handkerchief that she held in her hand, she displayed almost no emotion.

"Was it common practice for Mr. Young to take the children along when he went on these bank errands?" Schwartz asked.

"He would do it occasionally. The children loved it. They knew the trip always meant a stop at the variety store for treats," she said, a noticeable wistfulness coloring her soft voice.

Schwartz walked to the prosecution table where he picked up a stack of glossy black and white photographs. Returning to the witness stand, he handed to Christal—one by one, in all their vivid, graphic detail—the morgue photographs of the slain victims.

Christal, on more than one occasion, had already seen and had even identified these same pictures, yet she couldn't help but be perceptibly shaken as she studied each photo. The gallery fell silent as she proceeded to identify each victim:

"Guard. That's my husband, Guard."

Schwartz asked rhetorically, "Did you ever see Guard again?"

"No."

"That's Jean," she said.

"And did you ever see Jean again?"

"No," she replied.

"That one is Judy."

"And did you ever see Judy again?"

"No."

When shown the last photo, a trace of a smile crossed her face. "That's little Michael," she said.

"And did you ever see Michael again?"

"No."

Although understandably under enormous stress, except for the twisting and wringing of the handkerchief, Christal did not appear especially anxious, even forcing a nervous smile as she braced herself for Schwartz's next question. But not wishing to subject her to further distress, the prosecutor turned and nodded to the defense table, indicating he had completed his questioning of Christal Young.

After a hurried consultation among the three defense lawyers, Morris Durrant announced, "We have no questions for this witness, your honor."

Judge Curler thanked Christal for her testimony and with the same dignity and poise that she had displayed when taking the stand, she stepped down and returned to her gallery seat.

Elliott, Bridges, Cooley

Next to take the stand, store manager Dorothy Elliott was asked to describe the scene at the supermarket that Friday afternoon when Guard and the children left the store.

"Do you recall his parting words? Can you tell us what those last words were, Mrs. Elliott?" Schwartz asked. "What were the last words any of you heard?"

"It was something to the effect 'I'll be back in a flash with the cash.' Something like that," she said.

Under Morris Durrant's cross-examination, Mrs. Elliott's testimony would prove to be crucial for the prosecution when, contrary to earlier statements made by Emmett Perkins that he had never—in his life—been in Chester, she was able to state categorically that she had seen Santo and Perkins in Chester together, "many times."

Reno shoe store owner Ralph Parker described to the court how "big spender" Jack Santo had visited his store and purchased several pairs of shoes on October 11, the day after the murders.

Jerry and Helen Bridges told how they discovered the Young's car the afternoon of the day it had gone missing. Mrs. Bridges recalled seeing the green sedan while she and Jerry had been out hunting. She said that while they were walking in the area adjacent to the logging road, she noticed the green sedan which had apparently either been driven or pushed into the underbrush.

"As we were walking away I thought I heard some children holler. It was the same holler or scream I hear when my children are outside playing," she said, adding, "I didn't realize those sounds were coming from that car."

"At that time, did you inform your husband of what you had heard?" Schwartz asked.

"I told him I thought I heard children playing and he told me I must be imagining things."

State Highway Patrol Officer Jeff Cooley took the stand to tell his story. He related how on that Friday night, even though he'd been down with the flu, he had crawled out of his sick bed, and together with a friend, they had walked Highway 36 from Chester to Westwood. He said they had taken turns between driving and walking as they searched up and down the highway looking for the missing Young car. First one would drive the pickup, he said, as the other carried a lantern while walking alongside. Then they would alternate.

Cooley said that in the morning after he had finally returned to bed he was awakened by Helen and Jerry Bridges pounding on his front door. After first reiterating to the court the couple's account of how they had led him to Guard Young's partially concealed car, Cooley mesmerized the hushed courtroom as he described the raising of the trunk's lid and discovering what he thought at the time, were five bodies.

"And when you saw what looked like five bodies, what did you do?" Prosecutor Schwartz asked.

"Well, as we were all looking at them, I could see a child toward the back of the trunk," Cooley answered haltingly, "crouched down near the back; she had her head up, and was trying to raise herself up." He went on to describe how the terrified little girl tried to sit up above the other bodies, whimpering and squinting in the bright sunlight. Telling the court how he had reached out for her and how she had clung tightly to his arms, he lifted her from the trunk. "I learned later that her name was Sondra Gay."

At the mention of her daughter's name, Christal exhaled a soft sigh and dabbed at her eyes with a handkerchief.

"She was all covered with blood, her clothes and all, and I could barely make out her face," Cooley said, his voice beginning to quaver.

"And did it appear to you, Officer Cooley, that anyone else was alive?" Schwartz asked.

"Mr. Young was lying on top of the others and I could see part of a rope that had been tied around his hand and arm; there was some kind of a cloth on his face. It was a white cloth. I think it was a blindfold, but it had slipped down and covered his face from the nose down."

"Just to be sure," he said, I checked to see "if any of the others were still alive."

"And when you turned your attention back to the car and the trunk, Mr. Cooley, what did you find?" Schwartz asked.

"They were dead," Cooley answered. "They were all dead."

Cooley said he rushed Sondra Gay first to Dr. Greenman's office in Chester, only to learn that she would have to be taken to the hospital in Westwood.

So with Mrs. Greenman sitting beside him while holding Sondra Gay tightly in her arms and the doctor following closely behind in his own car, Cooley drove to Westwood where he delivered the blood soaked Sondra Gay into the capable hands of the emergency staff at Community Hospital in Westwood.

Dr. Greenman

Some of the trial's most graphic and dramatic testimony would come from Dr. Roger Greenman, the Young family's personal physician as well as the Plumas County Medical Examiner. Dr. Greenman testified that he was somewhat astonished to see that when he had finally gotten a chance to more closely examine Sondra Gay's wounds at the hospital, he found that despite having sustained a vicious beating, none of her injuries appeared to be life-threatening.

After ministering to her wounds, he prescribed a mild sedative and then in his official capacity as County Medical Examiner, he left the hospital immediately and arrived at the murder scene only minutes later. Schwartz asked him to describe the scene as he had found it.

"The first thing I saw was the Young car—it was on a side road, a logging road is what it amounted to, and I saw that the car had been driven or pushed into the brush which was just off the traveled part of that road. I don't know if they have names for those old logging roads."

"Could that be Malvich Road?" Schwartz asked for the record.

"Yes," Dr. Greenman answered. "That sounds about right."

"Alright, Doctor. What was the first thing you saw with regard to these individuals?"

"I saw that they were bunched up in the trunk of the car. They had been packed in like sardines—all rolled up."

"Now can you tell us very briefly, Doctor, what did you determine to be the cause of the death of Guard Young?" Schwartz asked.

"His head was bashed in—he had been hit in several places. And he had a tremendous hemorrhage over the vertex or over the cerebrum and he was dead as a result of brain injury—damage to the brain tissue."

Schwartz pressed on. "And in your expert opinion in your post-mortem examination, the cause of Judy Young's death was what?"

"The same thing," Dr. Greenman said. "She had taken a number of blows to the head." The prosecutor allowed his witness to expand. "I think the little fellow, as I recall . . . no . . .," correcting himself as he consulted his notes, "he also had been hit several times."

"By the 'little fellow,' you are referring to whom?"

"Michael Saile."

"And in your expert opinion, Doctor Greenman, in your post-mortem examination—the cause of Jean Young's death was what?"

"The same thing," Dr. Greenman replied. "She also had been bashed over the head with a heavy object."

"And again, in your expert opinion Doctor, could you describe how great a force would have been necessary to cause all those injuries?"

The twelve members of the jury listened in unconcealed revulsion to Doctor Greenman's response.

"It would have been the kind of force you'd get if you had swung a baseball bat," Dr. Greenman said, eliciting an audible gasp from the gallery.

"There were deep grooves left in the skulls of all of the victims so it had to be a blunt object and wielded with much force or else it had to be very heavy."

When shown the three-pound, eighteen-inch length of pipe that had been placed in evidence, Dr. Greenman was asked if it could have been the murder weapon to which he answered, "Yes sir—definitely."

As the jury recoiled at the doctor's graphic portrayal of how he had found Guard and the four defenseless children, they were even further appalled on learning about the length of time the victims had been made to suffer.

"You have testified that you arrived at the murder scene on the morning of October eleventh at approximately 10:30 or 11:00 a.m. Isn't that right, Doctor?"

"Yes, that's right," Dr. Greenman said.

"And when you examined the bodies at that time, Doctor, were you able to make a determination as to the time of death?"

"Not too accurately," Dr. Greenman answered, "because the bodies were all very cold, and there was rigor mortis. I would say they had been dead for approximately eight hours."

It didn't take a genius to calculate that if the attack had occurred around 3:30 p.m. and they had been stuffed into the trunk of the car shortly thereafter, they had lain in the trunk of the car, agonizingly clinging to life until one or two the following morning—another ten to eleven hours.

It was this revelation and the realization that the victims had likely been subjected to hours of painful suffering that sent shockwaves through the courtroom.

Although news of the actual times of death had come as a shock to jury and spectators, from earlier interviews with investigators, Christal had been aware of the hours of agony that Guard and the children had endured and hearing it again did not make it any less painful.

While Dr. Greenman's graphic testimony rattled even the most dispassionate of those hearing it, Emmett Perkins sat detached and icy cold, paying scant attention to the trial proceedings. He pretended instead to be absorbed in the newspaper he had ostentatiously spread across the table before him. With exaggerated gestures he would turn the pages while courtroom spectators, frowning and shaking their heads, looked on in horrified incredulity. Christal simply tried to ignore him.

But Jack Santo's lawyer, Morris Durrant, had become clearly agitated. The accumulated shock at the doctor's vivid testimony and the display of the grisly photographic exhibits—the images of the bludgeoned bodies of the children—all proved too much, even for the seasoned defense lawyer. Himself the father of a seven-year-old daughter, Durrant buried his face in his hands and began to sob loudly. The astonished Judge Curler called a brief recess so that the defense lawyer could compose himself, and as the bailiff helped him from the courtroom, no outward reaction from the others at the defense table was evident.

Christal of course, was fully aware that Morris Durrant, as defender of accused killer Jack Santo, represented her worst enemy, yet she couldn't help being moved by the sincerity in his unexpected display of humanity. Convinced that this flood of compassion was genuine, in her typical affinity with anyone in obvious distress, Christal's first instincts were to join him in the hallway in order to offer solace. However, before she could act on her consolatory impulses, Mr. Durrant had regained control of his emotions and had re-entered the courtroom to resume his place at the defense table. His client exhibited little if any concern, expressing his disdain for the entire process with simpering smirks while co-defendant Emmett Perkins, stoic and apparently unmoved, continued to flip through the pages of his newspaper. Harriet, like the courtroom spectators who filled the gallery, simply appeared bewildered.

Calvin Baccala

In all, the prosecution would call no fewer than forty witnesses; yet when it came to establishing a time line of events leading up to the murders, none would be more critical to their case than Chester rancher Calvin Baccala. Mr. Baccala would testify that on the afternoon of October 10, 1952, he had seen a big green sedan and a smaller blue car, both parked on State Route 36 near the spot where the bodies had been found.

"On that day, Mr. Baccala, did you have occasion to be traveling on State Route 36?" Prosecutor Schwartz asked.

"Yes. I was going to Susanville from my ranch in Soldier's Meadow," he explained.

"And your purpose in going to Susanville was what?"

"To get a chain for my chainsaw," Baccala answered.

"Mr. Baccala, on October tenth 1952, at about what time did you leave Susanville to return to your home?"

"Around fifteen minutes to three."

"Alright, Mr. Baccala," Schwartz said, "at about 2:45 you left Susanville and what route did you take on your way back home?"

"Highway 36," Baccala said.

"Did you make any stops?"

"No, no stops. I was going to the town of Chester, and I had to go through there to get home."

Baccala testified that he had departed the Susanville shop at around 2:30 p.m.—testimony that would later be called into question when the shop's owner took the stand to swear that Baccala had arrived at the shop at 11:00 a.m., lingered for a little while, then left the shop shortly before noon—not at 2:45 p.m. as Baccala was claiming. The implication being, of course, that assuming the shop owner's recollection was accurate, Baccala, could not possibly have seen the two cars parked alongside the highway at 3:25 or 3:30 p.m. as he had testified. If the shop-owner's testimony was to be believed, Baccala would have passed that spot hours earlier.

Schwartz walked to the defense table where he picked up a large poster-board on which the surveyor's map of the murder scene had been mounted. After placing it on the easel in front of the judge's bench, he turned back to the witness:

"On your way back home to Chester, did you have occasion, Mr. Baccala, to see any automobiles parked along Highway 36?"

When Baccala answered in the affirmative, Schwartz asked him to step over to the map.

"Would you stand over here and put your finger on—excuse me, I think we have a pointer—would you stand over here so the jury can see the whole map and place your pointer—bearing in mind that this is the Plumas-Lassen County line—approximately where you saw the cars?"

Using the pointer, Baccala indicated the relative positioning of the two cars. "I was there and the cars were parked over here," he said. "One—the green car—was parked off the right-hand side of the highway and the other was parked in front of the green one."

"And in which direction were they facing?" Schwartz asked.

"Toward Chester," Baccala said. "Both of them."

"Alright sir," Schwartz said. "I'm going to take this map down for a minute and just for the purpose of illustration—this is not to scale of course—I am drawing two lines to indicate the highway on which you were traveling and where you testified you saw the two cars."

He placed the map back on the easel. "Will you take this chalk, and please bear in mind that the top line here is the northerly edge of the highway and the bottom line is the southerly edge, and sketch in for us the positions in which you saw these two cars." Baccala complied.

"Alright sir, can you tell us anything in the way of description about those cars, either by color or by style?"

To Schwartz's dismay, Baccala answered, "Not much, no."

"Now wait a minute," Schwartz said, trying to recover. "Let's do this for the purpose of the record. Let's say the car you have drawn, which is off the highway, we'll call car number one and the car you have drawn that is parked partially ahead of car number one is car number two."

Baccala watched intently as Schwartz marked the map. The prosecutor continued, "Now, did you notice the color of car number one?"

"Green. A green color."

"And the make; do you know the make of car number one?"

Baccala said that he didn't know the make and when Schwartz asked if he knew the color and the make of car number two, he said, "I don't know the make but it was a kind of blue color."

This would prove to be a minor sticking point with Morris Durrant, Santo's defense lawyer, when, during his cross examination, he would force Baccala to admit that in his Grand Jury testimony, he had testified that he "couldn't remember" the color of car number two. "Can you tell us why you are now able to recall this detail when you couldn't remember it when you testified to the Grand Jury?" Durrant asked.

"I don't know. Mr. Keane helped me to remember," Baccala replied.

"I see. The district attorney helped you to remember," Durrant repeated, his tone laced with sarcasm. "What else did the district attorney help you to remember?" Durrant's condescending style in his treatment of prosecution witnesses, which at times, could have been described as bullying, had prompted a stream of angry objections from the prosecutor's table.

Despite repeated admonitions from Judge Curler, Durrant's tone would become only marginally more deferential.

Prosecutor Schwartz continued with his direct. "Mr. Baccala, when you saw these two cars along the highway, what, if anything, did you do?"

"Well, I slowed down a little bit."

"You slowed down. Why did you slow down, Mr. Baccala?"

"I was thinking that maybe they had a wreck; maybe they needed help."

"I see," Schwartz said. "How fast would you say you were traveling after you slowed down?"

"Maybe about ten. Something like that."

"Ten miles an hour?"

"Yes," Baccala said as Schwartz encouraged him to expand on his truncated answers.

"Alright. And could you tell us what you saw there as you slowed down—just go ahead and tell us, if you would, everything that you were able to see."

Baccala recalled seeing two men standing beside car number one. One of the men he recognized as Guard Young whom he knew as the owner of Young's Supermarket; the other, a much shorter man but one he did not recognize.

"Alright then, you saw these two men standing there. Could you see what they were doing as they stood there?" Schwartz asked.

"They were just talking. They weren't doing anything. Just talking."

"Did you see anything else as you drove by the two cars and the two men standing there who were just talking?"

"I saw kids," Baccala answered. "There was a little boy outside the car and I could see two girls—little girls—in the back seat of the blue car."

Schwartz asked Baccala to step down and with the pointer, would he please indicate to the jury the spot where he had seen the two men and the little boy.

"And now could you point to the car in which you saw the two little girls that you say were in the back seat."

He pointed to car number one which was the car he had earlier described as being a "kind of blue color."

Baccala returned to the witness stand whereupon Prosecutor Schwartz continued to press him on what he had seen.

"Now Mr. Baccala, this little boy you saw between the two cars—can you tell us what the little boy was doing?"

Baccala thought for just a moment before replying, "I think he was running. He looked like he was running around."

"Running around the car?"

"Yes. Around the back of the green car."

"And did you see anything else?"

"In the blue car I saw a man sitting in the front—behind the wheel."

"That would be car number one," Schwartz said, clarifying by pointing to the car on the map. "Did you see anything else?"

Baccala stunned the courtroom with his next revelation. "In the other car—the blue one—I saw a woman in the back seat with the little girls."

"You saw a woman?" Schwartz repeated as he looked at the jury.

"Can you tell us what this woman that you saw—can you tell us what she looked like? Can you describe what you saw?"

"She was wearing a hat but I could see she had long hair. Black hair. It was kind of stringy."

"Alright, Mr. Baccala. Would you recognize that woman if you saw her again?"

"Yes," Baccala said. "Yes, I would."

"And do you see that woman in this courtroom today?"

"Yes."

"Would you point her out, please?"

"That's her," he said, pointing to Harriet Henson at the defense table.

"You are pointing to the defendant Harriet Henson. Are you sure it was Harriet Henson you saw in the back seat of car number one—the blue car—on the afternoon of October tenth 1952?"

"Yes, I am sure."

At the defense table, Harriet, obviously jolted by Baccala's devastating accusation, began to whisper angrily into the ear of her attorney, William Lally, whose other ear was tuned to the witness's testimony that was now placing his client at the scene of the murders. He began to scribble furiously on his long yellow notepad.

The state's direct examination of Calvin Baccala had consumed an entire day, even running over into the morning of the following day when, after a short mid-morning recess, Baccala was finally handed over to the defense for cross-examination.

Santo's lawyer, Morris Durrant, took turns with Winslow Christian and William Lally, attorneys for Perkins and Henson, at firing questions at Baccala, all designed to rattle him or otherwise punch holes in his twelve hours of direct testimony.

Christian pounded on Baccala's time and distance account and his seemingly faulty recollection of his return drive to Chester after leaving Susanville:

Pacing back and forth in front of the witness stand, Christian's voice echoed through the courtroom and grew louder with each succeeding syllable. Mr. Baccala," he began as he looked at the jury before turning to face the witness; "you're testifying that you don't know how many miles it is between Susanville and Chester, is that right?"

It was apparent to Christian that Baccala had become comfortable under the prosecutor's soft-ball approach, so in his cross, the first thing on his "to-do" list was to shake this witness out of his comfort zone.

"And you have also told this court that you have no idea how long it normally takes you to drive that distance, isn't that right?" Christian fired at Baccala.

"Yes, I think so."

Christian stopped pacing and while standing with feet planted and spread slightly apart, his arms folded threateningly across his chest, he faced the witness. "Would you tell us how long you have lived in this area, Mr. Baccala—this Chester area? Can you tell us that?"

"I've lived here for, maybe, I think, fifty-four years," Baccala answered nervously.

"Fifty-four years? Wouldn't you say that fifty-four years is an awfully long time for a person to live in this area and still not know how long it takes to drive from Susanville to Chester?" he asked mockingly. "Wouldn't you say so, Mr. Baccala?"

"Yes, I guess so," Baccala answered.

After peppering the witness with one or two more questions in an effort to provoke some small slip on Baccala's part that could be used to discredit his damaging testimony but eliciting little of relevance, Christian deferred to his defense counsel colleague William Lally, and that was when the real fireworks began.

Since Baccala had specifically named his client as a participant in this crime, Lally would challenge that testimony in a more rigorous cross-examination.

"Mr. Baccala," Lally began, "in your testimony to Mr. Schwartz, you stated that as you passed the two cars that you saw parked alongside the road of Highway 36, as you passed them, your speed, I believe you said, was ten miles an hour. Is that correct?"

"Yes, ten miles an hour. That's right."

"How far from those two cars do you estimate you were when you saw them?" Lally continued.

"How far? I don't know. Not very far, I guess."

"Well, would you say you were—what—two hundred feet? One hundred feet?" Fifty feet? It's an easy question."

Baccala began to squirm in his seat. "I . . . uh . . . I dunno. I'm not very good at distances. Not a hundred feet. A lot less. Maybe more like ten feet. I don't know."

"Ten feet? Mr. Baccala, from where you are sitting to the back wall of this courtroom, I would estimate the distance to be about fifty feet. Would you like for me to measure it?"

Baccala looked puzzled. "No, I don't think so. It was a lot closer. Maybe half of that. Yeah, about half of that."

Lally pounced. "Half of that, you say. Okay, Mr. Baccala, there is a woman seated next to the aisle several rows back, about halfway to the back wall. She is wearing a pink hat. Can you see her?"

Baccala, peering out toward the gallery, squinted and frowned before suddenly brightening as he discovered the lady in the pink hat.

"Yes, I see her. She has on a pink hat," he said triumphantly.

"That's right, Mr. Baccala. She's wearing a hat, just like that woman in the car was wearing a hat, the woman that you say you saw sitting in the back seat of that blue car, is that correct?"

"Yeah, I guess so," Baccala answered, but not at all sure where Lally was leading him.

"Alright now, Mr. Baccala, would you say that that is about the distance from which you were able to see that woman?"

Before Baccala could answer, Lally fired another question.

"Would you tell us, Mr. Baccala, what is the color of that woman's hair?"

Baccala's eyes narrowed in the brightly lit courtroom and after a few moments of uncertain silence, he admitted, "I can't tell. I think it's a light color, but I really can't tell for sure."

"I see. You can't tell. Even though you're both sitting perfectly still, not moving; even though you have as much time as anyone would need to study the subject; even though the light is good; even though, by your own estimate, the lady in the pink hat is sitting at approximately the same distance from you now as was the woman you saw in that green car on October tenth who also was wearing a hat and whose hair you say was black, and you're absolutely certain of that. Even after all of that, you're saying now that you can't tell us what the color of her hair is. Is that correct, Mr. Baccala?"

Baccala nodding, mumbled, "Yes."

Lally steamrolled on. "All right, Mr. Baccala. Let's see how you were able to identify Mrs. Henson. I believe you did this in a statement that you gave when you were interviewed by Agent Horton, is that correct?"

Baccala replied in the affirmative and Lally asked, "Did he show you a photograph of Mrs. Henson?"

"Yes. He had a picture of her and I identified her."

"Only one picture?"

"Yes."

Lally bore down. "Only one picture and you're sure, by seeing that one picture, you're sure it was Mrs. Henson who you saw in that car. Is that right?"

"Yes."

"But isn't it also correct, Mr. Baccala, that you have a history of trouble with your eyes? You've been wearing eyeglasses ever since you were a teenager, isn't that right?"

"Yes, I guess so," Baccala said. "But I can see fine with my glasses."

"And you're having trouble right now, aren't you?"

Prosecutor Milton Schwartz objected to the defense counsel's "browbeating" of his witness to which Judge Curler agreed, sustaining the objection.

Lally tried a different tack. Returning to the defense table, he picked up a sheaf of papers and approached the witness. He held out one of the sheets and offered it to the witness. "Mr. Baccala, this is a transcript of the Grand Jury proceeding that was held on January twenty-eighth 1954, during which you testified about your vision. Would you read the first paragraph aloud, please?"

But even after slipping on a pair of glasses, Baccala still had considerable difficulty making out the words typed on the sheet of paper. Obviously under a great deal of stress, he tried to explain. "These are the wrong glasses."

Lally offered to help. "Would you like me to read it for you?"

Again, Schwartz objected and again his objection was sustained but Lally was confident that he had made his point and so, after having been on the witness stand for more than twelve hours, Calvin Baccala was excused.

To counteract the possible damage that Baccala's admission of his less than perfect eyesight might inflict on their case, the state called to the stand Dr. Carl Ciapella, an eye care professional practicing in the city of Chico.

After first establishing the doctor's bona fides as an "expert" witness, Schwartz asked, "Doctor, you have recently had occasion to examine Mr. Baccala's eyesight, have you not?"

"Yes, that's correct."

"Alright, Doctor, now without getting too technical, could you tell us what you found?"

"Mr. Baccala tested out—with glasses—twenty-forty in both eyes."

"And can you tell us—again, without getting too technical—what, exactly does 'twenty-forty' mean?"

"It means that twenty feet is the standardized distance for these tests. That's the top number. A person with average vision would have a score of twenty on the bottom number—that would be your twenty-twenty."

"I see," Schwartz said. "And so twenty-forty would mean what, Doctor?"

"Twenty forty simply means that at the standard distance of twenty feet, Mr. Baccala's vision, with a score of forty on the bottom, would mean that his vision is twice as—as poor, I guess is one way to

257

say it—as a person with a score of twenty which would be average. Twenty-twenty versus twenty-forty."

"Alright then, Doctor Ciapella, based on that analysis, with a score of twenty-forty, in your professional opinion, was Mr. Bacalla's twenty-forty vision adequate for him to see—at a distance of twenty-five feet—the things he has described in his testimony here today?"

"Yes. In my professional opinion, yes it was."

The uneasy tension that had filled the courtroom and had started to build from the moment Judge Curler brought down his gavel had now climbed to an almost palpable level. And no one was feeling it more than Jack Santo.

Engrossed in the doctor's testimony and plainly troubled by the realization that his lawyer's "poor eyesight" strategy had just been rendered moot and most probably was not going to work, Santo had been paying little notice to events that were taking place outside his own narrow sphere of awareness. He was visibly shaken when at the far end of the table, a matron who had been guarding Harriet Henson suddenly dropped a large and very heavy ring of keys to the floor. The loud sudden noise created by the key ring crashing against the hard parquet floor startled Santo so much that he literally jumped out of his chair. When he realized what had actually happened, he looked sheepishly around the room and, relaxing his white-knuckle grip on the edge of the table, he quietly sat back down.

Christal Remembers

Each day at the trial's conclusion, Christal would return to her hotel room to mull over the day's events, trying to sort through the searing jumble of emotions generated by everything that had taken place that day: Dr. Greenman's graphic testimony and the continuing, almost overwhelming grief over the deaths of her husband and children; the knowledge that this bitter sense of loss would never leave her as long as she lived.

Yet, at the same time, she could exult in the satisfaction of knowing that those responsible for this monstrous act were about to face the consequences; consequences for which, over the past year, they have been able to avoid.

All in all it had been a terrible day. Those gruesome photographs, the doctor's descriptions of Guard's and the children's bodies were images that never seemed to go away. She thought about how they were once actual people—real, smiling, laughing, loving, happy people—but now reduced to grotesque images on small sheets of glossy paper.

In the courtroom, although it had been a constant struggle for Christal to contain that sorrow—to keep it bottled up lest people think she was playing for their pity—she had managed it with some success. But alone in the solitude of her hotel room, recalling and reliving those joyous family times in Chester, there would be no one here to witness her grief. She closed her eyes and prayed and she could hear the sounds of her children's laughter and Guard's strong, soothing voice. The sounds of how it was before it had all been so cruelly wrenched away. Tears rolled silently down her cheeks and she was thankful that there was no one there to see them.

It was going to be an emotional battle every day for as long as this trial lasts—of that she was certain. She would put up with the crude antics of Emmett Perkins, the intimidating stare-downs of Jack Santo and the sometimes icy cold aloofness of Harriet Henson. To be sure, it would be difficult, but for the sake of justice and for her family, she was determined to see it through.

"They tricked me; they got me drunk and they tricked me."

FOURTEEN

Prevaricators

Key to building the state's case would be the establishment of a time line placing the defendants at the crime scene at the time of the murders. In addition to Calvin Baccala's testimony, which, if believed by the jury, would go a long way toward accomplishing that goal, it was expected that the prosecution's case would be aided immeasurably by the direct testimony of Lucille Shea.

Under gentle prodding by prosecutor Milton Schwartz, Lucille began by tracking the hour by hour movements of houseguests Jack Santo and Harriet Henson on that fateful Friday. Guided by Schwartz's skillful prompting, she traced her and her husband's activities, as well as those of Santo and Harriet on that particular morning. She stated that her husband had departed the house for Westwood at around 8:45 a.m. heading for Westwood to transact some personal banking business and while there, to pick up a golf trophy. Shortly thereafter, she said, at around 9:30, Jack Santo, in the company of Emmett Perkins who had arrived at the house earlier that morning, left in Perkins' car.

"When Jack Santo, who was now, as you have testified, accompanied by Emmett Perkins, left the house at nine-thirty on the morning of October tenth, 1952, did you know where they were going?" Schwartz asked.

"No," she replied. "He didn't offer and I didn't ask. I figured it was none of my business."

"I see. Now at that point, Mrs. Shea, that would have left just you and Mrs. Henson in the house. Is that correct?"

"Yes," Lucille said, "that's correct."

"And did Mrs. Henson stay—let me ask it this way—Mrs. Henson had occasion to leave at some point, didn't she?"

"Yes."

"Can you tell us at about what time Mrs. Henson left the house?"

Lucille, taking a somewhat roundabout route, began to answer. "Well, Jack and Perk . . ."

Schwartz interrupted. "By Perk', you're referring to whom?"

"Emmett Perkins," she replied. "They got back about eleven o'clock and my husband had come back a few minutes before that. We sat around, had a few drinks and then Larry—excuse me—my husband went in to take a nap."

"Alright, Mrs. Shea, after Mr. Shea went in to take a nap, what happened then?"

"Well, we talked a while. Jack and Harriet had a few more drinks and then at sometime around two-thirty, maybe a little later, they all left."

Had the prosecutor at this point had the presence of mind to question Lucille Shea about the conversation that had taken place in that house on that day, i.e., the aborted plan to rob Frank Locatell, and in its place, the implementation of "Plan B," the entire nefarious scheme might have been exposed right then and there. Unfortunately, Schwartz chose instead to drive her testimony in another direction and in so doing, changed the defendants' glowering scowls into self-satisfied grins.

"Alright now, you say they all left at two-thirty. And can you tell us, Mrs. Shea, when was the next time you saw them?" Schwartz asked.

"Actually, I wasn't there when Jack came home," she explained. "I had gone into town to run some errands and it was after four-thirty when I called home. I remember looking at my watch and Larry told me that Jack had just gotten home a half hour ago. He told me they were anxious to get started on the Reno trip and would I please hurry up and get home."

Schwartz pressed her on the time-line issue. "So Larry informed you that Jack had come home around four, is that it?"

"It must have been around four when Jack got back," she said.

"All of them? Did they all come back around four?" Schwartz continued to probe.

"No," Lucille replied. "Larry told me that Jack was alone. I never saw Harriet or Perkins again."

"Alright, now let's be sure we have the rest of this right," Schwartz said. "Your husband, Mr. Shea, had gone in to take a nap; Jack Santo, Harriet Henson and Emmett Perkins left the house at two-thirty that afternoon and an hour and a half later Mr. Santo arrived back at the house—around four you say. He was alone, as you have testified, and you never saw either Harriet or Perkins again. Is that right, Mrs. Shea?"

Lucille answered, "Yes, that's right."

As a stoic Christal, eyes glued to the witness stand, continued to assimilate Lucille's account of the various events and activities that had taken place on that ill-fated day, she was struck by this woman, who up until now, had only been known to her as Mrs. Shea, a store customer and to all outward appearances, nothing more sinister than a typical Chester housewife. But with each answer to the prosecutor's questions, Lucille's innocuous "just another housewife" persona began to unravel like someone pulling at a loose thread on a wool sweater. Christal was seeing another side of this woman—a darker side—and it made her wonder about the three other women: Henson, Pearney, Graham—all now hopelessly enmeshed in their own webs of lies and degradation. It brought to mind the time-worn cliché: "There but for the grace of God go I"—trite, but in this case, she thought, apropos.

She studied the pathetic collection of bottom-feeders now sitting around the defendant's table and was struck by the way Santo and Perkins were reacting to the testimony of the state's witnesses—their body language swinging wildly from apathy and dispassion to dismay and confusion, yet still managing to maintain a carefully contrived façade of defiance and false bravado.

Questioned about the weekend Reno trip she and Larry had taken on the evening of the murders in the company of Jack Santo and his girlfriend Bernadine Pearney, Mrs. Shea related that the purpose of the trip was simply to attend a golf tournament, explaining that it was something her husband, an avid golfer, had been planning for several weeks prior.

"Where did you stay while you were in Reno?" the prosecutor asked.

"I don't remember the name of the hotel. It was downtown; I think it was the 'Frontier' or something like that."

"Alright. Do you remember how many nights you stayed at that hotel and how the bill was settled?" Schwartz persisted.

"We were there one night—Friday only. Jack and Bernadine had the room across the hall from us and I think he paid the bill."

Schwartz dug a little deeper. "Mr. Santo and Mrs. Pearney occupied the room directly across the hall from your room, is that right?"

"Yes."

"Together? In the same room?" His mock incredulity was designed to get a reaction from Harriet, but all Harriet could do as she listened to Lucille's answer was to glare at Schwartz, who seemed to be enjoying her discomfort. "And Jack Santo paid the entire hotel bill—your bill. Is that right?"

"Yes," Lucille said, trying her utmost to avoid Harriet's withering stare.

She went on to detail the fancy restaurants, the posh nightclubs, the gambling and the lavish entertainment—all at the expense of the suddenly affluent Jack Santo.

Having wrung as much damaging information from the witness as he thought possible, at lease for the moment, Schwartz deferred to the defense's cross during which, despite Lally's vigorous questioning, Lucille managed to remain unshaken and unscathed.

"Mrs. Shea," Lally asked, "do you recall a statement you made to Sheriff Melvin Schooler on December fifteenth in which you said, 'On October tenth, 1952, Harriet did not leave the house; she was there all day.' Do you remember making that statement?"

"Yes."

"Were you lying when you made that statement? Mrs. Shea," Lally asked, "Or are you lying today?"

"I lied when I said that because I was just trying to protect a friend," Lucille said, unflustered. "I didn't realize the implications at the time."

Throughout her cross-examination, Lucille, while deftly parrying Lally's questions, affected an air of poised, steely confidence. For his part, Lally chose a scatter-gun approach as he picked away, probing for holes in her testimony, but at times, becoming obviously frustrated by her elusiveness.

Through his persistence however, Henson's attorney was still able to score a couple of minor points. Lally never missed a chance to call attention to the "slave-master" relationship that had existed between his client and Jack Santo. Lucille's testimony presented just such an opportunity. She testified that on Thursday, the day before the murders, Harriet had expressed a desire to leave Chester and return to her home in Auburn.

"And how did Mr. Santo respond to that?" Lally asked.

"He told her to 'quit yakking and go fix a couple of drinks.'"

Lally continued to press, this time with reference to the testimony of Calvin Baccala who had earlier described the hairstyle of the woman he said was in the back seat of the murder car—the woman he had identified as Harriet Henson.

Harriet's defense received a boost when Lucille reconstructed the activities of the two women on the day of the murders. Almost as an afterthought, Lucille testified that before leaving the house, Harriet had "put up her hair."

"How did Mrs. Henson put up her hair?" Lally asked.

"I've never been one to notice too well what people wear or how they fix their hair," she said before adding, "she borrowed a scarf—a bandana—and she tied it around her hair." It was just a throwaway remark but it tended to undermine the testimony of Calvin Baccala, one of the state's star witnesses, who had testified that the woman he saw in the back seat had "long dark stringy hair," while adding—not insignificantly—"she was wearing a hat."

Under Morris Durrant's questioning, Lucille conceded that she and Larry had not gotten married until a month after the murders had occurred. "Was this an attempt to avoid having to testify against each other?" Durrant wanted to know.

"Certainly not," Lucille protested. "We had been living together as man and wife ever since we came here from Iowa and we just figured it was about time we made it legal."

Lucille was questioned by Durrant about her husband's business dealings with Jack Santo.

"Jack sold Larry guns from time to time and once he bought some wedding rings from Jack," she explained matter-of-factly.

Hoping he could trap her into admitting that they had once trafficked in stolen cars, he asked, "Are you and your husband still the owners of a gray 1950 Oldsmobile?"

Before she could answer, he added, "That would be the car that your husband purchased from Mr. Santo and, by the way, is that car still in your possession?"

Like brushing away a fly, Lucille answered, "No sir, we disposed of it at the end of November in 1952."

Durrant shot back: "So you sold it after owning it for only a few months? Why would you do that? Was it because you could feel the law breathing down your neck?"

"We didn't sell it, Mr. Durrant," she said. "We delivered it back to Jack Santo. He had promised to get us ownership papers and they never arrived so Larry began to get worried."

Durrant quickly changed the subject. "Were you or your husband in the habit of lending money to Jack Santo during those occasions when he found himself short of funds?" he asked.

"They would lend each other money," Lucille said. "If one of them happened to be broke, it wasn't unusual for them to help each other out."

"But it was more usual for Jack Santo to be the one who was 'short of funds,' isn't that right?" Durrant persisted.

"I guess so," Lucille said.

"Are you aware of any recent loans your husband may have made to Mr. Santo? Was there any amount that might account for Mr. Santo's sudden display of wealth?"

"No," she said. "Jack hadn't borrowed any money from us."

Overall, Lucille Shea emerged from the defense counsel's scathing cross-examination relatively undamaged. Passing the defense table as she strode down the aisle to exit the courtroom, she nodded defiantly at the three defendants—even forcing a weak smirk of acknowledgment from Harriet.

Larry Shea

Of the forty witnesses the state would ultimately send to the stand, none was more devastating to the defense's case—particularly that of Emmett Perkins—than the testimony of Lucille's husband, Lawrence *Larry* Shea.

Shea's description of the events surrounding his bank errand on the morning of October 10 had the effect, among other things, of putting the lie to Emmett Perkins' alibi in which he claimed not to have been in Chester or Westwood on that day. On the stand, Shea stated that around nine o'clock that morning he had driven into Westwood to complete a personal banking transaction and to pick up his golf trophy which he had left at the jeweler's to be engraved. He had arrived in Westwood before the bank opened and decided to wait.

After running into an old friend who also was waiting, and while the two were engaged in casual conversation, Shea said Jack Santo and Emmett Perkins drove up and parked in front of the bank.

"Now after Jack Santo and Emmett Perkins parked their car, did you observe what they did at that point?" Prosecutor Schwartz asked.

"Well, about that time, some other people were gathered around outside the bank and Jack came over to me and he wanted to know about one of them," Shea answered.

"And what did he want to know?"

"He asked me if that was the guy who owned the Red and White Market in Chester."

"And what did you say?" Schwartz asked.

"I said 'yes, that's him. That's Frank Locatell.'"

"Very well, Mr. Shea, can you tell us what you observed—with respect to Mr. Santo and Mr. Perkins—can you tell us what happened then?"

"I went into the bank and deposited my checks and when I came out, Jack and Perk were gone."

"I see," Schwartz said. "They were gone, and so what did you do at that point?"

"I drove home. When I got there, Jack and Emmett were sitting in my driveway in the same car I saw them in at the bank. They were just sitting there talking."

"Did you join them, Mr. Shea? Did you go over to their car and enter into the conversation?"

"No," Shea said. "I just went into the house and they came in about fifteen minutes later."

"Mr. Shea, would you please tell the court exactly what Mr. Santo said to you after you had both gone back into the house." Schwartz, of course, knew exactly what was coming.

Averting his eyes from the dagger-like stares that were coming from the defense table, Shea cleared his throat before answering.

"Jack said, 'Damn, that Locatell guy drives like a maniac.'"

"He said, 'damn, that Locatell guy drives like a maniac?'" Schwartz repeated.

"Yes, I told him. 'I don't see what you're yelping about. I don't think I ever rode with you when you were driving under ninety.'"

"Alright," Schwartz asked, "what else did he say?"

"And he says, 'Just the same, if we had caught him, we'd have really been in the chips.'"

Schwartz jumped on Shea's answer. "Why would he say 'we'd be in the chips' if he could have caught Frank Locatell? Did you know what he meant by that statement?"

"I sure did," Shea said.

Schwartz would leave the partially answered question to dangle in the air, planning to use it to greater effect during his closing arguments.

"Now at that point, Mr. Shea, did Mr. Santo have anything else to say? Was there further conversation about what he intended to do since his attempt to overtake Mr. Locatell had been thwarted?"

Although not noticeable to Schwartz, Shea was beginning to sweat. This was the question he'd been dreading. How much did they know, Shea wondered; how much could he tell them? After the Locatell plot had fallen through, if his participation in *Plan B*—the plot to rob Guard Young—were to be exposed now, what would happen to their chances of a deal with the D.A.? The last thing in the world Shea wanted was to be one of those poor suckers who were, at this moment, sitting at the defendant's table, only steps away from the gas chamber and glaring at him with murder in their eyes.

"No," he said. "That was about it. We just drank for a little while and then I took a nap."

"And so you went off to take a nap while leaving Mr. Santo in the living room with Mr. Perkins, Mrs. Henson and Mrs. Shea, and they were just talking?"

"Yes. I don't know what they were talking about. I just could hear them talking until I dropped off to sleep," he said, wishing the prosecutor would now change direction. He breathed a quiet sigh of relief as, obligingly, Schwartz did exactly that.

"I'd like to turn your attention now, Mr. Shea, to a three hour meeting which took place between you and Bernadine Pearney on July twenty-fifth, 1953, at the Wagon Wheel Motel which is located, I believe, in Truckee, California. Do you recall taking part in such a meeting?" Schwartz asked.

"Yes, I do," Shea answered. "That's when they bugged the room."

"In fact, you now know that a wire recording of the conversation between you and Mrs. Pearney was made during that meeting?"

As noted earlier, this questioning referred to the incident in which Plumas County authorities arranged to have Bernadine Pearney lure Larry Shea to a motel room tryst during which she would ply him with liquor in hopes that in his intoxicated state, he would admit to his involvement in the Guard Young murders. The whole thing had been secretly recorded and the resulting one hundred and sixty-five page transcript of their conversations would ultimately show that the scheme was only partially successful.

"They showed me the transcript and I was shocked," Shea said. "They tricked me. They got me drunk and tricked me."

Schwartz's motion that the entire transcript be entered into evidence drew angry objections from defense counsel. After a short sidebar conference, the objections were overruled.

Reading aloud from the transcript, Shea could be heard giving Bernadine a blow-by-blow account of what had happened on the morning of October 10, 1952, while he waited for the bank to open.

"Now Mr. Shea, when you told Mrs. Pearney you had run into Jack Santo and Emmett Perkins in front of the bank, were you telling her the truth?"

"Yes," Shea said, "but she tricked me," he added, glancing nervously at the defense table.

"Do you now stand by that statement, Mr. Shea? Are you now testifying that you are absolutely certain that it was Emmett Perkins whom you saw on that morning of October tenth?"

Shea answered in the affirmative and Schwartz mentally checked off another score. One more piece of the mosaic that he would use in his summation. Perkins' claim that he had never been in Chester or Westwood so he could not have possibly committed these crimes, had again been thoroughly dismantled, first by Dorothy Elliott, then by Lucille Shea and finally confirmed by Larry Shea.

For what seemed like several minutes, Schwartz continued to flip through the pages of the transcript until he finally came to the page he was searching for.

"Alright now, Mr. Shea," he said. "Let's see what you had to say about the evening of October tenth, 1952." His eyes scanned the page from top to bottom. "It seems you devoted a considerable amount of your time with Mrs. Pearney talking about your weekend party in Reno."

Shea objected mildly to the word *party*. "I wouldn't call it a party," he said.

"You wouldn't call it a party? What would you call it?"

"Lucille and me, we went to a golf tournament. That's the reason we were in Reno."

"Alright then, you and Mrs. Shea drove to Reno to attend a golf tournament on the evening of October tenth, 1952, the day of the Young family murders, correct?"

"Yes, that's correct."

"Did Jack Santo come with you?"

"Yes."

"Did he come alone?"

"Well, he was alone on the drive down, but after we got there he hooked up with Bernadine at the Reno bus depot. But, yeah, he was alone on the drive down."

Schwartz went on to draw further defense-damaging admissions from Shea that tended to corroborate Lucille's testimony. In addition to the golf tournament, their Reno weekend consisted of dining, drinking, gambling and "big room-big name" casino entertainment at Harrah's as well as at Harold's Club. The entire weekend, he said, had been financed by Jack Santo.

"Was Mr. Santo in the habit of lavishing this kind of largesse on his friends—even those as close as you and Mrs. Shea?" Schwartz asked.

"No," Shea said. "I don't think so."

For Larry and Lucille Shea, although not active participants in the murders of Guard Young and the three children, certainly by any legal definition, would have been considered "accessories"—both before and after the fact—to four counts of murder. The fact that they had managed to avoid charges for their involvement in the crime had begun to raise serious misgivings in the Santo camp.

The three defendants could now only sit and watch as Shea began his contorted attempt to wiggle off the hook, leading Santo to consider the possibility of a sell-out by the Sheas in exchange for their cooperation with the D.A. They knew just about everything—Santo himself had seen to that. To Santo, it appeared that the Sheas were trying to have it both ways. Jack recalled Perk's warning that Larry would be trouble. Should've listened to him, Jack thought. Should've taken care of both of them when we had the chance.

Larry pondered the question. Of course the Sheas knew full well where Jack's money had come from. He could have easily dispelled all the speculation by simply admitting the awful truth that Jack Santo had shared with them on the drive to Reno. But in so doing, he realized, they would be jeopardizing their own chances for survival. The Sheas had to walk that fine line between cooperation by providing the testimony Schwartz would need to obtain convictions, yet at the same time, being careful to avoid saying anything that would incriminate himself and Lucille. It was a delicate balancing act but they seemed to be pulling it off.

Perkins' attorney, Winslow Christian, would now have to mitigate the damage that had been inflicted on his client by prosecution witnesses who had testified to seeing Perkins in Chester and Westwood, not only on the day of the murders but, according to Dorothy Elliott, "many times" prior.

"Let's go back to your testimony regarding the morning of October tenth, 1952," Christian began. "You have identified unequivocally Mr. Perkins as the man you saw in front of the bank that morning and then again, later on, sitting in a car parked in your driveway. Was that your testimony?"

"Yes," Shea answered.

"Now let me ask you, Mr. Shea, are you acquainted with a newspaper reporter by the name of John Keyes?"

"Yes."

"How do you know John Keyes?"

"He's a reporter for the Call-Bulletin in San Francisco. I've had a couple of interviews with him," Shea explained.

"Yes, that's right," Christian said, referring to his notes, "And in one of these interviews—I believe you were telling him about the interview you had just had with investigators from the California Department of Justice—do you recall telling Mr. Keyes, and I'll quote: 'If they want Perkins in Westwood, I'll put him in Westwood.' Do you recall saying that?"

"No," Shea snapped back. "I never said that."

Christian didn't let up. "Are you acquainted with a William Gambell, Mr. Shea?"

"Yes. He's another reporter. For the Sacramento Bee, I think."

"That's correct, Mr. Shea. And in your interview with William Gambell, I believe you stated—again let me quote: 'I'm the guy who fingered them. They asked me and I gave it to them.' Do you remember saying that?"

Shea stammered his response. "Yeah, but I meant 'unwittingly'. I unwittingly fingered them."

Christian continued to hammer on Shea's credibility, or more accurately, his apparent lack thereof.

"Now, Mr. Shea," he said, "you have testified that on the evening of October tenth, 1952, you had occasion to visit Reno, Nevada in order to attend a golf tournament."

"Yes."

"And you have also testified that on that trip you were accompanied by Mr. Santo. Isn't that correct?"

"Yes."

"Do you recall that in a statement given to Sheriff Schooler on December fifteenth, 1952—that would be during the same interview that was referred to in Mrs. Shea's testimony—do you recall telling Sheriff Schooler that on the evening of October tenth, 1952, you drove to Reno with Mrs. Shea, in order to attend a golf tournament? Do you recall that, Mr. Shea?"

Shea's answer was a terse "Yes."

"And do you recall that at that time you told Sheriff Schooler that you and Mrs. Shea had made that trip alone—that you had not been accompanied by Jack Santo?"

"Yes, that's right, but I had a reason."

"Yes," Christian interrupted. "I'm sure you did." He glared at the witness.

"So I'll ask you the same question that Mrs. Shea was asked. You admit that you lied to Sheriff Schooler. So, we've established the fact that on occasion—when it suits you—you lie. You are, in fact, a liar. Can we all agree to that?"

Schwartz jumped from his chair. "Object, your honor. We object to that!"

"Overruled."

Christian continued, "Why should we believe that you aren't lying now?"

"I told you," Shea shot back, "I had a reason to tell them that. I was trying to protect Jack from getting in trouble with Harriet. It's just something I used to do a lot. He was always putting me in that kind of a jam with all his women." Shea's remark elicited a laser-like glare from Harriet directed at Jack whose only response was a lame, sheepish grin.

Christian would not let up. "It does appear, Mr. Shea, that you and Mrs. Shea have a very difficult time of it when it comes to telling the truth."

Shea squirmed uncomfortably as Christian concluded his cross. "What other lies have you told to us today? Mr. Shea? Is your name really Lawrence Shea?"

Schwartz leaped to his feet again to object but before Judge Curler could rule, Christian had started back to his table. "I'm sorry, your honor," he said. "I'll withdraw that question."

Larry Shea stepped down from the witness stand, smug in the knowledge that, despite their culpability in the commission of this most heinous of crimes, it now appeared that they would avoid being prosecuted for it.

Christal, from her front row seat, eyed him with utter revulsion as their eyes made contact. In her mind, there was not the slightest doubt of Shea's involvement in the murders of her family and the fact that he was in this courtroom as a witness and not as a defendant was almost more than she could bear.

As her stress levels continued to build and with the agonizingly slow pace of the trial as it lurched from witness to witness, it was becoming increasingly difficult for Christal to listen to the lies and distortions of the defense lawyers while watching the crude antics of Santo and Perkins, both sitting so near she could almost reach out and touch them.

Adding to her torment, Christal would return to her hotel room each evening, the day's events fresh in her mind but yearning for the company and comfort of the family she had left in Utah. It would only be a matter of days before she made the decision to send for her children and when they arrived in Chester, she moved the family into the apartment that had been formerly occupied by Rosemary Saile and her son Michael. It would be their home for the duration of the trial.

On trial days, Vance Young would provide Christal with the use of his car which allowed her to make the forty mile commute to and from the courthouse in Quincy at her convenience.

Meanwhile in San Francisco, Mary Young, Guard's mother, had been following the first days of the trial in a state of unsettled anguish mixed with feelings of helplessness. She tried to imagine the emotional turmoil that Christal must be experiencing and it wouldn't be long before she would decide that Chester was where she needed to be if she was going to help her son's widow cope with what had to be the most difficult time of her life.

Placing a long distance call to her son Vance who had moved into Guard's and Christal's former Chester apartment in order to better manage the supermarket, she informed him of her intention to catch the next bus to Chester and asked him to meet her at the bus depot.

She packed two suitcases and very early the next morning, Mary boarded a Greyhound bus for the four hour ride to Chester where, on her arrival, she was warmly greeted by her grandchildren and a smiling daughter-in-law—especially after informing Christal and Vance that she would be more than happy to assist with the day-to-day operation of the supermarket as well as help with the children's care during Christal's absence.

Bernadine Pearney

To the muted wolf-whistles and snickers of approval emanating from a small clique of male spectators, the blond, tall and strikingly attractive Bernadine Pearney mounted the two steps to the witness stand. To their disappointment, the former Jack Santo girlfriend's tenure on the stand, though telling, would be brief.

Corroborating testimony from previous witnesses as to the events of the Reno weekend spending spree, she related how she, along with Lucille and Larry Shea, had been wined and dined by Jack Santo and how he lavished on her a new wardrobe including shoes, boots, dresses and a fur trimmed coat. She testified that throughout the entire weekend, Jack had picked up every tab while leaving unusually large tips, paying for everything—even the clothes, to the astonishment of the sales clerks—with crisp, new twenty dollar bills.

"It was more money than I had ever seen him with," she told the prosecutor. "He had money in his shirt pockets, coat pockets, pants pockets—he had money everywhere."

Prosecutor Schwartz asked, "Now Mrs. Pearney, going back to the period just prior to that weekend in Reno, when, as you say, Mr. Santo had 'more money, than you had ever seen him with,' had there been a recent incident in which you loaned money to Mr. Santo?"

"Yes," Bernadine said.

"Would you describe that incident?"

"I was in Auburn about a week before the Reno thing," she said. "Jack told me he was broke and asked me if I could lend him some money. So I did."

"How much did you lend him?"

"Fifteen dollars I think it was."

"I see," Schwartz said. "And then a week later, he had more money than you had ever seen him with. Is that right?"

"Yes, I guess so."

Schwartz questioned Pearney about Santo's reaction on the night he first saw the early edition newspaper headlines reporting the Chester murders.

"It was Lucille who saw the papers first," Pearney said. "She didn't say anything. When I saw them I said, 'Oh, look, it's Chester, Jack.'"

"And what did Mr. Santo do or say at that point?" Schwartz asked.

"He grabbed my arm and he said, 'Come on, let's get out of here.'"

Schwartz followed up. "Didn't that make you suspicious, Mrs. Pearney? I mean, here he is with all this new-found wealth and now you see there has been, not only four murders, but a robbery as well; all in Chester. Weren't you even just a little bit suspicious?"

"Well, it did make me wonder a bit. I asked him where he had gotten all the money and he told me he had done a robbery in Redding, so I—you know—just let it pass."

She described the July meeting with Larry Shea at the motel in Truckee, how she wired herself with a hidden recorder and after pouring a quart of whiskey into him to loosen his tongue, how she wire-recorded their three hour conversation during which he incriminated not only himself, but the other defendants as well.

"Can you tell us how it came about that you and Mr. Shea would have this meeting?" Schwartz asked. "Were the two of you romantically involved in any way?"

"No, romance had nothing to do with it," she said as she glanced nervously over at Santo. "Sheriff Schooler wanted me to do it—him and the state's CII. They're the ones who set the whole thing up. I was supposed to meet with Larry to help figure out a good alibi for Jack."

"An alibi?" Schwartz asked. "An alibi for what?"

"For the Chester thing. Sheriff Schooler figured that Larry would be willing to help out his friend Jack, because he knew Jack was worried about being fingered for the Chester murders. Schooler thought that if Larry got drunk enough, he might say something."

When Morris Durrant, Santo's attorney, took over the questioning of Bernadine Pearney, he immediately seemed to shoot himself in the foot.

Apparently forgetting the old lawyer's cliché that a lawyer should never ask a witness a question to which he doesn't already know the answer, Durrant's first question elicited an answer from Bernadine that he neither expected nor wanted.

Probing into Santo's peculiar reaction on seeing news of the murders splashed across the early edition headlines, he asked, "Since, as you say, you were somewhat suspicious, why didn't you go to the police?"

"I was afraid to," she answered.

"You were afraid?" Durrant asked mockingly. "What on earth were you afraid of?"

"There was another time," she said, "when Jack and I were arguing about something and I threatened to go to the police. He told me that if I did, he might not be here but there are other people who would take care of me."

Durrant, taken aback by Pearney's unwelcome remark, might have been well-advised at that point to let the matter rest. With his help, she had managed to poke another small hole in Santo's defense. Still, he reasoned, it was a hole he'd be able to climb out of during his closing argument. Thus, instead of just moving on, Durrant chose to keep digging.

"What do you suppose he meant by that? 'Take care of you?' How would he take care of you?"

Casting another quick glance at the smoldering Santo, Bernadine said, "Well, it was pretty clear to me. I had heard him say this before, to other people, never to me. It was a threat."

Durrant, now realizing where this line of questioning was leading, finally decided to switch topics.

"At the time you met and recorded your conversation with Mr. Shea at the motel in Truckee, were you acting at the time as an employee—that is, an agent employed by the state of California?"

"An agent? Me, an agent?" Bernadine said, obviously flattered.

"Yes," Durrant said. "Did you receive payment from the state?"

"Well, I guess you could say that. They paid me for renting the room and they paid me the same amount I would have got if I had worked on my job. Is that an agent?"

"I have nothing further for this witness," Durrant said as he returned to the defense table, his voice tinged with just a hint of frustration.

Other Witnesses

The procession of witnesses called by the prosecution included what many observers would consider—if not irrelevant—certainly minor, but prosecutors were convinced, these lesser-light witnesses were absolutely essential to the successful prosecution of their case.

State's witness Wayne Brown, Sheriff of Nevada County would attest to the integrity of the procedure involved in the wiring of Harriet Henson's jail cell, as would the testimony of Assistant State Attorney General, Thomas Martin.

Modesto truck salesman, Jack Furneaux, an acquaintance of Harriet Henson, testified that he had been approached by Henson who offered him a $1,500 bribe to provide her with an alibi for Jack Santo.

Of course, not all of these peripheral "small-bore" witnesses would produce the desired effect for the state. Things did not go as well as they had hoped when, during William Lally's cross-examination, State Criminologist, Everett Chamberlain, was questioned about a bloody handprint that had been discovered on the fender of Guard Young's sedan.

"And were you able to identify that print with any person connected to this case?" Harriet's attorney asked.

Chamberlain's response, to the dismay of those at the prosecutor's table, was an unequivocal, "No, I was not."

The trial was entering its fourteenth day when Harry Cooper was called to the witness stand. The announcement seemed to cause a visible stir around the defense table; in particular, it seemed to rattle Jack Santo. If Santo was concerned that Henry Cooper's testimony might somehow be the nail that could seal the lid on the prosecution's case, he didn't know the half of it.

Schwartz began, "Would you state your name and occupation, please?"

"Harry Cooper, special agent, employed by the State of California, Department of Justice, Bureau of Criminal Identification and Investigation."

He spoke with the self-assurance and the authority of a man who was no stranger to a courtroom proceeding.

"Bureau of Criminal Identification and Investigation?" Schwartz asked. "Would that be more commonly known as the 'CII'?"

"Yes, that is correct."

Harry Cooper identified himself as the agent who, with the help of Nevada County Sheriff Wayne Brown, and with the full knowledge and acquiescence of Harriet Henson, had installed a wire recorder in Henson's Nevada County Jail cell, the purpose of which was to clandestinely record conversations between Henson and her one-time lover, Jack Santo; conversations which they hoped would link Santo to the Chester murders.

Santo and Perkins had been transferred from their death row cells at San Quentin to the County Jail in Nevada City where they were scheduled to stand trial for their role in the Edmund Hansen murder.

Jack had been placed in a cell as far from Harriet's cell as was possible and because they'd now be cut off from all contact with each other, it was hoped that Jack's need for a sounding board—someone in whom he could confide—would continue to grow and fester.

Authorities had long been aware of Jack Santo's anti-social— almost paranoiac—temperament. Separating him from Harriet was a deliberate attempt by Brown and Cooper to exploit what they assumed was his growing sense of distrust of his former lover. Not surprisingly, the plan worked almost to perfection.

In return for what she understood was an explicit promise of immunity against prosecution in the Chester murder case by Agent Cooper, Harriet had allowed Sheriff Brown to wire her cell, after which, under the pretense of Brown's making a "humanitarian gesture," Jack was permitted to visit Harriet in her cell while the hidden wire recorder continued to run.

"Now Mr. Cooper," Schwartz began, "I'm going to have portions of that recording played here and, as I'm sure you'll agree, some of it is a bit garbled and hard to understand so I'd like to ask you to help us with those parts."

"Certainly."

Having been re-recorded from the original wire recording onto magnetic tape, the conversations now crackled to life. A male voice, which Cooper identified as being that of Jack Santo's, could be heard over the background noise and static:

"Dammit, Harriet. Why did you have to tell them that you left Chester with Perk? Why couldn't you have said you took a bus or something?"

Harriet had responded, "I didn't think it would be such a big deal. How should I know that Perk wasn't supposed to be in Chester?"

Fast forwarding the tape, Schwartz stopped at a later exchange with Harriet speaking: ". . . that Perkins is an animal. Why did you let him—I mean, why . . ." Jack had cut her off with "Harriet, you know me better than that. If I had known those children were along, I wouldn't have done it."

Jack Santo sat at rapt attention absorbing every incriminating word, his eyes darting first from the recording device to the witness stand and then to Harriet, hearing his own self-convicting words being played back for all to hear.

Christal listened to Santo all but admit to his involvement in the murders of her family. As she watched him stare at the playback of the tape while displaying not the slightest trace of shame or remorse, she was filled with a revulsion that came close to making her physically ill. Had there been any doubt or uncertainty in her mind before this moment—and there may have been—it had been completely dispelled by this tape.

Schwartz shut off the recorder and turned back to his witness. "Mr. Cooper, could you help us to understand what, exactly Mr. Santo was referring to when he said to Mrs. Henson 'I wouldn't have done it'?"

"We took that to be an admission of guilt," Cooper said, prompting an immediate objection from defense attorney Morris Durrant. After a lengthy discussion in Judge Curler's chambers, Durrant was overruled on technical grounds.

On cross-examination, none of the three defense attorneys was able to controvert any portion of Agent Cooper's testimony and after parrying a few innocuous questions, he was excused.

Judge Curler peered over his bifocals as he addressed the prosecutor's table. "Call your next witness, Mr. Schwartz."

Milton Schwartz rose and said, "Your honor, at this point the state will rest."

FIFTEEN

Pendulum

As attorneys for the three defendants huddled with their clients in last minute preparations for the presentation of their case, at the defense table, a loud argument broke out between Jack Santo and his attorney Morris Durrant. Their disagreement had become so heated that Judge Curler was forced to call both attorney and client into chambers. After a lengthy *in camera* hearing during which it had become clear to Judge Curler that the rancor that existed between Morris Durrant and his client had grown so bitter, not only did it threaten to disrupt the proceedings, he feared that any escalation might very well lead to a mistrial. Reluctantly, Judge Curler granted Durrant's petition to withdraw from the case. He called a five-day recess during which time a replacement would be appointed.

For Christal, it was a welcome break from the emotionally grueling first two weeks of the trial but she also knew that those five days would come and go like a gust of wind and suddenly the recess would be over and it would be time to resume the daily Chester to Quincy commute.

While enjoying the brief recess, Christal had been preparing herself for her return to the courtroom and the presentation of the defense's case in what promised to be a litany of wild accusations, claims, counter-claims and specious arguments by the defendants' lawyers—all borne of desperation and which were, for the most part, patently preposterous.

But even in the darkest recesses of her worst nightmares, never could she have imagined what one of those defense lawyers had in store.

With the loan of brother-in-law Vance's car, Christal drove the eighty mile round-trip to and from the Quincy courthouse and on frequent occasions she would be joined by store cashier, Dottie Elliott. Today, after having already testified as a prosecution witness, Dottie wanted to be in the gallery as one of the spectators when the attorneys opened their defense,

When the trial resumed on Monday, April 19, courtroom spectators and jury members alike were surprised to learn that Morris Durrant, Jack Santo's attorney had been replaced at the defendant's table by Sacramento lawyer, Theodore Elges, who had then been granted the five-day recess in order to give him time to study the case and to bring himself up to speed.

As defense attorneys now prepared to begin their presentation, they would start by introducing a string of witnesses who, though intended to bolster arguments that would establish their clients' innocence, in the final analysis, did little to achieve that objective and in some perverse way, may have actually accomplished the very opposite.

A motion asking for a directed verdict of acquittal on behalf of his client was introduced by Winslow Christian claiming that the state had failed to offer any evidence whatsoever that would connect his client, Emmett Perkins, to the murders. Judge Curler quickly denied the motion and with that, Christian rose to open his client's defense.

From the outset it had become clear that the main thrust of the defense's strategy would be the impeachment of Larry Shea's testimony. They intended to impugn—or at least call into question—his account of their clients' activities around the time of the murders by characterizing his entire testimony as self-serving and motivated by the prosecution's promises of leniency with regard to other unrelated criminal charges.

To that end as his first witness, Christian called bank manager John Woods to the stand.

Christian had subpoenaed the Sheas' bank records and now as he showed them to Woods, he asked, "Mr. Woods, do you recognize these documents as the statements issued by your bank for the months of August, September, October, November and December of 1952 and January, 1953 and belonging to the joint checking account of Mr. and Mrs. Lawrence Shea?"

Woods glanced perfunctorily at the papers. "Yes," he agreed.

"Now, do you notice, Mr. Woods, that during the months of August and September, 1952 and the month of January, 1953, on the first day of each of those months, there is a cancelled check in the amount of $175.00 reflecting a payment to Sierra Mortgage Company, which, I think we can safely assume, represents a monthly mortgage payment?"

When Woods concurred with Christian's characterization, he was asked, "But if you will also notice, Mr. Woods, there are no such payments for the months of October, November and December. What does that suggest to you?"

It was a calculated question by Christian, knowing that it would almost certainly draw an objection from Schwartz, but it was one he wanted the jury to hear and consider.

As expected, Judge Curler immediately sustained Schwartz's objection to Christian's "asking for a conclusion" but unconcerned with Curler's ruling now that he'd gotten the desired result, Christian continued to bore in.

"In fact, there was no debit activity in Mr. Shea's account, of any kind, in any of those months; isn't that right Mr. Woods? No mortgage payments, no utilities payments, no phone bill payments. No checks to any account, for any amount?"

"Yes, that's right."

Since the prosecution had already rested its case, there would be no opportunity for Schwartz to call Shea back to the witness stand in order to rebut or explain the apparent anomalies in his checking account. This, of course, would allow Christian, in his closing arguments, to offer to the jury whatever explanation he deemed would be helpful to the defense.

John Keyes, newspaper reporter for the San Francisco Call-Bulletin, was questioned about his relationship with Larry Shea and in particular, about an interview he had conducted with Shea soon after Shea had been interrogated by agents of the California Bureau of Criminal Identification and Investigation.

"Mr. Keyes, in your interview with Lawrence Shea, did he say anything to you about the state agents—or any other law enforcement officer, for that matter—did he say anything about their employing 'coercive' tactics in that interrogation?"

"Well, yes, he said that they told him that if he didn't cooperate, they'd arrest him for having venison in his deep freeze. He said they told him that they'd nail him every time he turned around."

"Who told him that?" Christian asked.

"The CII agents. He didn't mention any names—just the CII agents."

Keyes' answers drew an immediate objection as "hearsay" from the Prosecutor's table but the objection was overruled and Christian was allowed to continue.

"Now Mr. Keyes, in your interview with Mr. Shea, as he described to you his interrogation by CII agents, did he tell you that they asked him about Emmett Perkins?"

Again an objection from the prosecution and again it was overruled.

"Yes, he said they asked him about Perkins and he told them 'I do not know Mr. Perkins. I have never met Mr. Perkins.' He said 'they brought me a picture and showed it to me.'"

Christian prompted, "And did he say anything else about Emmett Perkins, Mr. Keyes?"

"He said he told them, 'What do you fellows want from me? If you want Perkins in Westwood, I will put him there.'"

After a few more questions—all harmless—the witness was turned over to the prosecution.

Prosecutor Milton Schwartz rose to cross-examine and in an obvious attempt to undermine the reporter's credibility, he attacked:

"Mr. Keyes, shortly after the interrogation of Mr. Shea, isn't it true that you advised Mr. Shea that in order to avoid any more tough questioning by the CII, he might want to get out of town for a while?"

"No, I don't remember saying anything like that," Keyes replied.

"Well, isn't it true that you then took Mr. and Mrs. Shea on a week-long trip to Reno?" Schwartz persisted. "What was the purpose of that trip, Mr. Keyes, if not to avoid more questioning?"

"I just wanted to get them sequestered so other newspapers wouldn't be able to find them," Keyes explained.

"Do you recall how much you had to drink on that trip?"

Keyes, obviously flustered by the question, asked, "How much did I have to drink?"

"Yes, Mr. Keyes. How much alcohol did you consume on that trip?"

Keyes tried to recall. "Well, we bought a fifth in Chester before we left and we drank that. I think we bought another fifth in Susanville."

"And then of course," Schwartz added, "you had several more in Reno, wouldn't you say?"

"I guess so," Keyes said.

"And how much have you had to drink before you took the stand this morning?" Schwartz's question elicited a violent objection from Elges which was immediately sustained by Judge Curler.

Schwartz, satisfied that he'd squeezed as much defense-damaging information as was possible from the witness, turned and headed back to the prosecutor's table. With an almost imperceptible grin, he addressed the bench.

"I have nothing further for this witness, your honor."

Keyes stepped down from the witness stand at which point, court was adjourned for the day.

The evening rush hour traffic on the return drive to Chester was unusually light and Christal, anxious to get home where she'd be able to kick off her shoes, relax and hug the kids, increased her speed.

Dottie began to think out loud. "They're a part of it," she proclaimed with no lack of certitude. "You can't tell me that they could all have been staying in the same house that entire weekend and the Sheas had no idea what was going on."

Christal had also been thinking about the Sheas and the part they may have played on that Friday night leading up to the murders, but even so, she wasn't ready to pronounce them guilty. Not yet anyway.

"You know, Christal," Dottie said, "I remember Lucille Shea. I never knew what her name was, but I know she has been in the store. I'm almost positive . . ." her voice trailed off as she suddenly realized just how recently it had been.

"In fact," she exclaimed, "I remember now. She came in that very afternoon," she said with an almost triumphant note in her voice.

"What very afternoon?" Christal asked.

"The afternoon of—uh—the uh—murders." It wasn't a word that Dottie was comfortable using, particularly in Christal's presence.

"I made change for her because she wanted to make a phone call and she didn't have a nickel.

"Well, Dottie," Christal said, speaking with an objective detachment one would not expect from someone so personally tied to the event, "it certainly does look bad for them. I don't know if the Sheas had a hand in the actual murders—in fact I doubt that they did . . ." She hesitated before adding, "But without their testimony—the Reno trip and everything—I'm not sure we'd even have a case, much less get a conviction."

Christal pondered the irony in the possibility—even the probability—that a member of their tight little community, someone the Youngs may have known and probably trusted, could have done something so unspeakably evil.

They drove for another ten miles with only the soft purr of the car's engine breaking the silence before Dottie, staring blankly out of the window, spoke again.

"What the hell kinda people are they?" Her gaze was fixed on—though not really seeing—the passing scenery.

"What must have been going through their twisted minds when they looked into the children's eyes and heard their screams?" Dottie caught herself, suddenly realizing that she might be painting too graphic a picture.

"I'm so sorry, I shouldn't have said that," she said, only half contritely. But instead of reacting, Christal's eyes remained stoically locked on the road ahead. Without a visible response from Christal, after a short pause, Dottie continued.

"And that Reno trip," she spat it out. "After murdering four people, they're up there in Reno having the time of their lives, spending the stolen money, just like nothing happened!"

"I'd much rather have it this way," Christal said, ignoring Dottie's imagery. "They haven't been convicted of anything yet, Dottie. Not just Larry and Lucille Shea; this applies to all of them. If the police have the right people, there's nothing I'd like more than to see them convicted and be given the punishment they deserve." After driving another half mile, Christal finished her thought, "But if they're convicted on tainted evidence—or perjured testimony—then I will take no satisfaction from that."

They rolled into Chester and the moment Sondra Gay and little Wayne wrapped their tiny arms around their mother's neck and began to cover her face with wet kisses, all the stresses and tension that had been building inside Christal over the past two weeks seemed to miraculously vanish.

The Final Two Weeks

Eyebrows were raised when the decision by defense attorneys to call Barbara Graham to the stand was announced. In the sensational 1953 Mabel Monohan murder trial in Los Angeles just a year prior, Graham had been convicted of first degree murder and sentenced to death. She had been brought from her cell at the California Institute for Women in Corona by an armed escort to testify as a character witness for Santo and Perkins; a defense counsel's move deemed by some trial watchers as a major tactical blunder.

The courtroom buzzed with anticipation as her name was called, particularly among those familiar with the Monohan case, conjuring up lurid images of sultry gun-molls pistol-whipping helpless old ladies.

While Barbara Graham's mere courtroom presence might very well produce the opposite of counsel's desired effect, It was the opinion of defense lawyer Theodore Elges, that the overall positive aspects of her testimony, given voluntarily and with nothing to gain, would outweigh the perceived negatives created by her notoriety.

After Graham had been sworn in, Elges began his questioning by asking her about a jailhouse interview that had taken place while in the Los Angeles County jail where she was being held in the Monohan murder case.

With the approximate date of the interview having been established as "sometime in May or June of 1953," Elges came to the point:

"Can you tell us, Mrs. Graham, the name of the person who conducted that interview with you?"

"His name was Ray McCarthy," Graham answered unhesitatingly.

At the mention of CII Agent Ray McCarthy's name, District Attorney Jack Keane, who had been sitting at the prosecutor's table in an advisory capacity, rose to ask for a sidebar at the judge's bench. A small furor erupted over whether or not the defense was intending to call McCarthy as a witness.

Agent McCarthy had earlier been suspended from active duty by Attorney General (and future California governor) Edmund G. Brown on charges of misconduct with regard to the Chester murder case. Brown had filed charges claiming that McCarthy had placed a 2:00 a.m. person-to-person telephone call from San Francisco to Bernadine Pearney, a key witness in this trial and who, at the time, had taken up temporary residence at a Quincy hotel. The call in question had been made a few hours prior to Pearney's appearance before a Grand Jury during which she was to testify in the Chester multi-murder case. Attorney General Brown was alleging that McCarthy had warned Pearney to "keep your mouth shut."

Agent McCarthy had admitted to making the call but denied that it was meant as a threat, explaining that he had only intended to caution her against talking to newspaper reporters. Santo's attorney Elges indicated to the court that the defense had indeed subpoenaed Agent McCarthy, but said that the decision had not yet been made to actually call him as a witness.

In the end, since McCarthy was not called, court spectators were left to speculate on the significance of the telephone call and wonder to what extent McCarthy's testimony might have helped in Jack Santo's defense. After being assured by Elges that at that time there had been no decision made yet on McCarthy, the judge ordered the lawyers to return to their respective tables and after the court reporter read back the last line of testimony, Elges resumed his questioning of Barbara Graham.

"And can you tell us, Mrs. Graham, in what capacity was Mr. McCarthy acting?"

"He was a special agent with the CII."

"And at that time, Mrs. Graham, did Special Agent McCarthy make you any kind of an offer?" Elges asked.

"Yes. He asked me if I would like to be free and at home with my children. He said that if I would put Jack Santo and Emmett Perkins in Chester on October 10, 1952, he was in a position to offer me complete immunity in the Monohan case."

Elges paraphrased, "He offered you complete immunity in the Monohan case and all you had to do was lie about Santo and Perkins by placing them in Chester at the time of the Young killings—is that what you're saying?"

"Yes. That's what he said."

Elges, turning to face the jury, pounced. "Are you telling us that a law enforcement agent for the State of California was deliberately suborning what he knew to be false testimony—in other words, he was encouraging you to commit perjury? Is that what you're telling this court and this jury?"

Somewhat taken aback by Elges' exaggerated feigned outrage, Barbara Graham, with just a trace of a smile, said, "Yes, I guess so. He had a deal to make but I didn't want any part of it."

Prosecutor Schwartz sprang to his feet to object on grounds of what he deemed to be hearsay testimony, but after a forty-five minute discussion in Judge Curler's chambers, the objection was overruled and Elges, with Graham still in the witness box, once again, picked up his questioning.

"And so, as a result of your refusal to lie to save your own skin," Elges continued, "you made no deal with Mr. McCarthy, and because of that, you ultimately were convicted of murder for which you are now under a sentence of death. Do I have that right?" Elges asked, his eyes fixed icily on the jury, wanting to be sure he had their full attention.

Barbara Graham answered in the affirmative and Elges moved his questioning to a particular conversation she once had with Santo and Perkins.

"Now at the time you were sharing living quarters with Emmett Perkins—that is, before your arrest in the Monohan case—you once had occasion to ask both Jack Santo and Mr. Perkins if either had anything to do with the Chester killings, isn't that right?"

"Yes," Graham answered. "I asked them if they had done such a thing, and they said 'no—absolutely not.'"

"And what did you conclude from that?"

"Knowing them as I do," she said, "I believed them. I still believe them."

After a few more questions from attorney Elges followed by the prosecutor's unremarkable cross-examination, Barbara Graham was thanked for her testimony and excused. Stepping from the witness stand she was immediately met and handcuffed by a gruff matron, and after an exchange of warm smiles with Santo and Perkins, and while curious gallery spectators looked on, Barbara Graham was led from the courtroom.

Although it is somewhat rare in a criminal trial and almost always against the advice of his or her lawyer, a defendant will on occasion, take the witness stand to testify in his or her own behalf. In exercising their self-incrimination rights, most defendants more often than not, will choose to let others speak for them rather than subject themselves to a bruising cross-examination. In such cases, when a defendant decides not to testify, the jury is instructed by the judge that, under the U.S. Constitution, all defendants are entitled to exercise that right and in so doing, no conclusions should be drawn by the jury as to their guilt or innocence simply because of their reticence to testify.

With the trial entering its final stages, it was not clear whether any of the three defendants would be taking the stand. Perkins' attorney Winslow Christian petitioned the Court and was granted a few moments to discuss the matter with his client. Following a ten minute recess, he called Emmett Perkins to the witness stand.

Emmett Perkins

That Winslow Christian would allow defendant Emmett Perkins to testify in his own behalf, thereby subjecting him to what he had to know would be a merciless cross-examination, the astonished prosecutors could not believe their good fortune. It was as if Christian were handing them the cyanide pellets with which to execute his client.

Schwartz sat back in a smug silence, salivating as he watched and listened to Emmett Perkins—almost certainly against the vehement advice of counsel—tell his story and by so doing, proceed to pave the road that would lead him straight into the San Quentin gas chamber.

On the stand, Perkins told how his troubled life of criminality had begun in 1925 when as a teenager, he was convicted of grand theft after stealing a car. In his thick Texas drawl, exaggerated perhaps in what some suspected might have been a clumsy attempt to charm the jury, he related how, as a child he had been pampered by his mother and how shortly after the family moved to Fullerton, California, she

289

had permitted him to quit school and at one point, even bought him a car.

It was around this time he said, while cruising the mean streets of Fullerton and surrounding Southern California townships, that he had become a full-fledged juvenile delinquent—a criminal in every sense of the word.

"I stole some cars and they sent me back to juvie," he said, "but I got paroled again, but the next time I did an armed robbery and I got caught, and that time they put me in San Quentin."

Inexplicably, Christian allowed Perkins to continue to expand on his extensive history of—some would say pathological—criminal behavior despite the fact that this narrative would have the potential to inflict serious—if not fatal—damage to whatever chance he might have had to win an acquittal.

"So after being arrested, you're now in San Quentin on a charge of armed robbery," Christian continued to plow on. "And how long were you there?"

"They paroled me—I think it was in '30, but they sent me to Folsom in '32 on a parole violation rap—I mean charge."

The gallery sat in rapt silence as Perkins reeled off his litany of crimes and incarcerations. "I got arrested for robbing a bank in '37. I got twenty years for that one, but I got paroled again in '46."

Probably one of the most revealing aspects of Emmett Perkins' testimony—though probably not intentional—was the manner in which he exposed what many people often characterize as this country's "revolving door" prison system, i.e., the seeming ease with which hardened criminals are granted parole over and over again despite their criminal histories. The jury stared open-mouthed as they listened to Perkins' unashamedly frank responses to Christian's gentle questioning.

Christian had apparently chosen to confront his client's criminal history on his own terms rather than to allow the state to frame it in such a way that the jury would think he was attempting to hide it. His best shot, he probably calculated, would be to show that even in a crime-filled career stretching over decades, Perkins had never actually physically hurt anyone. He knew it was a weak argument but it was all he had.

"After you were paroled from Folsom in 1946, did you continue to commit crimes, Mr. Perkins?"

Perkins thought for a couple of seconds. "Well, I don't think it was actually a robbery or nothing like that, but I got sent back to San Quentin that same year on a concealed weapons charge—and, oh yeah—resisting an officer."

"And were you paroled for that offense too, Mr. Perkins?" Christian asked.

"No," Perkins answered. "I did the whole stretch. I think it was two years."

"So, in the commission of all of these crimes to which you have testified here today—in none of them—is it true that you have never killed anyone?" Christian asked.

"Yes, that's true," Perkins responded adamantly. "Definitely. Never."

"Nor have you ever hit anybody over the head?"

Again, Perkins responded with a resounding, "No! Never!"

Christian took a deep breath and turned to the prosecutor's table. "Your witness," he said.

Milton Schwartz, like a sprinter coming out of his starting blocks, sprang immediately to his feet and without wasting any words on niceties, he went straight to Perkins' record.

"Mr. Perkins," he began, "Would you please tell the court your current address."

Perkins was clearly rattled by the sudden change in tenor; from his own lawyer's gentle approach to the prosecutor's aggressive, even hostile, demeanor and after a long moment's hesitation, his answer came in a voice barely above a whisper. "San Quentin," he said as he began to squirm uncomfortably in the straight-back witness chair.

"San Quentin Prison," Schwartz emphasized, his tone as disdainful as he could possibly frame it. Turning to face the jury, he almost spat the words out. "You're incarcerated in San Quentin Penitentiary. Is that right, Mr. Perkins?"

Again, Perkins hesitated before answering and again, his answer was only barely audible above the ambient courtroom background sounds.

"Yes."

"Was that a 'yes', Mr. Perkins?" Schwartz prodded. "Speak up so the jury can hear you. Was that a 'yes'?"

Looking directly at the jury, Perkins cleared his throat before answering. "Yes!"

"And what was the charge and conviction that sent you to San Quentin?" Schwartz asked.

"Murder," Perkins said.

"Yes, murder," Schwartz continued his belittlement. "Murder in the first degree. How many charges of first degree murder, Mr. Perkins?"

Perkins again cleared his throat. "Well, there's two counts" he said, but quickly added "but I didn't do no murders. It wasn't me that did them murders. You can look it up."

"No, of course not," Schwartz said, his voice thick with sarcasm. "But you were convicted and you are now residing on death row for committing those murders, isn't that right Mr. Perkins?"

Perkins slumped in his chair. "I guess so," he mumbled.

"So Mr. Perkins, when you tell the jury that you have never killed anyone, is that because you just have a short memory?" Schwartz stared steadily at the jury, his eyes shifting from juror to juror, like needles boring holes into their brains. It was apparent to some that with the mere presence of the man now sitting in the witness box, heavy courtroom security notwithstanding, every member of the jury was on edge.

Schwartz was relentless. "Had you forgotten that you had just killed two—possibly three people, Mr. Perkins? Had it just . . ." he paused as if groping for the right phrase, "you know, slipped your mind—that you had murdered Mrs. Mabel Monohan and Edmund Hansen and probably Baxter Shorter—all in cold blood?"

Under Schwartz's withering cross, Perkins' combativeness was beginning to show; his fidgeting became more pronounced and his now shouted responses to Schwartz's questions drew a stern admonition from the judge.

"Mr. Perkins, there's no need for you to yell. We can all hear you. Please lower your voice and just answer the questions."

Perkins looked up at the judge and grunted an insincere "sorry,"

Turning back to his tormentor, and speaking in a more modulated tone, he said, "I never killed anyone. It wasn't me. I wasn't there. Look at the records. Y'all will see that both times, there was never any proof that I was even there. Someone else did them murders. It wasn't me."

Schwartz turned to face the defendant. "You weren't there—just like you weren't in Chester when Guard Young, his daughters and the neighbor boy were all brutally murdered. You weren't there, is that right, Mr. Perkins? You're never there. It's always somebody else."

Schwartz's volley brought a vehement objection from Winslow Christian. "He's being argumentative, your honor." Judge Curler agreed, sustaining the objection.

"So, Mr. Perkins, since the time you were released from custody in Los Angeles in 1925, by my count you have been charged with nine felony counts ranging from first degree robbery to six counts of first degree murder. Isn't that true?"

Perkins' again raised his voice as he responded angrily, "You're including the charges in this case," he said. "I didn't do those murders. I don't know anything about any of those murders."

"Do you deny that you were in or around Chester on October tenth, 1952?" Schwartz asked.

"Yes, I mean I wasn't—I wasn't even in Plumas County when those murders happened."

Schwartz fired back. "Then tell us, Mr. Perkins. Where exactly were you on October tenth, 1952?"

"I . . . uh . . ." Perkins stumbled trying to find an answer but all he could come up with was a feeble, "I don't remember."

"Were you drunk on that day? Too drunk to remember?" Schwartz persisted.

"No," Perkins answered. "I don't drink—leastwise, not enough to get drunk."

Schwartz turned and as he walked to the Prosecutor's table, he addressed the Court. "I have no further questions for this witness, your honor," he hissed with undisguised, contempt and with that, Perkins stepped down and resumed his place at the defense table.

Harriet Henson

William Lally, attorney for Harriet Henson, next called Pauline Parelli to the witness stand. The owner of an Auburn drive-in café,

Mrs. Parilli testified that Harriet Henson had once worked briefly in her café as a part-time waitress during the month of October in 1952.

"And during that time, Mrs. Parelli, can you recall Mrs. Henson's hairstyle?" Lally asked. "That is, can you recall if her hair was long and stringy as has been testified to in this court?" Lally asked.

"No, she had short hair," Mrs. Parelli replied without hesitation. "I remember because she never had to wear a snood which was required of all the girls with long hair who worked at the cafe."

"A what, Mrs. Parelli? A 'snood'?"

"Yes, a snood. It's like a hairnet for women with long hair."

"I see. And you're saying that in early October, 1952 which would have been only days before these murders took place; you're saying that Mrs. Henson did not wear a 'snood' because at that time, she did not have long, stringy hair as was testified to earlier," Lally continued to hammer. "You're saying her hair was short?"

"Yes, that's right."

Mrs. Parelli was then excused and the defense announced that it would call on one more witness. It would not be Jack Santo. Against the advice of her attorney, Harriet Henson was sworn in. She would be the trial's final witness.

In an obvious play on the sympathies of the twelve jurors, Lally used the opportunity to extract from Harriet the story of what her life had become as Jack Santo's mistress; a cruel existence of servitude and abasement in a master-slave relationship where her life was not her own. It was an account that corroborated an earlier statement made by Lally in his opening remarks in which he had characterized their relationship as "unfortunate," describing Harriet as "a girl who loved unwisely."

Harriet related a harrowing story of abuse and degradation at the hands of her former lover, and how she had always worked to support him, even after he had begun a relationship with Bernadine Pearney.

"One time he ripped my blouse off and then he hit me in the mouth," she said. "He called me a 'cop-lover.'"

Frequently her testimony would be drowned out by bursts of loud, raucous laughter emanating from Santo and for which he was constantly admonished by Judge Curler.

"Was he in the habit of using physical force against you?" Lally prompted. "Were there other instances?"

"Once in front of Bernadine he tied me to a bed," she said, "and snuffed out a cigarette on my leg," eliciting audible gasps from female courtroom spectators.

Whenever Harriet invoked Bernadine Pearney's name, her voice would grow stronger and her green eyes would flash with anger through her heavy-rimmed glasses.

"Jack always went to see Bernadine around the first and fifteenth of the month," she recalled bitterly. "He wanted to get part of her paycheck."

Again, Jack guffawed heartily at Harriet's remarks, this time prompting Judge Curler to interrupt her testimony and issue a stern warning. "Mr. Santo, one more outburst like that and you will be removed from my courtroom for the duration of this trial. Are you clear on that, Mr. Santo?"

Apparently taken aback by being publicly scolded, Jack could only mutter, "Sorry, Judge."

The judge continued to glare at the chastened defendant for a full ten seconds before finally speaking. "Please continue, Mr. Lally."

Lally questioned Harriet about Jack's relationship with Pearney, wanting to know why she would put up with such a situation.

"I asked him many times to break it off with her, but every time he'd tell me he couldn't end their relationship because she knew too much and he was afraid she'd talk."

"Talk about what?" Lally asked.

"I don't know. He didn't say," Harriet responded.

In relating her movements on the day of the murders, she told the jurors that she had come to Chester with Jack and stayed in the Shea home; that she had remained in the home all day but that Jack had left sometime that morning with Perkins. She said he was gone for several hours.

"And what time did they return?" Lally asked.

"Well, Jack came back sometime around four o'clock."

"Alright, Mrs. Henson. Mr. Santo returned at around four o'clock. Tell us what happened then."

"Well, we had a little spat—I don't remember what it was about—but he told me to leave."

"Mr. Santo told you to leave?"

"Yes. He told me Perk was going to drive back to L.A. and on the way, he could drop me off at my house in Auburn," Harriet said, failing to mention the key parts of what had actually happened on that day. She described the drive to Auburn with Perkins as uneventful, again omitting any conversation about the murders.

Lally summarized, "So Mr. Perkins dropped you off at your home in Auburn and then he continued on to Los Angeles—is that right?"

"Yes."

"And at that time—did he—that is, before continuing on his way, did he do or say anything else?"

"He gave me a wallet and a money sack and told me to burn them," Harriet said. Of course she left out the part about receiving two thousand dollars as her cut of the loot.

Henson's testimony was delivered in an emotionless monotone. It was almost as though she had become numbed by the horror in which she now found herself inescapably embroiled.

When it came time for Prosecutor Milton Schwartz to cross-examine, he exhibited little, if any, empathy for the witness and her heart-wrenching story as elicited by her attorney. Personally, Schwartz was convinced that this woman who was now claiming to be the "unfortunate girl who loved too unwisely" was, in fact, lying through her teeth or at the very least, not telling all she knew about the Chester murders.

"Mrs. Henson, how far would you say the city of Auburn is from Chester?" Schwartz began.

Harriet appeared puzzled by the question. "I don't know," she replied. "Maybe a hundred miles."

"Well, you're close," Schwartz said. "It's actually a little over a hundred and fifty miles."

"Okay," Harriet conceded, still unsure where Schwartz was going with the question.

"So, during that one hundred and fifty mile drive—that I think we can safely assume would have taken several hours—are you saying during those several hours, no conversation took place between you and Mr. Perkins?"

Harriet now began to squirm uneasily. This was probably the kind of questioning her lawyer had warned her about should she choose to testify. She eyed the sheaf of papers being held in the prosecutor's hand, fairly certain that they had something to do with that one hundred and forty-eight hours of police questioning she had undergone during which she had made a number of self-incriminating statements.

"Well," she said haltingly, "there was a lot of small talk. He said 'something pretty rough' had happened that day."

Harriet's obvious reference to the Chester murders and to "something rough" happening that day, however vague, caused her to inadvertently cast a glance at Christal, who had been listening attentively to every word of her testimony. It was just in time to see Christal's expression change from the emotionless stoicism that had been her trademark reaction to the trial's events up until that time, into a faint but discernable grimace accompanied by more than just a few tears. Still gripping the small white handkerchief—and with the emotional pain once again making its unrelenting presence felt—she dabbed at her eyes.

"Something pretty rough had happened that day?" Schwartz repeated. "Did he explain what he meant by that?"

"No, he didn't say and I didn't ask."

Saving for last what he thought would be his best shot, Schwartz asked, "one more thing Mrs. Henson. Can you tell us—that is, would you describe the car—the car in which you accompanied Mr. Perkins on that drive from Chester?"

Harriet hesitated before responding. "It was just a car, nothing special about it. Just a blue sedan."

"A blue sedan?" Lally repeated. "A blue Oldsmobile maybe?"

"Maybe," she replied.

It was all Christal needed to hear. If Harriet was being truthful, there could be no further doubt in her mind—or in anybody else's—that Emmett Perkins was one of the people who had committed the murders. But what about Harriet? Could this woman possibly have been a participant in the slaughter of her family?

When, after twelve grueling hours on the witness stand, Harriet finally stepped down, to many it was apparent her testimony had done little to further her own cause, but if believed by the jury, it could have dealt a devastating blow to the cases of her co-defendants.

As she walked back to the defense table—"shuffled" would be more accurate—she couldn't help but take one last look at a now composed

Christal whose eyes were glued on the woman who, according to the evidence that had been offered so far, had taken part in the massacre of her family. As Harriet completed the short journey by stepping in front of the gallery, their eyes locked.

It would be difficult for anyone other than Christal herself to say exactly what went through her mind at that moment, but court observers in post-trial interviews have described her facial expression during that exchange as being one of sympathy or even pity.

Closing Arguments

On the morning of May 5, 1954, Prosecutor Milton Schwartz rose to deliver his closing arguments. As is the law in most states, California included, he would have an opportunity—a second chance, as it were—to rebut the defense's final arguments before the jury begins the deliberation process. To most lay observers, this law may seem to give the prosecutor a huge and even unfair advantage, but because the burden of proof always rests with the prosecution while the defense is not required to prove anything at all, it's a law that's intended to "level the playing field."

So, aside from being able to challenge the state's final arguments through the normal objection process, the defense would not have an opportunity to rebut the alleged facts or arguments introduced by the prosecutor in his final summation. For this reason Prosecutor Schwartz wisely decided to save his heavier blows for his rebuttal.

"The state is not interested in revenge," Schwartz began. "The state is not avaricious. But this is a situation where these people balanced the difference between money and life. These defendants have desecrated the sacred principle of our right as citizens to be secure."

He cited the evidence that had been presented: the testimony of Calvin Baccala which put the three defendants at the scene of murders; the testimonies of Lucille Shea and Dorothy Elliott and even that of Harriet Henson, putting the lie to Perkins' denial of having been in Chester on the day of the murders; the testimony of Bernadine Pearney who related the story of Jack Santo's wild Reno spending spree, and most damning of all, the devastating testimonies of Larry and Lucille Shea.

Facing the jury box as he paced from one end to the other, occasionally gesturing with a pointed finger in the direction of the defense table, Schwartz let his voice dramatically rise and then fall as he roared on. "They must be destroyed like mad dogs—not permitted to live—when they can take the lives of four people for $7,000."

When the defense got its turn, William Lally began by asking the jury to return a verdict of not guilty for his client, Harriet Henson. Co-defense lawyers, Christian and Elges glared icily at Lally when, beginning his summation, he homed in on the contentious relationship that had existed between Jack Santo and his client.

"You may have a duty to convict Jack Santo," Lally declared. "You may have a duty to convict Emmett Perkins. But you have a duty to send Harriet Henson home, acquitted of any responsibility for these murders."

Referring to Lucille Shea's direct testimony, he reminded the jury that on the morning of the murders and before leaving the house, Mrs. Henson "had put up her hair and tied it with a bandana," contradicting what he termed, the "dubious" testimony of Calvin Baccala who had identified Mrs. Henson as the woman sitting in the back of the car and who, he said, was wearing a hat.

"Now let's examine the credibility that we shall give to the witness, Mr. Baccala," Lally said. "He states that he thinks he left Susanville heading to Chester at 2:45 p.m. on October tenth, 1952. However he doesn't know the mileage between Chester and Susanville nor how long it takes to drive from one to the other—even though, by his own admission, he has resided in the Chester area for fifty-four years and has probably made that drive dozens, if not hundreds of times.

"He's never noticed how far it is to Susanville, but he's observant enough to remember—months later—with no circumstances to impress on his mind—that after coming over the hill and traveling at a speed he estimated to be ten miles an hour, he observed two parked cars. He observed their color. He observed one of the two men standing there as someone whom he knew and, moreover, he observed a woman in the back seat of one of the cars—observant even to the point of being able to describe this woman's facial features—even the color of her hair, never mind that she was wearing a hat," Lally said, his voice thick with mocking skepticism.

"He says the woman that he saw sitting in the back seat of that car had long, stringy black hair, yet you heard Mrs. Parelli's sworn testimony that Mrs. Henson had short hair, and, even though Mr. Baccala was observant enough to notice—poor eyesight and all—that that woman he saw had long, stringy hair, Mrs. Parelli is absolutely certain that Harriet Henson had short hair." Lally paused briefly in order to let his characterization of the conflicting testimony sink in.

"And is it credible that Mr. Baccala, in all his years of living in this area has never, not once during those fifty-four years, had occasion to observe the distance between Chester and Susanville? Do you find that credible?" Lally paced as he spoke, letting his eyes scan the jury panel, all the while affecting an exaggerated expression of disbelief.

"How should we account for the discrepancy in Mr. Baccala's testimony as to the time of day he allegedly passed these cars? We have Mr. Baccala telling us that he drove by these two cars that were parked beside the highway at between 3:00 and 3:30 p.m. He testifies that he went directly from that machine shop in Susanville to his home after passing through Chester without stopping; a thirty-five mile drive that should have required no more than forty-five minutes to an hour," he said, locking his eyes on each juror while making his point. "Yet we have the owner of that shop who remembers very clearly that Mr. Baccala left the shop 'shortly before noon' and not at 2:30 or 3:00 as Mr. Baccala has testified."

Lally's eyes searched up and down the jury box for the one juror on that panel for whom, he hoped, this seemingly irreconcilable contradiction would generate the reasonable doubt that would ultimately lead to Harriet Henson's exoneration.

"So, since it would have been virtually impossible, ladies and gentlemen, for Mr. Baccala to have seen my client sitting in that parked car at 2:30 or 3:00 p.m. as he has so testified, Mr. Baccala is either lying or he is just plain mistaken, but in either case, he casts a cloud of doubt on his testimony—a reasonable doubt, I would submit to you—and therefore, his entire testimony must be disregarded."

Winslow Christian, attorney for Emmett Perkins, would focus his attack on Larry Shea and the supposedly incriminating testimony the state had elicited during their direct questioning. He mentioned the criminal charges that were still pending against Shea and said the prosecution's strategy was to "keep those jail doors clanging" while Larry Shea was on the stand.

Christian argued that if, after weighing all the evidence, the jury considers Shea an accomplice in the murders, his testimony must therefore be disregarded. He cited Shea's bank account and the lack of activity indicating that, in all probability, he had access to a large amount of cash during and shortly after the time that the murders were committed.

"If Mr. Shea did not need to write out checks to pay his monthly bills—as was his normal practice each and every month except for the two months immediately following the murders—how, then, do you suppose he was able to pay those bills in October, November and December?"

Pausing dramatically for effect, his voice modulated but firm, Christian said, "I submit to you, ladies and gentlemen, that he paid those bills with cash—ill-gotten proceeds from the robbery and the killing of Guard Young and the three children."

He consulted his notes. "You heard Larry Shea in his own words, you heard him say in an obvious slip of the tongue, that when Jack Santo expressed his disappointment in failing to overtake the first grocer they had intended to rob—I believe his name was Locatell—Frank Locatell," he said, again reading from his notes, "and Santo declared 'if we could have caught him, 'we'd be in the chips.'"

Christian looked up from his notes. "Did you catch that? 'We' would be in the chips. Not 'I' would be in the chips—he said 'we' would be in the chips. What does that suggest to you?"

After pausing again to give the jury a moment to absorb the question, he continued to drive home the point that Shea was indeed a co-conspirator. "It's obvious to me, as I'm sure it must be to you, that Mr. Shea was expecting to share in the proceeds of that day's activities. And that is why, ladies and gentlemen, that is why, as an accomplice in these crimes, Mr. Shea's entire uncorroborated testimony must be thrown out."

It was obvious that Christian had chosen not to revisit his scurrilous and completely unfounded suggestion that Christal Young had been involved in some kind of illicit relationship with an unidentified "Mr. X"; a decision for which Christal, understandably, was more than grateful.

In his rebuttal arguments, Prosecutor Schwartz characterized the defense's testimony and closing arguments as "a long series of buck-passing." Reiterating his demand for a verdict of guilty he asked that the jury fix the penalty for each of the three defendants at death. He emphasized that "Harriet Henson is just as bad as the others."

The prosecutor continued, "The state does not want Jack Santo and Emmett Perkins convicted on the testimony of Harriet Henson. Her testimony is not worthy of belief."

His eyes darted from juror to juror, briefly making contact with each, driving home the point that the state had presented evidence sufficient to result in convictions even without Henson's testimony.

Citing the evidence against Perkins, his only comment was that "the worst possible witness against Emmett Perkins was Emmett Perkins."

Referring to Perkins' claim of not being in Chester on the day of the murders and Harriet's conflicting account of how Perkins had driven her from Chester to Auburn on that day, Schwartz, reiterated, "We don't need Mrs. Henson to confirm that Emmett Perkins was in Chester when these murders were committed. There is ample evidence from other sources."

"As for Mrs. Henson's testimony; while she says that on the drive from Chester to Auburn, she and Perkins had only engaged in "small talk," is it likely that—and remember, he had handed her Mr. Young's wallet and a bank money bag with the instructions to destroy them— is it likely that she would ask no questions and Perkins would make no comments as to the circumstances under which he had come to be in possession of these items?"

"Of course, by not asking questions and—if we are to believe her self-serving account—not getting answers, you, the members of this jury would be left to conclude that at that point, she was completely unaware of the four brutal murders that had taken place that very afternoon."

After once again pausing for dramatic effect, Schwartz continued. "Ladies and gentlemen of the jury: use your common sense. Harriet Henson knew about those murders. She knew about them for one reason—she was there."

Schwartz spent more than two hours in his rebuttal citing the mountain of evidence the state had been able to amass against the three defendants. He emphasized the money angle, pointing to the testimony of Bernadine Pearney, who told how Jack Santo borrowed fifteen dollars shortly before the murders but flashed large amounts of money in Reno a short time later.

After nearly three days of final arguments, both sides were harboring fears, not altogether unwarranted, that in trying to sort through the flood of evidentiary minutiae, the jury was in danger of being pushed to the brink of information overload. The trial had turned into a baffling maze of complexities: multiple murders with multiple murder scenes; three defendants with three individual agendas, some in bitter conflict. There was contradictory testimony, unethical behavior by law enforcement officials, as well as members of the press. There were attorneys breaking down after being overcome by emotion and attorneys squabbling with their clients as well as amongst themselves.

In various stages of exhaustion after having somehow survived the month-long ordeal, the lawyers returned to their respective tables, each wondering to himself what more, if anything, he could have done: in the prosecution's case, to put three vicious killers in the gas chamber, and in the defense's case, to save their clients' lives.

On May 5, Judge Ben Curler read his final instructions to the jury before declaring a recess for the lunch break. At 2:30 p.m. the jury returned from lunch and immediately retired to begin their deliberations.

Each defendant was facing charges of four counts of murder in the first degree, one count of attempted murder and four counts of armed robbery. Jurors were given two options in deciding punishments for each defendant if found guilty: life imprisonment or, absent mitigating circumstances, they could recommend the death penalty.

The Jury Deliberates

As the jury filed from the courtroom to begin deliberations, an emotionally drained Christal decided to return to Chester where she could be with her children while awaiting the jury's verdict. Of course there was no way for anyone to know how long the jury would be out and Christal wondered if it would even be necessary for her to attend the reading of the verdicts. There was also the problem with reporters. Media people would be falling all over themselves trying to get her to say something—no matter which way the verdicts went— and she just didn't have the stomach for it.

She decided to wait it out in Chester with the children, reasoning that since Dottie would be going back to Quincy for the reading of the verdicts, Dottie could call her when those verdicts were reached.

In Christal's mind, there was no doubt that the right people were on trial for the murders. The evidence against them, she was absolutely convinced, was so overwhelming and so compelling there was not the slightest question as to their guilt. Surely the jury would see what she could see: these were the monsters who had taken her husband and children from her.

Christal's thoughts went out to Rosemary, Michael's mother. She made a mental note to herself that the moment she was informed of the verdicts she would call Rosemary to give her the news.

She would have to wait at least another day to make that call. At around 10:00 p.m. that night, the jury requested transcripts of the testimony of Calvin Baccala and of Harry Cooper, the CII agent who had made the wire recording of Harriet Henson's jailhouse conversation with Jack Santo. By midnight, still unable to reach unanimous agreement, the jury of seven men and five women were locked up for the night.

The following morning, after having endured twenty-one tortuous days of convoluted, often contradictory testimony; after sifting through piles of evidence; after having been forced to suffer the boorish antics of Jack Santo, the sickeningly bizarre who-cares demeanor of Emmett Perkins and the pitiful self-serving sobs of Harriet Henson, and after nine hours of sometimes tumultuous debate, the jury advised Judge Curler that it had finally reached a unanimous agreement.

When word got out that a verdict had been reached, the courtroom became a scene of controlled chaos with spectators scrambling for seats vacated during jury deliberations and reporters dashing to and from hallway telephones while trying vainly to read the expressions on the jurors' somber faces as they took their seats in the jury box.

Three of the five women jurors were clearly in tears while the seven men wore blank expressions.

As the three shackled defendants were ushered into the courtroom, armed guards seemed to be everywhere. Spectators were searched as they entered the courtroom and as rumors about another escape attempt had begun to circulate throughout the courtroom, the atmosphere, as it had been at the onset of the trial, grew ever more strained.

The tension was being fed by credible reports that, far from being a groundless rumor, a clumsy attempt by Santo to smuggle a note to outside confederates had been intercepted by the ever alert Sheriff Schooler only hours prior to the jury's returning with its verdict.

The note, penciled on San Quentin letterhead, had obviously been written while Santo and Perkins were being held in San Quentin's death house, making all the more real their fantasy that somehow, they would successfully be able to pull off an escape and thus avoid the beckoning gas chamber:

Every body will turn out to a good fire up there – even if two were made, all the better. Don't wait as the trial might not be long. & that will be the last go round. Ah Revoire.

(Reverse Side)

Sunday nite – 10 p. m. or week nite 1 a.m. on [sic] should be two men – one sawed off & (2) .38 or .45s – Tell the Man - to think twice - don't try to be a hero – shakedown may be armed. Take elev. to 3rd floor or stairs. Take man with you to show you where.

Impress – No false move. Good conversation will stop trouble – very easy with two one can do –

5 gal kerosene to an outlaying building – will make it like getting money from home. It will take away the pinto job if it is around. Eyes open – Home free. Should have rented in advance a house stocked with food etc. Enough for (1) week. Either in Oreville [sic] or Trucky [sic]- unless otherwise taken care of elsewhere. Shouldn't have to stay on the road any longer than necessary to start with. Should let it cool for 4 or 5 days. But come is the main thing. Bring h.p. rifle along if possible – be sure and go the kerosene route – it will clean house for sure. Be sure (S) has an address where we can drop off some loot for you – Get word to (S) not to take any long shots – we will take care of that later just come and get us and we will look after the loot.

Memo & destroy - VIVA

On that same sheet Jack Santo had sketched a crude but roughly detailed map of the courthouse area including the jail. The map depicted the streets coming in and out of *Quency* with a caution to watch for Pinto Cars, most probably a reference to police vehicles. His instructions on the map were hardly any more coherent or explicit than were those on the rest of the note:

Park car in the rear of the courthouse – can leave the building the same way – But enter from the side door. Collect the man and come up to our floor (3) There may be a ginney up there not for sure but be on the lookout – very easy with just a little moxey.

There was one last addendum: *Get out to (S) this fellow's name & add where some loot can be left for him.*

The identity of the mysterious *"(S)"* was never disclosed by the authorities.

The Verdicts

A hush fell over the courtroom as the foreman handed the jury's findings to Judge Curler who scanned them before handing them to the court clerk. Although there were few—if any—courtroom spectators who, for even a millisecond, seriously thought that any of the defendants would be acquitted, nevertheless, the entire gallery was perched on the edge of their seats as the court clerk began to read. It would require a full half hour, as one by one, the clerk intoned each count and verdict.

As they listened to the clerk's monotone, Santo and Perkins glared at the jury in frozen-faced silence while a completely devastated Harriet struggled to maintain her composure.

Of the four charges of first-degree murder, Jack Santo and Emmett Perkins were found guilty on all counts with a recommendation of death on each count. Harriet Henson was found guilty on all counts but with a recommendation of life imprisonment.

The jury's inability to reach a speedy verdict had nothing to do with whether or not the defendants had committed the crimes as charged. As the public would learn later, a unanimous guilty verdict for all three defendants had been reached within the first hour, as were death penalties for both Santo and Perkins. But it had taken seven out of the nine total hours of deliberation for the jury to finally decide that Harriet Henson should be spared the gas chamber

While Santo and Perkins were returned to their cells in manacles, Harriet, uncuffed and sobbing loudly, was led by a matron from the courtroom through the side door. The three defendants would be held in the Plumas County Jail until formally sentenced which would not occur for another nineteen days.

Special afternoon editions would soon hit newsstands in every town in Northern California, many bearing headlines that simply proclaimed "Guilty!" A reporter for the San Francisco Examiner wrote:

Quincy, May 6—Jack Santo and Emmett Perkins, as brutish a pair of cutthroats as ever invaded the Sierra, collected a fresh batch of death sentences here today when a jury found them guilty of the Chester massacre. Santo paramour Harriet Henson received four concurrent life sentences for her part in the gruesome murders.

Although the pronouncement of the sentences would not formally take place until May 24, the judge's statement, absent any mention of mitigating or extenuating circumstances, seemed to make their fates a foregone conclusion. In California, a judicial override of a jury's recommendation in a capital case, although permitted by California law, is extremely rare and for a crime that included the wanton slaughter of three innocent children, the possibility of such a jury override by Judge Ben V. Curler fell somewhere between slim and zero.

California law also mandates automatic appeals on death sentences, but unless their appellate lawyers could find some kind of a procedural technicality on which to base a nullification of the verdicts, Jack Santo and Emmett Perkins would die in San Quentin's notorious gas chamber and Harriet Henson, barring a parole, would spend the rest of her natural life in prison.

Newspaper reporters, again with their notepads, pencils and microphones at the ready, prowled the courthouse hallways, as well as the outside front and rear entrances, seeking someone of note to interview.

Few jurors could be found and those who were, had nothing to say. In the hallway just outside the courtroom door, one reporter was able to corner District Attorney Milton Schwartz.

"I'm satisfied with the verdicts," Schwartz said, and in reference to Harriet Henson's escaping the death penalty, he added, "I guess the jury believed that Santo and Perkins engineered the deal and Harriet just went along with it."

On the other hand, William Lally, Harriet's lawyer was disconsolate. "I am very disappointed," he told reporters. "I must have failed somewhere because that is the only way they could convict a person who is not guilty."

He was asked if he believed that his client was a victim of circumstance. "I feel that they convicted her only because of her close association with Jack Santo. As I said in my summation, she loved him too well and much too unwisely."

Christal's decision to remain in Chester during the reading of the verdict dealt a blow to the mob of reporters who were walking around like hungry, prey-stalking predators.

After searching into every nook and cranny of the building—upstairs and downstairs, peeking into every empty room and office—for even a glimpse of the wife and mother of the murdered husband and children, they finally came to the realization that Christal Young was not even in Quincy. She had somehow slipped past them while they were looking the other way.

But one enterprising reporter from the Sacramento Bee noticed that Christal had not been in the courtroom at all, even for the readings of the verdicts. He was somehow able to obtain the phone number where she could be reached and on the long shot that she would agree to talk with him, he called her for a telephone interview and she obliged.

"I have a feeling of relief that the seemingly endless investigation, questions, and wondering are over." Christal spoke in soft tones, muffled occasionally by undulating waves of emotion. "I'm grateful I can now go back to Provo with my children and move on with my life there."

The reporter asked her if she agreed with the death penalty for Santo and Perkins. "No penalty," she said, "could bring me satisfaction. I can't answer your question as to whether I think that the payment of their lives is just punishment," adding, "I could never be one to ask that one life be taken for another."

"Do you have any wish to be on hand when the sentences are carried out, Mrs. Young?" the reporter asked, apparently unfamiliar with the intellectual make-up of this remarkable woman.

"No," Christal answered without the slightest trace of hostility. "I have no wish to watch people die. I will be glad only when the time comes that Mr. Santo comes forward and says he's sorry and tells all he knows."

"Do you really think that will happen?" the reporter pressed.

"I think that day may come, but I don't know when," she said.

In typical fashion and as the interview came to a close, Christal again dipped into what many regarded as her bottomless reservoir of graciousness.

"I just want to thank everyone for the kindness and thoughtfulness shown me and my family during this time. It has made it so much easier for me."

Easier indeed.

"Why are good people always so sure they're right?"

SIXTEEN

Punishment

Occupying 275 acres of sprawling, high-priced real estate overlooking the northernmost shores of San Francisco Bay, California's San Quentin State Prison houses the largest death row inmate population in the entire Western Hemisphere. As of December, 2012, the condemned unit at San Quentin was home to 734 male inmates, a figure far exceeding those of second place Florida's 407 followed by Texas at 308.

With a total inmate population of 4,260, a staff of 1,832 and an annual operating budget of $164 million, San Quentin (or "Q", as it's more commonly known among inmates) is the second largest prison in the United States, surpassed in size only by its sister California facility at Folsom whose population presently exceeds 7,000.

The only correctional facility in the state with an execution chamber, San Quentin opened its gates in 1852, and by 1937, the year in which the state changed its method of execution from hanging to lethal gas, 215 people had met their fate by hanging. The infamous Green Room gas chamber was installed in 1937 and until 1995 when the United States Supreme Court ruled that execution by gas constituted "cruel and unusual punishment," another 196 had been executed, not including two federal prisoners who had killed an Alcatraz Prison guard during an aborted breakout attempt in 1946.

California's worst of the worst have passed through these gates of hell, more commonly known as San Quentin's execution chamber. These are criminals who are responsible for some of the most heinous crimes ever committed in the Golden State.

Some accepted their fate with calm stoicism. Farrington Hill, a murderer of no particular note, strode peacefully into the Green

Room after enjoying his last request—a Strauss Waltz played by a hastily assembled San Quentin prison band.

As was the custom at San Quentin, each afternoon before an execution, the condemned prisoner would be walked from his death row cell on the top floor to a holding cell located on the ground floor directly behind the gas chamber

Robert Pierce, a murderer who had vowed that he would not go easily, had promised his fellow condemned inmates, "You're gonna get a real show when they take me downstairs." When the Catholic chaplain arrived at the holding cell to accompany him to the chamber, Pierce grinned and revealed to the startled chaplain a deep wound in his neck that was now gushing blood.

Despite having been thoroughly and repeatedly searched, Pierce had somehow managed to conceal in his prison garb a shard of mirror glass with which he intended to kill himself by slitting his own throat.

While the guards tried to attend to his wound, Pierce struggled and bit at them as he tried to fend them off. They managed to get his arms pinned while wrapping a prison shirt around his neck in an effort to stanch the flow of blood.

Witnesses watched in horror as the bleeding prisoner was dragged, kicking and screaming into the gas chamber. "Lord, I'm innocent," he howled. "Don't let me go like this. Oh, God!"

Fellow prisoner Smith E. Jordan was then brought into the chamber and strapped into Chair A, within arm's reach of his partner in crime who was now occupying Chair B. The pair had been condemned for the robbery and murder of an Oakland cab driver—a brutal crime from which the total proceeds amounted to seven dollars.

While Jordan sat quietly, a fiercely struggling Pierce emitted a stream of invectives and curses at the spectators and had even managed to get his bloody right arm free. As he was furiously working to free his other arm, he was finally and mercifully felled by the gas.

Prior to 1955, only two women had been put to death in San Quentin's gas chamber: The first in 1941 when Louise Peete, a former socialite, prostitute and murderer of a string of husbands was executed and in 1947, a harridan by the name of Juanita Duchess Spinelli was likewise dispatched.

The Duchess, besides being a cold-hearted killer, was an ex-wrestler, a grandmother, a mother of three and the mastermind of a gang of San Francisco teenage robbers. She had been condemned to die for the vicious cold-blooded murder of a nineteen-year-old member of her own gang.

In his book, *88 Men and 2 Women,* San Quentin's Warden Clinton Duffy described Juanita Spinelli in a few unflattering but well-chosen words:

"The coldest, hardest character, male or female, I have ever known. She was a homely, scrawny, nearsighted, sharp-featured scarecrow. Duchess was a hag, evil as a witch, horrible to look at, impossible to like, but," he added, "she was still a woman and I dreaded the thought of ordering her execution."

Before the advent of the gas chamber, hangings posed a problem for some witnesses, "So many witnesses fainted that we had to station extra guards around to help carry them out," Duffy wrote.

But "hanging Fridays" were big days in the hillside village outside San Quentin. In the 1920s, the village saloons—Figaro's, LaCante's and the back room of Kinney's grocery—filled up with spectators after the 10 a.m. executions. Since the law forbade using gas on anyone who had originally been condemned to hang, the gallows at San Quentin were used for the last time in 1942.

Major Raymond Lisemba, alias Rattlesnake James, named for the method he used to kill his victims, had kept himself alive with appeals for several years. When his execution date finally arrived, the gallows had to be spruced up and a new holding cell built. Afterward, Warden Duffy told reporters that hanging was thankfully now in the past. "This was the most terrible experience of my life and I pray to God I shall never have to repeat it," Duffy said. A month later, guards found the old gallows demolished, presumably by one of the prisoners. Duffy knew which inmate was responsible but took no action. Duffy felt the death penalty was wrong. He said it was "applied unfairly to only a fraction of murderers and even at that," he said, "it did not deter many killers."

For evidence he offered Alfred Wells. While serving a burglary term at San Quentin, Wells helped install the new gas chamber. He explained its working to the other inmates, vowing, "That's the closest I ever want to come to the gas chamber." After he was paroled, Wells got into trouble again. When his family objected to an affair he was having with his half-sister Violet, he killed his half-brother, the brother's wife and another woman.

Short, deformed, slender and slowed by a limp, Wells fled and in 1941 became the target of the biggest manhunt in Southern California up to that time. A posse of more than 1,000 men scoured the desert between San Bernardino and Las Vegas for the man the press had labeled the notorious "Hunchback Killer."

Wells eluded capture for a month before being apprehended in a hobo camp in Spokane, Washington. He was sent to death row where he knew better than most what awaited. He tried to stab guards, flooded his cell, lit fires and made himself a nuisance by howling the nights away. "Officers and inmates alike hated him," Warden Duffy wrote.

On June 29, 1972, in Furman v. Georgia, the Supreme Court ruled that because the death penalty was being applied in an "arbitrary and capricious manner," it not only violated the Eighth Amendment's proscription against cruel and unusual punishment, it also denied the due processes provided by the Fourteenth Amendment and was therefore declared unconstitutional. In California as a result of this 1972 ruling, 107 condemned inmates had their death sentences commuted to life in prison; among them six members of the notorious Charles Manson Family (including Manson himself). In 1969, all six had been sentenced to die for the vicious murders of seven people, one of whom was actress Sharon Tate, the eight-month pregnant wife of famous film director Roman Polanski.

Among the more than 700 inmates currently residing on San Quentin's death row, some of the most depraved killers ever to prey on the citizens of California are still awaiting their turn in the Green Room; among them, Richard Allen Davis, the kidnapper-rapist-murderer of Petaluma schoolgirl, Polly Klaas. After brazenly abducting the twelve-year-old from her bedroom, Davis raped and murdered her before dumping her body in a ditch alongside a major California freeway.

Others include Richard Ramirez, the aptly dubbed *Night Stalker*, a devil-worshipping predator who in 1984, on one murderous year-long rampage, held hostage an entire terror-stricken state leaving in his wake a bloody trial of thirteen randomly selected murder victims; David Westerfield, child killing rapist of his seven-year-old neighbor,

Danielle Van Dam as well as David *Trailside Killer* Carpenter, the cold-blooded ambush murderer of seven unsuspecting Mount Tamalpais hikers. Carpenter was convicted and sentenced to death in 1988. More than twenty years after being sentenced to die, David Carpenter continues to languish on death row.

Richard Farley, a Silicon Valley defense laboratory engineer, who in 1988, armed himself with a Benelli semiautomatic shotgun, a 22-caliber rifle with scope, a pump action shotgun, a Sentinel 22 WMR revolver, a Smith and Wesson 357 Magnum revolver, a Browning 380 ACP automatic pistol, a Smith and Wesson 9mm pistol, a twelve-inch buck knife, a smoke bomb and more than a thousand rounds of ammunition before embarking on a murderous workplace rampage. He stalked the hallways, going from office to office, randomly shooting and killing seven co-workers and seriously wounding four others before finally being corralled by Santa Clara police.

Cary Stayner, the pathologic *Yosemite Killer* is currently a guest on San Quentin's death row. In 2002 Stayner killed three women, two of them teenagers, before stuffing their bodies into the trunk of their car and setting it afire. Not yet satisfied with his murderous handiwork, he then went on to murder and decapitate a female Yosemite Park Ranger.

Media star Scott Peterson awaits his appointment with the lethal needle for the murder of Laci, his eight-month pregnant wife and their unborn son, Connor.

Charles Ng, maniacal sex slave torturer, rapist and murderer—a monster who enjoyed capturing his debauchery on videotape and who in 1999 alone, tallied no fewer than eleven victims—still sits on death row more than a decade later.

The Extreme Penalty

In the capital punishment environment of today—particularly in California—after a death sentence has been imposed, it can be—and often is—years before that sentence is carried out. If, during that time, the inmate is able to control his behavior, follow the rules, get along with guards and other inmates, and in general keeps his nose clean, he can be considered for *Grade A* prisoner status.

Although most of his time will be spent in his 5' x 7' cell, the condemned Grade A prisoner is allowed five hours of outdoor recreation time each day. He is granted privileges which *Grade B* convicts are not. As a Grade A prisoner, he has access to a telephone, books, tapes and even television to keep him company. As he waits for his execution day to arrive—which could still be decades away— he will while away the hours by reading or watching his favorite television show. He might enjoy a movie or a ball game or maybe play cards or chess or he may choose to avail himself of any one of a myriad of other leisure activities.

Statistics show that he is much more likely to die of old age than execution but if he's still alive when his date with the executioner finally arrives, he'll be escorted by the warden and a chaplain (if he so wishes) into the green execution chamber at which time he'll be strapped to a gurney and given a series of three painless injections. He will drift peacefully into a deep sleep and in about eight minutes, without having had to experience the slightest amount of pain or discomfort, his heart will cease to beat.

In today's America, there is a vociferous and stubborn body of opinion advocating the "ultimate punishment" for society's most egregious of lawbreakers. Often citing the biblical admonition "an eye for an eye," the pro-death penalty lobby argues that the only appropriate way to deal with the *Night Stalker* and others of his ilk is to simply put them to death.

But when death penalty advocates argue for what they believe is the *extreme punishment*, they might not be fully aware that they're also making an argument for the gurney, the needle and that sweet, painless slumber as described above.

The appeals process in twenty-first century California, because of its complex, enormously expensive and frustratingly time-consuming procedural track—which by law, the courts must follow before a death sentence can be carried out—almost always means that a condemned prisoner awaiting execution will languish on death row for years, even decades. It is a little known fact that, of all the deaths that have occurred on San Quentin's death row, only eighteen percent have actually been the result of an execution. Shockingly, eighty two percent have been due to either suicide or natural causes. The betting odds that a condemned prisoner will pay for his crime by being executed are slightly less than one in four.

* * * *

In 1954, unfortunately for Santo, Perkins and Barbara Graham, such was not to be the case. Scarcely a year and a half had elapsed since their conviction for the 1953 murder of Mable Monohan and having exhausted all remaining avenues of appeal, the three execution dates were set for June 3, 1955.

Even so, from the moment the Monohan sentences were handed down, the three convicted killers had been convinced that their executions would never take place.

"I'm glad they convicted Barbara," Santo told Willie Jones, a fellow Grade A prisoner as they sunned themselves in the exercise yard. "When they gave her the death penalty, that was the best thing that could happen for me and Perk."

"How so?" Willie asked.

"Because they don't execute women," Santo said confidently. "In the whole history of California, I think only two women have ever been executed. They just don't believe in executing women."

"So how does that affect you? Just because they give her a break, you guys are still on the hook aren't you?"

"One thing about the system in this state, Willie. It tries to be fair." Grinning smugly, Jack took a deep drag from his cigarette. "They aren't going to gas Barbara so they won't gas me and Perk."

His audience of one stared into Jack's eyes, marveling at the man's self-assuredness. "Bullshit! They're going to gas her and they're going to gas Perkins and they're damn sure going to gas you!" Willie sneered as he turned and walked away.

On their return to San Quentin's death row and according to prison protocol, both Santo and Perkins had been moved from their relatively comfortable accommodations in the Grade A unit into the Grade B unit which is known for its much harsher conditions. The Grade B unit is reserved for those inmates who prison officials deem to be threats to themselves, to other inmates, to guards, or who may be targets of other inmates.

Word gets around quickly inside prison walls, even in the seclusion and isolation of condemned row, and now because the two convicts had been convicted of killing innocent children, each bore a stigma that, historically, would have marked them for violent reprisal.

Inexplicably, both Santo and Perkins got on well with other inmates and the jailhouse loathing usually reserved for offenders of their ilk failed to materialize. Their behavior while in the Grade B unit was notably trouble-free and it would be scarcely a month before both found themselves back in their original cells in Grade A.

As their execution date drew nearer, Perkins had grown sullen and uncommunicative with fellow inmates, choosing instead to keep to himself, finding all the camaraderie he needed—or wanted—by either watching television or just sleeping.

Declining to be interviewed about the Chester massacre and stubbornly refusing to discuss anything that related to any of the crimes for which he and Santo had been condemned, he would respond simply with a terse, "Look at the record. It's all in the record."

Jack Santo, on the other hand, was garrulous to a fault and anxious to persuade anyone who would listen that he had been wrongly convicted, protesting endlessly about his innocence and speaking confidently about what he called his "sure-thing" reprieve.

"I may have done a lot of crimes in my lifetime, but I always drew the line at murder," he would repeat *ad nauseum.* He had new lawyers now and when his appeals were heard, the very least that was going to happen, he had convinced himself, would be a new trial. While Perkins appeared to be resigned to his fate, spending most of his time sulking in his cell, Santo would devote most of his waking hours in communication with his lawyers while holding out hope for a new trial.

The Appeal

Sitting down with paper and a soft lead pencil in hand, Jack Santo, for someone with no more than an eighth grade education, scrawled a surprisingly literate eight-page letter to Allan Sapiro, the San Francisco attorney appointed by the California Appellate Court to handle his appeal.

Despite his obvious confusion regarding the date of the Guard Young family murders—he refers to the date as October 11 rather than October 10 and makes other factual errors as well—for the most part, Santo displays a lucid coherency and a detailed understanding of the trial and court procedures in general:

Dear Mr. Sapiro:

Your letter of April 18th, 1955 at hand and I wish to express my gratitude for your early reply. Also we received the copy of the briefs. I notice that the briefs are quite lengthy which denotes that much time was spent on them. If you will make the trial and Grand Jury transcripts available to me, I shall be glad to go through them & set out re-page, date & etc. so as to save you time. In case that does not meet with your approval I am setting down certain facts – facts that are a matter of record.

Re-the Grand Jury & trial transcripts which I had in front of me all during the trial. However it is my understanding that these matters should have been filed with the opening brief, & that it is necessary to get permission from the court to file additional information and that it has to be filed so that the Att. Gen. can answer it.

I believe we are within our rights to charge the defense attorneys with prejudicial negligence, as they made little or no effort to offer these facts – by records, in our defense. In fact they refused to subpoena witnesses and also to bring these different points to bear – and their main witnesses impeached themselves one or more times each.

Lucille Shey [sic] testified before the Grand Jury that on October 11th [sic] 1952- Larry Shea, herself & Jack Santo did not go road hunting. In [sic] the trial records show that she said we did go hunting - in the direction of Malivich Road. [sic] Again changed it towards the meadows. As you pointed out, she changed her story every time Larry did because she didn't want to make him out a liar.

Re: Baccala – on page #35 line #10 forward of the Grand Jury Transcript states clearly as Mr. Swartz [sic] brings out pointedly the positions of the cars. The light green one that he recognized as Mr. Young's was on the highway near the centerline facing towards Chester & Swartz [sic] pinned him down on it, and that the darker car was off the side of the road and behind the green car.

*Now in the daily transcript – 6ᵗʰ day on page #11 Swartz [sic]
led the witness Baccala to place the dark car on the highway & tend
[sic] to show that it had nosed the light green car off the highway. Mr.
Perkins and I both pointed this out to our defense attorneys & even
made conversation with Harriet Henson's attorney & they would not
call the prosecution on that gross and malicious error.*

*And you will notice that the grand jury transcript was used, not
only once, but different times to impeach the witnesses and should
have been admitted into evidence.*

*The judge should also be charged with misconduct as he clearly
stated when my attorney asked that the Grand Jury Transcript be
admitted into evidence so that the jury could read it. The judge stated
"We can't do that because if we do allow it, we will be in trouble."*

*Baccala fixed his time at arriving where the aforementioned cars
were, by a transaction in a business house in Susinville [sic]. The state
produced the business house owner – He stated that the transaction
that Baccala referred to took place on Oct. 18ᵗʰ, 1952, a week later than
the eventful day Oct. 11ᵗʰ, [sic] 1952.*

*We begged our attorney to comment on this pointing to Baccala's
own statement – that he saw one of the men seated behind the wheel
of the car that would mean he had a close & reasonably clear vision
of him. And the other was closer to him than Mr. Young, he testified
that one of the men was standing between the highway ad Mr. Young.
Mr. Young was standing by the rear door opening which puts two men
in between Baccala & the woman he states he saw in the back seat of
the car. When Baccala was confronted by Perkins & myself, he stated
that he had never seen us before.*

*It is incredible to say the least – when Baccala was asked to locate
Harriet Henson in the courtroom, he was lost & didn't locate her until
after Mr. Swartz [sic] had made a motion in her direction, & there
being no other female in that direction, he pointed to her & in reality
she was close to being right in front of him.*

*Larry Shea denied the hunting trip on Oct. 11ᵗʰ [sic] even after
making a deal with the CII & the D.A. Then after they found out we
could prove the trip was taken, he stated "Yes we did take a road hunt
that evening but in the opposite direction stated by Lucille Shea."*

*Bernadine Pearney was impeached with the Grand Jury Transcript
also, re – She made the statement that Lucille and Larry Shea, herself*

& I were walking down the street on the forenoon of Oct. 12ᵗʰ, [sic] 1952 & noticed the headlines of the crime. She changed her statement to late in the afternoon then said she didn't remember. But she remembered emphatically before the grand Jury.

Raymond McCarthy of the CII was suspended for thirty days for threatening Pearney before she testified before the GJ. We prevailed on our attorneys to expose this coersion [sic] but they refused to do so.

Harriet Henson told conflicting stories and changed them at will. Showing that she never made any such trip with Perkins – 1ˢᵗ she said he purchased the beer, then that she did, next he got the cigs then she did. Many changes. She stated to the CII officer that Perkins gave her $1000 & gave her a tan wallet to destroy.

After Mrs. Young testified that Mr. Young's billfold was black engraved & initialed, she returned to the stand and said it was dark brown. No comments from the defense attorneys.

State agent Horton testified that Harriet told him that Perkins gave her $1000 – after they checked up on the figures, they didn't get the answers they needed so they changed it to $2000. Same as their changing the positions of the cars. Two CII agents testified that the Sheas and Henson & I were interrogated on this case early in Nov. 1952. Shea and Henson testified that we met in Oroville ten days or two weeks after Nov. 24 to prepare a story – about 3 weeks after we had already given our version of our activities.

When Shea was asked why he stayed in the same room on that hunting trip he stated that we did not stay in the same room. I asked that the other couple Mr. & Mrs. Joseph Baranowski of 1924 No. Marengo Pasadena Calif be subpoenaed as well as the court owners to prove him a liar. The attys. refused. No effort on their part was exerted to show these witnesses were lying when there were positive facts to prove them as such. One atty. could be called inept, but four of them let these points go by after having had them pointed out only points to the handwriting on the wall.

The judge would have to be biased to allow that which went on at the trial. The state brought in a fingerprint expert with a print when asked on the stand if it could be fixed to anyone, he stated that it was not readable, that it couldn't be fixed to anyone. I charge that the state used him solely to confuse and bias the jury.

The daily transcript should show that I asked for a change or rather to dismiss my defense attorney because he would not cross examine properly & that he refused to subpoena witnesses. I asked to be allowed to defend myself, the judge said that he would not allow it.

I hope having pointed out these points that are a matter of record will help both you and Mr. Barber to file the necessary additional papers to the opening brief. You have only to ask and I'll be glad to catalogue & furnish you additional facts to substantiate any of these contentions.

Both Mr. Perkins & myself send you each our best regards. Hoping to hear from you at your convenience.

Sincerely, J.A. Santo
Cc Mr. Teets

The Last Interview

Rarely availing himself of the perks allowed Grade A inmates, such as the five hours a day each prisoner is allowed to spend in the exercise yard, Emmett Perkins saw no visitors and granted no interviews. Jack Santo, conversely, was a veritable talking machine, especially to reporters. Stanley Wilson, a staff writer for the Sacramento Bee had developed a kind of bond with Santo and they frequently spoke with each other at length. Wilson thought that since Santo's appeal in the Monohan killing had been denied and with his execution for that murder looming ominously, Santo might finally be willing—maybe even eager—to get the whole thing off his chest.

In past conversations between the two, no matter how hard Wilson tried to manipulate the interview so as to elicit some sort of a confession or at least an admission of culpability, Jack would go off in another direction, usually continuing to insist that he was the victim of "perjured testimony" and a double-crossing mistress.

The final Santo interview began innocuously enough, going back to Jack's early years and establishing the fact that he was born in Lewiston, Washington of Castilian Spanish Catholic extraction, the youngest of six boys and two girls.

He said he had quit school after the eighth grade and left home at fifteen. He grew up wandering up and down the West Coast, working as a ranch hand, a welterweight professional boxer and a better than fair auto mechanic.

He told of how he had opened a garage in San Francisco and though it was successful, he had to sell it five years later when his wife had taken ill, forcing them to move to New York so that she could get the medical care she needed. But she died anyway and he moved back to California where he opened the Stucco Paint and Roofing Company in Pasadena.

Jack relished this opportunity to tell his story. He was human, he reminded Wilson, and hardly the kind of person who would go around killing kids and old ladies.

He had been forced to sell his business when a competitor ratted him out for lying on an application for a contractor's license by omitting the fact that he had once served some prison time—for what, he couldn't remember. It resulted in the loss of his license, his business and whatever community-respect he still may have enjoyed.

Bitter over his continuing bad fortune, Jack moved to Nevada County in 1939 and bought a 700-acre ranch where he raised hogs and cattle. It was here that his luck seemed to turn. After struggling to make a go of ranching and not doing very well at it, he was ready to throw in the towel when, in 1943, the hog market crashed. This time, as fate would have it, the market's collapse came just before all the buildings on the property had mysteriously caught fire and burned to the ground allowing him to collect a generous insurance settlement.

With his newfound wealth, Jack moved to Auburn, did some home building and got into gold prospecting, eventually taking over the operation of the Big Chief gold mine. With credentials now certifying that he was an actual gold miner, he was able to slide very effortlessly into the illegal gold trade, otherwise known as *high-grading*.

Meanwhile, the insurance proceeds from his ranch fire enabled him to purchase the Higgins Corner roadhouse where he met and hired Harriet Henson as waitress and sometime manager. The state law that prevented ex-convicts from obtaining liquor licenses compelled him to purchase the bar in Harriet's name.

"How about Perkins?" Wilson asked. "How did you guys hook up?"

"Perk used to run a private card room down in L.A. and I'd drop in from time to time. He introduced me to Bonnie; that's the name Barbara went by then—you know her as Barbara Graham—she used to hustle for him. She'd hang out in fancy hotel bars and steer suckers to the game. She's a high class broad, that Barbara. When she gets dolled up, I'll tell you man, she's a real looker."

Maybe, Wilson mused, this might be the way to get the interview headed in the direction of the actual crimes. "Even good-looking women can do bad things, Jack. Don't you agree?"

"Aw man, you know yourself that Barbara is a little girl. A hundred fifteen pounds if she's an ounce, and she's accused of killing that old woman—of dragging the body around the house and beating her over the head with the butt of a gun? It never happened, Stan. Okay to call you Stan?"

"Besides," he added, "do you think something like that could have gone on if I was there?"

Wilson scribbled furiously as Santo prattled on. "That kind of stuff is completely out of my line," he said. "Sure, I've dealt in a little high-grading of gold, sold a few guns to people who wanted to do a little negotiating, but you can stop right there. I don't deal in murder."

Wilson would later write: "Although he denied complicity in any of the crimes for which he'd been convicted, Jack Santo expressed no sympathy for the victims or relatives involved."

In documenting this interview in the Sacramento Bee, Wilson wrote: "Turning to the point of his impending execution, Jack had this to say: 'I'm supposed to die so someone else can get out of hock.'"

At one point, Santo asserted that he was not afraid of dying, saying, "I don't know what there is to be scared of. Everyone has to die, No?"

Later in the interview, however, Jack made this statement: "Scared? Sure I'm scared. I'm just as frightened as a man who is drafted and sent to Korea to be slaughtered or maimed for life."

He continued to express his confidence that he would beat his race with death and the cyanide pellets. When he was asked if he had become acquainted with the two men now on death row for killing a fellow inmate, he answered, "Yeah, I know 'em," he said, "but I don't mix with 'em. They don't have very good reputations."

"What about Harriet?" Wilson asked. "It was her statements and testimony that put you and Perkins on death row. She blew the whistle on you."

Surprisingly, Jack replied, "I feel the same way about her as I always have." Without a trace of hostility, he said, "She was confused. She told that story about the Guard Young case because they said she would get off. It was a terrible thing for her to do, but I don't hold it against her. She was all mixed up. She lied herself into the Big House and she only has herself to blame. The girl simply is not guilty. She wasn't there and I know it. I warned her that the story she gave out would get her involved."

Peering through the interviewing room's screened grillwork, Jack added, "I wasn't going to see you but a guy can't help but get mad sometimes. Anyone who knows me personally in these counties—and I've been here fifteen years—knows I can be counted on for a fast buck."

"Gold? Sure, but these other things—murders or robberies—no." He paused. "I've never been picked up with a gun in my possession. I've been out of McNeil Island Penitentiary nearly thirty years. I did thirteen months there for auto theft. I've never done one day's time for even a misdemeanor ever since."

He went over all the points he had outlined in his letter to his appeal attorney.

"If you want to write about all this, all I ask is that you tell the truth. I don't want a word in the paper in my favor if it's a lie."

Jack intimated that he knew "a lot of the misdeeds of a lot of people" saying, "You can't have associations like I have and not know things," but served notice that at this point, he wasn't about to open up. Grinning almost boastfully, he said, "There are people shaking in their boots in L.A. wondering if I'm going to open up, but I won't. Believe me, I'm nobody's paid policeman."

Jack readily admitted that he'd like to escape—a remote possibility in San Quentin. "When we sawed through those bars in Nevada City, why, we could have gone right out. There was only one deputy and two trustees around and we could have brained them, but we didn't," he said, again proudly. "You can believe me when I say I wouldn't kill anyone for freedom." He added, "Sure I'd like to escape 'cause I can't get a fair shake any other way."

Disappointed that he wasn't able to coax Jack into admitting to his involvement in any of the murders, Wilson decided to zero in on Henson.

"How close were you and Harriet? Did the two of you ever plan to get married?"

"Nah," Jack said with a hint of a frown. "I'm not the marrying kind. She knows it. We just hit it off pretty good and I was a kind of a meal ticket for her." Wilson chuckled to himself. He knew that wasn't exactly the way Harriet would have described it.

"Jack, what kind of a girl is she?"

"She's a real decent broad, is what she is, Stanley," Jack said and Wilson sensed that hidden somewhere underneath that cold and brash exterior, maybe there actually was some semblance of a heart.

As Jack began to sketch out a biographical portrait of the woman with whom he had once shared his life—perverted though it was—Wilson could detect in the man's tenor just a trace of nostalgia, and in his own warped way, even melancholy.

For Wilson, his interview with Jack Santo would end in deep frustration since he realized that, for now at least, no matter how hard he prodded, this wily criminal had no intention of admitting to the crimes for which he had been condemned. It was going to take at least a second interview it now appeared.

But there would be no second interview because this was to be the final interview ever granted by Jack Santo.

While the murderous duo languished on San Quentin's condemned row, their female accomplices—Barbara Graham, sentenced to die for her part in the 1953 murder of Mabel Monohan and Harriet Henson—who had received a life sentence as an accessory in the four Chester murders—were being housed in the California Institution for Women at Corona. Although no record exists to suggest that they ever came into contact with each other during their simultaneous incarcerations at this facility, it's entirely possible—even probable—that they did. What might have transpired at those meetings of course, no one knows, but it's safe to say that the names Jack Santo and Emmett Perkins would have been at the top of any list of topics that might have been discussed.

While Barbara was being held at Corona, her appeals process had played itself out. After all possibilities for a successful appeal had been exhausted, she would be driven four hundred miles under guard to San Quentin's death house a day prior to her scheduled execution date and placed in a specially outfitted cell where she would spend her final hours.

Harriet Henson on the other hand, would remain at Corona to serve out her sentence and where, even though having been caught up in a number of minor rules violations, she would establish a reputation as a model, well-behaved prisoner. On one of those occasions she was charged with stealing a jar of peanut butter from the prison commissary and on another she had been written up for having a friend smuggle a small bit of nutmeg into her cell. On the whole though, her overall good behavior earned her sufficient good-time credit so that in July of 1961, after having served a total of seven years, Harriet Henson was granted conditional parole.

A Sentence of Death

Anyone, for whatever reason, who would be tempted to emulate the criminal behavior of Jack Santo or Emmett Perkins, or to a lesser degree, Barbara Graham, need only be reminded that when they are caught, the ultimate penalty will likely be the forfeiture of his or her own life. With all the new high-tech crime-fighting advancements now available to law enforcement authorities, the odds against their getting away with murder are greater now than ever before. The good guys are now able to employ tools never before available to crime fighters: DNA profiling—including the FBI's Combined DNA Index System (CODIS) a criminal database containing almost one billion DNA profiles which is in addition to the Integrated Automated Fingerprint Identification System (IAFIS), the largest biometric criminal database in the world, holding a criminal master file of over 66 million subjects.

One would think—and conventional wisdom would tend to agree—that in light of the vast array of high-tech tools and weapons that are now available to law enforcement, any individual with half a brain who has murder on his mind would be deterred from committing the crime which in all probability, will end up sending him to his own demise.

But such logic does not seem to apply when it comes to the crime of murder. The homicide rate in America continues to rise at an alarming rate. Statistics show that a majority of the murders that occur in the United States are committed in our southern states—those same states, paradoxically, where eighty percent of the country's executions take place. In the South, it would seem, the deterrent effect of a looming execution chamber has little—if any—impact on the overall murder rate.

By contrast, the lowest number of homicides in America occurs in the Northeast where inversely, only one percent of the country's executions take place. Clearly, these statistics show that if an individual is bent on murder, he will probably not be deterred by the threat of his own execution. The imposition of death penalties has not in any way reduced the number of murders being committed every day in American society. Using "deterrence" as a rationale for imposing the death penalty simply does not stand up to close scrutiny.

In 1994, the California Supreme Court ruled that execution by hanging, firing squad, the electric chair or the use of lethal gas (as in the San Quentin gas chamber) amounted to "cruel and unusual punishment" and was therefore proscribed by law. As a result of that ruling, lethal injection—even in many of the other states—became the method of choice by which a prisoner could now be put to death by the state.

In Idaho, Utah and Oklahoma, the firing squad remains an option and in Delaware, New Hampshire and Washington, a condemned prisoner can still be hanged. But as of 2012 of the thirty-seven states that still execute convicted murderers, all use lethal injection as their primary method.

When one stops to consider in simple terms just what an execution by lethal injection actually entails, it becomes obvious that claims of the death penalty being an "eye-for-an-eye" punishment acquires a hollow ring.

Convicted for the cold-blooded murders of seven human beings and having been sentenced to die by lethal injection, Jack Santo and Emmett Perkins, according to today's laws, would be strapped to a gurney and given an injection which, within thirty seconds, would desensitize their nervous system and send them into a sound sleep. They would then receive a second injection to induce muscle paralysis after which a third injection of lethal potassium chloride would be administered and in a matter of seconds, their hearts would cease to beat.

While their victims may have been forced to endure untold amounts of suffering before being overtaken by death as was the case with the victims of Santo and Perkins, the murderers, in receiving the so-called "ultimate punishment" for their crime—again, by today's laws—would be rendered unconscious and made to experience neither pain nor physical distress.

If it is society's intention to punish a condemned criminal by inflicting on him some degree of physical discomfort, it's clear that his execution by lethal injection would fall far short of that "noble" goal.

In 1954, the process with respect to capital punishment was quite different. At that time a condemned prisoner on San Quentin's death row could expect to have all of his chances for appeal—including those to the U.S. Supreme Court—to have been either upheld or denied within a couple of years at most.

In 1953, Jack Santo and Emmett Perkins had been sentenced to die for the brutal murder of Mabel Monohan and a year later, both had received four additional death sentences for the Chester murders. With their appeals in the Monohan case having been denied, their day of reckoning had arrived. Barring a reprieve from the governor, their executions were scheduled to be carried out on June 3, 1955, a scant two years from the date their sentences had been imposed.

As the hour grew inexorably near, the condemned men had finally been forced to face the inevitable. It was now apparent that there weren't going to be any last minute reprieves. Instead, there was to be a triple execution—a fact made dismayingly clear when on June 2, one day before their scheduled execution, they were joined on condemned row by Barbara Graham.

Throngs of reporters and news media people had begun to gather at the prison gates as the state trooper's car transporting Barbara pulled up. While she was being led to her cell, reporters elbowed their way into a position affording the best chance to snag that last Barbara Graham interview. There was still hope—even a smattering of expectation—that she would finally confess, expressing remorse for the crimes for which she'd been condemned and in so doing, go to her death with a clear conscience.

But Barbara would grant few interviews, and to the select few to whom she did speak, she said tersely, "If I were guilty, I would never admit it and let my children be branded with the stigma of having a murderer for a mother for the rest of their lives."

If, as Jack Santo had been boasting, he and Perkins were to be spared the gas chamber because of Barbara Graham's gender then time—that most precious of all commodities when one is counting off his remaining days—had run out. Even though their appeals for the Chester murders were still pending, all appeals relating to the Monohan murder had been denied. The execution date for the three convicted killers was now set for the following day.

For his last meal, at 6:30 p.m. on June 2, Jack Santo was served a dinner of fried chicken, avocado and tomato salad, pie and coffee. At midnight he was given a slice of banana cream pie. Perkins on the other hand, asked only for a piece of pie and a glass of milk and at twelve thirty he fell asleep. At 8:00 a.m. he had to be awakened by the guard who reported that neither inmate appeared to be agitated or disturbed.

It's Time

In those final days, Barbara had turned to religion and for solace, to San Quentin Catholic Chaplain, Father Daniel McAlister. It was to Father McAlister she had shrugged and said, "If it is God's will that I die, then, I will die like a lady."

And die like a lady she did. At ten o'clock on the morning of June 3, 1955, Barbara Graham was visited by Father McAlister. "It's time," he said softly.

"Thank God," Barbara said. "You know, Father, I'm alright. I feel pretty good. I don't feel any hatred for anybody. Just pity for the people who've done this to me—that they'll have to live with it."

Barbara had dressed for the occasion as if on her way to a job interview. She wore a trim beige colored wool suit with matching cloth covered buttons, high-heeled shoes, gold tear-drop earrings and around her neck, a crucifix dangling from a silver chain. Her hair, no longer bleached but now a reddish brown, flowed in soft curls against her shoulders and glistened in the harsh ante-chamber light. Barbara Graham would be a dazzler to the very end.

At a few minutes before 10:00 a.m., after having been already seated in the small preparation anteroom adjacent to the gas chamber, she would receive two brief stays from the governor's office.

"I can't take this," she sobbed. "Why didn't they let me go at ten? I was ready to go at ten!"

When she saw the large crowd of people that had already taken their seats in the witness area encircling the glass-windowed, morbidly green death chamber, Barbara turned to Father McAlister.

"I don't want to look at all those faces. Can I have a blindfold?"

A matron hurried to accommodate her last wish and at 11:34, Barbara, now sweating profusely, her lips moving as if in a silent prayer and before the blindfold was put in place for the final time, surveyed the faces of the people who had come to watch her die.

"Why are good people always so sure they're right?" she remarked, mostly to herself as she was led by two matrons through the hatch-like steel door. Her shoes were removed and both her ankles were strapped to the waiting chair as were her forearms and chest.

"Count to ten after you hear the pellets drop and take a deep breath and it won't hurt so much," one of the male guards advised her.

Barbara tilted her blindfolded face toward the sound of his voice. "How the hell would you know?" she said. They were the last words she would ever utter.

Award winning author Clark Howard, in his brilliant online essay *The True Story of Barbara Graham*, described Barbara's last moments:

The big air-tight door was swung shut and pressure locked. Witnesses saw Barbara swallow nervously. Several times she wet her lips. At some point, she moved her lips, perhaps praying. It was a full minute before she heard the plunger-like sound of a cheesecloth bag containing two golf-ball size pellets being lowered into a concrete vat of sulphuric acid directly beneath her chair.

She was startled by the faint, almost indiscernible sound and her body tensed while a doctor listened to her quickening heartbeat through a stethoscope/rubber hose arrangement that, after having been taped to her chest, was run through an air-sealed compartment to the chamber's exterior.

As the vapor's bitter almond odor reached her olfactory senses, her nostrils flared and as Clark Howard vividly describes; *she drew in a deep, deliberate, tortuous breath. Almost at once her head nodded, her lips twitched and she slumped forward.*

Barbara Graham, who had sworn all the way to her grave—literally—that she was innocent of the crimes for which she had been condemned, was pronounced dead at precisely 11:42 a.m. on June 3, 1955.

The Bell Tolls

There was very little drama attached to the "last mile" walks of Jack Santo and Emmett Perkins and certainly there was nothing like the frantic media crush and the cruel series of delays that had plagued the final moments of Barbara Graham's life. During the time it took to purge the chamber of all traces of the deadly cyanide gas, Santo and Perkins sat quietly talking in the preparation anteroom.

A story in the Los Angeles Herald Express the following afternoon erroneously reported that Jack could be heard "screaming and weeping" as he was being readied for his appointment. On the contrary, both he and Perkins had spent the final minutes of their lives discussing cars and making jokes.

At 2:30 p.m., as they were being led into the chamber, Jack turned to Warden Teets and quipped, "Don't you fellows do anything I wouldn't do."

They were grinning and wisecracking as they were strapped into their respective chairs, and precisely at 2:32 p.m. the cyanide pellets were dropped. Santo's face twisted into a grimace: Perkins coughed as their heads simultaneously dropped against their chests and at 2:38 p.m. Jack Santo and Emmett Perkins were pronounced dead.

The official prison Execution Record describes their final moments:

> *2:25 pm: Water and Acid mixed:*
> Santo: Friendly, calm and resigned
> Perkins: Very calm and resigned. Shakes hands and thanks all for care and treatment.

331

2:34 pm: Gas Strikes Prisoner's Face:
Santo: Grimaces and strains at chair straps.
Perkins: Nods head, says 'this is it'. Makes little resistance.
2:36 pm: Prisoner Certainly Unconscious:
Santo: Head falls forward. Relaxed.
Perkins: Head and hands relaxed.
2:38 pm: Special Comments:
Santo: Dies very quietly.
Perkins: Dies very quietly.

The entire process was over in thirteen minutes and with their deaths, a nearly decade-long reign of terror had come to a quiet—albeit fitting—end.

It now remains for succeeding generations to ponder whether Jack Santo or Emmett Perkins had ever experienced a single pang of guilt or remorse as a result of the horror they had inflicted on their victims and their families.

Professionals are not unanimous in drawing a distinction between the *sociopath* and the *psychopath,* or whether either condition is the result of some kind of chemical imbalance in the brain that responds to medication.

In a dichotomy relating to the psychopath / sociopath distinction alluded to in the *Preface* section of this book. Clinical Psychologist Dr. Kelly McAleer, addresses the question on her blog *Forensic Focus:*

The age-old debate of psychopathy versus sociopathy is not one that can be answered easily. This is mainly because the words are often used interchangeably, and even when the terms are clearly defined by one scholar, another may disagree and choose to use the term in an entirely different fashion. Looking up these terms in dictionaries can lead to more confusion as the definition for psychopathy may include the word sociopathy in its description and vice versa!

She adds that in the mental health field there is some consensus that psychopathy is more of an innate phenomenon, whereas sociopathy, a state in which there may be a similar clinical presentation to psychopathy, is more the result of environmental factors (poverty, exposure to violence, permissive or neglectful parenting, etc.).

Dr. Martha Stout, a practicing clinical psychologist and former Instructor of Psychology at Harvard University, in her recently published best seller, *The Sociopath Next Door,* writes:

Most sociopaths are not mass murderers or serial killers. Instead, most are only life-sized, like the rest of us and can remain unidentified for long periods of time. The ominous truth is that a shocking average of 1 out of 25 U.S. citizens is one of the "remorseless." While varied, as sociopaths, they are completely devoid of conscience and can do literally anything to achieve their personal goals whatever they may be.

In his book, *Without Conscience*, Dr. Robert D. Hare states that: *The capacity to feel attachment and empathy towards another and to feel guilt and shame after doing something wrong is not associated with psychopathy; however it is suggested that sociopaths can emotionally attach to others, and feel badly when they hurt those individuals that they are attached to.*

Dr. Hare goes on to say that although the sociopath will still lack empathy and attachment toward the greater society and will not feel guilt in harming a stranger or rebelling against laws, he does not lack empathy entirely, as is typical with the psychopath. While it may be true, Dr. Hare says, that although both psychopaths and sociopaths are capable of committing heinous crimes, the psychopath can commit crimes against family members or 'friends' (as well as strangers) and feel little to no remorse.

The psychopath is charming and manipulative; able to use his charisma and his ability to intimidate others and can effectively mimic the feelings of "normal" people. The psychopath is organized in his criminal thinking and behavior. He's able to maintain emotional and physical control and display little or no emotion, even under situations most would find troubling or even threatening. He is keenly aware of what is right and what is wrong but he simply doesn't care.

Less organized in his demeanor, the sociopath is apt to be nervous, edgy, easily agitated and quick to anger and is more likely to spontaneously act out in inappropriate ways without regard for the consequences. The sociopath will lie, cheat, manipulate and hurt others, but differs from the psychopath in that, while the psychopath may exhibit the same kind of behavior, he would try to avoid hurting someone he cares about because in doing so, he could experience feelings of guilt or remorse.

Compared to the psychopath, Dr. Hare states, *the sociopath will not be able to move through society committing callous crimes as easily, as they [sic] can from attachments and often have 'normal temperaments.'*

Dr. Hare concludes: *So, while these two terms seem interchangeable on the surface because they share many of the same characteristics, they are more like two sides of the same coin.*

Looking at the differences may seem futile; however, looking at psychopathy and sociopathy as different constructs may prove to be helpful in understanding the etiology of these disorders, and in the development of effective treatment methods.

Be that as it may—psychopath or sociopath—to their victims it makes scant difference. Tragically, the seven people who lost their lives at the hands of Jack Santo and Emmett Perkins may not have been the pair's only murder victims.

In July of 1952, two months before the Chester massacre, a trail crew discovered the bodies of two General Motors executives who had been murdered somewhere in the woods of Crater Lake National Park. Both men had been shot in the head execution style, their mouths gagged with their own neckties and shoes removed of which one pair had been stolen. Sixty years later, FBI agents still haven't identified the killer or killers although Jack Santo and Emmett Perkins have always been at the top of their suspect list.

And there were other crimes as well. In 1953 a suspicious series of phone calls linked Jack Santo to a San Francisco gem dealer who was subsequently charged and convicted of being the "brains" in a $300,000 diamond robbery.

Santo and Perkins chose to live their lives on the darkest side of decent society, preying on its citizens and taking for themselves whatever they wanted. Without mercy or compassion, they simply killed those unlucky enough to get in their way. On that cold autumn day more than sixty years ago, Jack Santo and Emmett Perkins chose to sell their immortal souls for a few pieces of silver.

Yet Christal would have been among the first to say that in making their bargain with the devil, the killers had lost far more than she.

◆◆◆◆◆◆◆ *End* ◆◆◆◆◆◆◆

POSTSCRIPT

Many autumns have come and gone since that awful day in October of 1952 when, on the gentle slopes of the northern Sierras, citizens of the tiny California town of Chester were forced to glimpse firsthand the full scope and the frightening reality of pure evil.

It's now been over sixty years since five unsuspecting, innocent and totally blameless residents had been ruthlessly robbed, bludgeoned and left to die under the sprawling branches of Sequoia redwoods and quaking aspens that populate the western slopes of the Northern Sierra Nevada Mountains.

The old logging road alongside which Guard Young, his daughters Jean and Judy and playmate Michael Saile drew their final breaths is now barely a path and hardly recognizable. Most of the townsfolk of today's Chester are not even aware of its existence.

Chester itself hasn't changed appreciably. Collins Pine Lumber Company is still the town's major employer; except now, instead of its workers being forced to travel to Westwood for their banking needs, the town of Chester can boast of two banks. The Main Street lot on which Young's Supermarket once stood is now a retail sporting goods emporium. Most Chesterites who trade there on a regular basis are unaware that the building itself—which remains one of the town's most imposing structures—was originally built by Guard Young. In fact, one would be hard-pressed to find anyone in Chester under the age of sixty who even recognizes Guard Young's name. Memories of that tragic day in 1952 have long since faded from the town's awareness.

But Jeff Cooley, the eighty seven-year-old former California Highway Patrolman remembered. On that cold autumn day, Cooley had rushed Sondra Gay Young—battered, bleeding and barely clinging to life—to Westwood Hospital where she was lovingly nursed back to health. Cooley died in May of 2010 but eight months prior to his passing, in an emotional ceremony held before a small but appreciative audience at the Chico CHP Station, he had been awarded the *Superior Act Commendation*, one of the highest honors the California Highway Patrol can bestow on one of its fellow officers. Sondra Jones (nee Young) who had flown in from her home in Utah, looked on with teary eyes as a very proud Officer Cooley finally received the long overdue recognition for his life-saving act. This solemn yet joyful occasion would be the last time they would ever see each other.

Together they recalled the horrific events of that day: Sondra, at three and a half, only partially conscious and Trooper Cooley, in a state of anguished shock on seeing her tiny, blood covered arm reaching out from beneath a pile of battered bodies.

Without his quick and decisive action, Sondra reminded him, their coming together again on this day and on this occasion would not have been possible.

Many of the players in this real-life drama have long since faded into obscurity. Larry and Lucille Shea who, even while providing trial testimony that helped to secure the convictions of all three defendants, had nevertheless been suspected by most Chester townspeople of having had a hand in the four murders. Only a few months after the trial, the Sheas saw their home in Chester mysteriously catch fire and burn to the ground. Volunteer firefighters, after being uncharacteristically slow in responding to the alarm, stood by quietly and in the opinion of some of Shea's neighbors, deliberately allowed the Shea house to burn until it had been reduced to ashes.

After finally being harassed out of Chester, the Sheas relocated to Susanville, some forty miles east which became their last known address. From there, they disappeared from public view.

For her part in the crime, Harriet Henson was sent to the California Institute for Women to serve out her life sentence, but as mentioned earlier, after having served seven years, she was released on conditional parole.

Henson remained under the close supervision of parole authorities, merging seamlessly into the kind of ordinary lifestyle some might describe as humdrum but remaining nonetheless, trouble-free. In 1965 she met and married Valentine Matkovich and in 1969 with her new husband, she relocated to Duluth, Minnesota. In 1972, they moved to Texas where ten years later, Valentine passed away. Harriet, if still alive, would have celebrated her eighty-seventh birthday in January, 2011. Unfortunately, she too has vanished from public view.

Shortly after the trial, Mrs. Fern Watters, the Grass Valley waitress who had alerted authorities after overhearing Bernadine Pearney boast of her weekend Reno spending spree with Jack Santo, received a $6,000 reward which had been posted by the state of California, the United Grocers' Association and the Collins Pine Lumber Company.

* * * *

In September, 1954, Christal Young returned with her two children to her home in Provo, Utah where, during the following August, she married widower Clair R. Mathis. In May of 2001, after an extended illness, Christal Young Mathis died at age 88. She was returned to Westwood where she is now interred in the Young family plot.

Sondra Gay grew up in Provo and after marrying and raising her own large family, managed to find time to obtain her undergraduate, as well as a master's degree. She is a published author and while holding down a professorship at Brigham Young University, she has now earned a doctorate degree from that university.

A direct descendant of Lorenzo Dow Young, the brother of Brigham Young, early pioneer of The Church of Latter-day Saints, Sondra Gay exemplifies the ongoing legacy of high achievement that, for succeeding generations, has been a hallmark of the Young family.

In the 1976 Olympics, Sondra's little brother Dr. Wayne Young, captained the USA Olympic Gymnastics Team. His son and grandfather's namesake, Guard, also a gymnast, earned a Silver Medal as a member of the 2004 Olympic team and in 2010, was inducted into the BYU Sports hall of Fame.

Michael Young, son of elder Guard's brother, Vance, served in the first Bush administration in a number of posts and was named to the position of Chairman of the President's Commission on International Religious Freedom. In 2004 he was named President of the University of Utah.

The still tiny mountain village of Chester, while it may not have completely recaptured the innocence it had lost on that old logging road over half a century ago, has long since regained its rightful honor as one of God's favorite—and favored—places.

Authors' Notes:

In Chapter Sixteen of this book, we discussed the imposition of the death penalty and its efficacy in exacting what many believe to be the *extreme punishment* for the commission of society's most heinous of crimes.

Setting aside the specious notion that the threat of the death penalty has a deterrent effect on criminals who may otherwise be predisposed to murder, and setting aside too, the totally painless aspect of death by lethal injection as fitting punishment for those who commit such crimes, there is still the matter of economics.

Death penalty advocates continue to make the "cost-effective" argument: i.e. executions save the state money. They point out that the cost of an inmate's care and feeding over the span of a life sentence far exceeds the cost of his execution. A closer look at the numbers however, paints a far different picture.

A 2005 Los Angeles Times study comparing the cost of incarceration as opposed to execution revealed that the California death penalty system now costs taxpayers many millions more per year beyond the expense of simply keeping the convicts locked up for life. Even then, it fails to take into account the additional expense of post-conviction hearings in state and federal courts which are estimated to exceed several million dollars per inmate. In June 2011 the L.A. Times reported:

The additional cost of confining an inmate to death row, when compared to those of the maximum security prisons where inmates who have been sentenced to life ordinarily serve their sentences, is $90,000 per year per inmate.

With California's death row population of 734 condemned inmates (as of 2012), that would add up to over $66 million annually. Then there is this: Taxpayers have spent more than $4 billion on capital punishment in California since it was reinstated in 1978, or about $308 million for each of the 13 executions that have been carried out since then. *http://articles.latimes.com/2011/jun/20/local/la-me-adv-death-penalty-costs-20110620*

If it costs the state $308 million to execute a single prisoner, it should be readily apparent that the argument supporting the death penalty as being purely a matter of economics when compared to a life sentence is by all accounts, most definitely NOT the most cost-effective method of punishment.

In addition to the financial strains placed on the state's treasury with the imposition of the death penalty, the length of time an inmate spends on death row while awaiting execution has grown exponentially over the years. In the 1950s, Caryl Chessman, California's notorious *Red Light Bandit* was held on San Quentin's death row for twelve years, spending his time writing best-selling books, making movies, granting interviews, all while being granted no fewer than eight stays. After a twelve-year wait, he was finally executed in 1960. Up until that time, twelve years of stays for a condemned criminal waiting to have his execution carried out was practically unheard of but in today's over-clogged appellate court system—it's the rule rather than the exception.

Of the condemned inmates who have died on San Quentin's death row, only eighteen percent have actually been executed. The rest—eighty two percent—died of natural causes. It's a shocking figure but when one considers that in the California criminal justice system today, a condemned inmate will often languish on death row for twenty—even thirty—years while the appeals process creaks its way through the courts, the numbers are hardly surprising. An inmate entering the system at age fifty in all probability will reach the ripe old age of seventy and still will not have exhausted his entire menu of appeals.

It's something to think about.

ABOUT THE AUTHORS

Although Loren Abbey has written articles for various trade journals, quarterlies and magazines, *A Massacre of Innocents* is his first attempt at a full-length book. A former Silicon Valley electronics company executive, he is now retired and resides in Roseville, California.

Co-author Pam Zibura is a successful realtor who, with husband Tony, makes her home in South Carolina, just outside the historic city of Charleston.

Pam's keen interest in this book's subject matter coupled with a unique researcher's ability of unearthing those elusive, little known facts that add substance and texture to any narrative, were invaluable contributions in the writing of *A Massacre of Innocents*.

Printed in the United States
By Bookmasters